אמת

The Exorcist's
Handbook

Josephine McCarthy
with Peter McCarthy

Forward by Dr. John Plummer PhD

Golem • Media
BERKELEY, CA
www.golemmedia.com

Golem Media
BERKELEY, CA

Golem Media
1700 Shattuck Ave #81
Berkeley, CA 94709
www.golemmedia.com

Copyright © 2010 by Josephine and Peter McCarthy

ISBN: 978-1-933993-91-1

Contents

Acknowledgements 4

Note From Author 5

Forward by Dr John Plummer PhD 7

Introduction 9

Chapter One: The Life of an Exorcist:
How to Stay in One Piece 15

Chapter Two: The Tool Kit 32

Chapter Three: Working with Beings 45

Chapter Four: Beings You May Encounter 60

Chapter Five: Assessing a Potential Possession 78

Chapter Six: Working with Dead People 95

Chapter Seven: How to Conduct an Exorcism;
Removing Demonic Beings 108

Chapter Eight: The Exorcism of Non-Demonic Beings 124

Chapter Nine: Dealing with Curses 141

Chapter Ten: How to Deal with Magical Attacks 158

Chapter Eleven: The Clearing and Reconstruction
of a Sacred Space/Temple 171

Chapter Twelve: Issues of the Land and Beings of Nature ... 185

Chapter Thirteen: A Tailored
Divinatory Deck for Exorcists 199

Chapter Fourteen: Long Term Management of the Exorcist 226

Appendix 1: Understanding
and Working with the Abyss 231

Appendix 2: Tarot Layout
for Looking at the Health of a Person 239

Bibliography 244

Dedicated to Tim McCarthy

Who crossed the bridge
while doing something he loved

Acknowledgements

Thanks to Dr John Plummer for his wonderful guidance, Rev Margie McArthur, Karen McKeown, and Cecilia Lindley for their friendship and support. Thanks to Alan Richardson for his encouraging comments and to Adam Mclean for the amazing reference material he provides through his Alchemy website.

Note

This book is a collection of practical knowledge acquired through many years of work in the field of exorcism. There are many esoteric 'secrets' or Mysteries contained alongside the practical working techniques in this book as it is my belief that there is no reason to hide the Mysteries—people can only unlock the Mysteries when they are ready to absorb them. The true Mysteries can not be studied intellectually—they are a natural expression of power that must be experienced.

Therefore, putting some of the Mysteries within these texts offers guidance to an exorcist or magical worker who has sufficient knowledge to recognise what he or she is reading and therefore can use the text to fill gaps, confirm intuitions, and expand upon practical individual experience which in turn enables the Initiate to take the next step. The Mysteries can only be understood by someone ready to understand them—it is that simple.

Someone who has little magical/spiritual experience but is searching may feel a connection with the text but not understand parts of it. However, exposure to elements of the Mysteries can in itself trigger deep stirrings and help guide a seeker to find the right path that he is able to walk down. He will remember the text in years to come and will be able to return to it with deeper understanding.

The Mysteries themselves are simply a basic rule book and guide map to navigating the inner worlds, connecting with beings from other realms and, most important of all, learning how to connect and commune with Divinity—the Mysteries are a road map for the soul. It doesn't matter if you are a Christian, a Muslim, a Pagan, a Wiccan, or an Animist; the labels and surface manifestations of those labels are all just operating systems—they all potentially lead to Divinity and to Gnosis.

Once an Initiate makes a magical commitment to inner service, the Initiate is funnelled down a path of specialisation so that she can train and work in a specific area of magical/spiritual service.

This book covers one of those specialised paths—the path of the exorcist.

I have approached this book in a casual, personal way without any specific magical or religious path so that it is accessible to people from a variety of spiritual/magical backgrounds. Once you get past the surface manifestations of our spiritual constructs, the inner worlds and the beings that inhabit them are the same—our spiritual constructs/religions are simply Man's attempt to create an interface with Divinity. So the techniques and information within this book should work just as well for a Catholic exorcist as it should for a Kabbalist, a Pagan priest, or a Wiccan priestess—it's all a matter of being able to step past dogma and keep walking.

Exorcism is a difficult and somewhat obscure subject matter that does not sit well with theorising or intellectualising. It needs to be approached in a straight-forward matter with a good sprinkling of down-to-earth humour which is one of the greatest necessities for an exorcist. Humour is the one thing that will keep you sane in a crazy and difficult world. This book is littered with bad jokes and personal stories—the subject matter is heavy enough without making it unnecessarily serious too.

I have used a variety of inner visions in this book which is a working method used extensively in a variety of Western Mystery Traditions. The best and easiest way to work with these visions as they are presented in this book is to record them and play them back to yourself and let the recording guide you through the meditation. Once you have worked with a vision, you will be able to find your own way back to the inner realm without the use of a recording.

And finally, although I wrote this book, I have also credited Pete, as he contributed enormously to this book—both as a co-conspirator, advisor, through his practical work with me as an exorcist, and through joining me in exploratory work which helped to develop techniques that later appeared in this book. He is my fellow exorcist, magical partner, and best friend.

forward

by Dr. John Plummer

Exorcism is a topic that immediately leads into a fog of sensational and paranoid religious expressions, in which any direction or clear vision is quickly lost. Josephine McCarthy slices through this fog with a brilliant sword of a book. While McCarthy is conversant with scholarship on the topic, and knowledgeable regarding many religious, esoteric, and other spiritual traditions, it is her hard-won experience as an exorcist which animates her writing. With good humor and common sense, all sensationalism is brushed aside, so that the student exorcist can get down to work. This is very much a "how to" guide, in which decades of experience are shared far more openly than in any other treatment of the subject I have encountered.

McCarthy speaks to spiritual workers who may be called to exorcism as a major component of their vocation, for a period of time or for life. Her guidance will also inform priests, priestesses, ministers, and workers of many traditions who may encounter a need for exorcism more than occasionally, or who simply seek to understand these phenomena. The most compelling part of the book concerns the spiritual preparation of the exorcist. Much of McCarthy's guidance on this preparation could apply to any spiritual worker, exorcist or otherwise. She captures the very essence of spiritual initiation and the unconditional offering of oneself in service. Any remotely introspective reader is likely to swallow hard before some of the proposed visionary work. Yet it is the willingness to step forward, placing oneself and one's fate in the hands of Divinity, that sets one on a path of true spiritual service.

True wisdom challenges us and remakes us, and this is a wise book.

John Plummer, Ph.D.
Bishop, Mission Episcopate of the Theophany
Author, The Many Paths of the Independent Sacramental Movement

Introduction

There are many types of exorcists just as there are many types of faith. Demons, spirits, entities, ghosts, and angelic beings make no distinction between an atheist, a catholic or a pagan—they can set up shop if the conditions are right, and they can wreak havoc in someone's life, building, or mind.

Different types of exorcists have different approaches, from prayers all through the spectrum to beatings, and some methods on those spectrums work and some do not. It all depends on the method, the beings, and the circumstances.

The most effective types of exorcists are ones that are either able to pass equally and freely between all faiths and none, and to work without dogma. The other extreme is an exorcist who is fully and deeply immersed in one specific religious faith. The only problem with the strict religious exorcist is that the ceremony usually only works if the host and possessor are of that same religious steam. Some religious exorcists do not agree at all with that, and such arrogance can and does put people's lives in danger. (Ever found yourself chanting the exorcism of the *Ritual Romanum* at a non Christian host/demon? The only chance of success will be if it keels over from sheer boredom.)

What is an exorcist?

There are many branches, varieties, and lines of exorcists, and they all differ widely. This book approaches the details, information, and methodology of just one stream of this line of work.

An exorcist is a person who takes things out of hosts and puts them back where they belong. The host could be a person, place, a car, or a tractor—it doesn't really matter. The being or beings that are taken out could be demons, parasites, ghosts, angels, faery beings, basically anything with consciousness and intelligence (which rules out British politicians...good to know you will never be possessed by a cabinet minister).

Such work can be anything from time consuming to outright dangerous so it is not a line of service that many people are drawn to (or if they are, they tend to run screaming pretty quickly). Because you are working with conditional beings that will try to tempt or bargain with you, an exorcist needs to be grounded, clean, clear, and not connected to anything. You cannot go home to a family of vulnerable children in this line of work—you have to be able to let go of everything.

An exorcist also needs to be able to take a great deal of pain, have stamina, patience, the ability to go into a non-emotional state and stay in it, be a hermit, a vegetarian, sexually balanced, have a very strong connection with Divinity, and be slightly mad with a love of adrenaline sports!

The outer needs are knowledge of ancient history, religions, geography, geology, archaeology of languages, herbs, medicines and substances, human biology and anatomy, ancient myths and legends, animal psychology, ritual and magic with all its attendant beings in all its different forms, tribal cultures, music, sacred architecture, and human psychology.

It also helps if an exorcist is bloody-minded, stubborn, has a strong sense of purpose, is committed to service, has a warped sense of humour, and is not easily shocked.

The last thing on the shopping list of what an exorcist needs is connection into a spiritual line. Working alone in the human world is one thing, but working alone in the spiritual realm is a totally different thing altogether and not something that I would recommend.

Connection to a spiritual line means literally that: a consecration into a sacred line of humans who have dedicated their lives to the work of Divine service. That can be a priest/esshood, an apostolic succession or a genetic line of active mystics or priests. An exorcist needs to be able to draw upon the long and rich line of previous experience—the line of spiritual service and the line of fellow workers whom you can call upon if ever needed. Everything that has ever been learned by any one member of that line is accessible to all within that line. All apostles are one, all mystics are one—it is one of the deeper mysteries of the priesthoods regardless of where they are and what Deity guides them. The only downside is that, as an exorcist, you must not be tied only to that line. It must be a relationship where you have the freedom to work with any line/being that is needed.

The one major difference with this line of exorcism is that the being is given a chance to leave of its own accord and if it doesn't, it is taken back to where it came from without aggression and the access point that it got out from is sealed up. Most exorcisms are driven by fear and control—the exorcist is often afraid and is depending on faith, and the being is commanded, insulted, and harangued. This just usually tends to piss it off if it is big and nasty. Such action works from a standing point of moral superiority (which is laughable in our species), and domination. That in itself creates a weakness for the exorcist and puts her in danger— here, stand on this very high pedestal and let's see how long it takes you to be knocked off.

The exorcist who operates in that way is taking the position that he/she is superior to the being in the host. Such arrogance is begging to be slapped down and will provide endless rounds of energy for the being to feed from. It is much more effective to simply understand that the being just doesn't belong there. It is in a place that is not good for the host, so it must be removed and put somewhere where it is not likely to damage anyone.

What does an exorcist actually do?

The first step that an exorcist takes when called to a situation is to establish whether the affliction, if in a person, is mental illness or possession. The same attitude is taken when it is a place or object that is under scrutiny. 'Could it be something else?' is the first question that should be asked, and most of the time it is. This is where knowledge of the human body, the land, buildings, etc, comes into play, along with a liberal dose of common sense.

If the exorcist concludes that there is a possession, the next step is to ascertain what it is, where it has come from, and what drew it in. It is important to know these facts so that it is dealt with properly. Once she knows what it is, then she knows where it probably belongs and what it feeds from. It is also important to know what gave it access to the host in the first place to ensure that once it is out, it never gets back in again.

One thing to be aware of in this line of work, is that these beings are often highly intelligent and are not averse to cross dressing or pretending to be something else to prevent or interfere with their removal. You have to be able to approach these beings and assess them not from what they tell you, but from what they do and the very basic fact that they are in another being and they shouldn't be.

The reality of exorcisms

The exorcisms that are dramatised in films tend to be very exaggerated, overblown, and involve lots of dramatic shouting in Aramaic, wall climbing and spitting of black smoke. The other extreme that is put into the public eye is that possessions are simply mental illness or psychological issues—sometimes they are, most times they are, but some times they are not and it is the 'not' times that exorcists need to work on.

One of the great failures in today's exorcisms, besides the fact that many priests today don't believe in demons and spirits, is that most exorcisms in the Christian church tend to consist of prayers. That is really not going to do a lot for anyone. The other favourite method is one that tends to come out of Africa, and that is to beat the host half to death to force the spirit out. It seems to me to be a bit of a waste of time to beat and starve someone to death to cast out a demon—the host would probably be better keeping the bloody thing and not getting murdered by fanatics.

The most sensible way to deal with a demon or a very intelligent and dangerous spirit, is to go and deal with it in its own world—passing into the inner worlds and dealing direct with the being on its own terms (with help) and using inner patterns along with outer techniques to put it back where it belongs. It has its own dangers for the exorcist, which is why the worker must be well prepared and experienced.

Some tribal shamanic cultures have a similar idea, using both inner and outer methods to banish spirits, and the Tibetan form of magic handles demons pretty adeptly using inner and outer methods. Unfortunately some Shamanic methods have been hijacked by the modern day 'shamanistic therapy go-round' and blend low level parasite removal with psychological therapies and counselling. There is always someone wanting to make money from other people's misery.

If after reading this introduction you still want to be an exorcist then I suggest you find one that is already working and has been for a long while, is still in one piece (that is always a good sign that he knows what he is doing...) and ask to be apprenticed. If he wants to charge you money, walk away. If he falls about laughing and asks you if you are insured, you are probably on to a good bet.

The approach of this book is haphazard and contradictory, but every method of action described works well without leaving too much of a mess. It is all written from first-hand experience, and I have put in my mistakes (hence some contradictions...the rules might say one thing, but dang, if the other works, use it!) as well as my successes as mistakes teach us so much. The haphazard quality of the book reflects the true working dynamic of operating behind the scenes in the inner worlds. Although the universe can seem harmonious, when you're up to your neck in nasties and you pull out whatever tool works, it might look like a haphazard method of working from a reader's point of view. But trust me, you won't give a shit so long as it all works—the universe truly does work in mysterious ways. (The chaos magicians would love that one....)

If you are already working in the field, then I hope this book gives you some good ideas, but if you blow yourself up, I didn't write this book and you can't sue me because I don't have any money!

Chapter One
The life of an exorcist—how to stay in one piece

Making the decision to be an exorcist is one that usually creeps up on a priest/ess or magician over a period of years—you don't suddenly wake up one morning and decide to quit tennis and take up demon bashing, or most people don't anyhow.

It is a calling that finds you rather than the other way around. Such calling is born out of the simple ability to do a job and that ability being recognised in the inner worlds. Things start to be put into your path for you to deal with and the subsequent need to adjust your lifestyle begins to bear down on you quite aggressively.

The actual development of the base line skills also tends to creep up on you as you realise that you're magical or spiritual path is taking you in a very specific direction in a quiet but consistent way. Anyone who suddenly decides that she wants to save the world from demons and is evangelical about it is probably not a good candidate for the job—that is a messiah trap.

The work of an exorcist will challenge your whole idea of good and evil, and you will come to realise that the world is very complex, intricate, and not everything is as it appears. Angelic beings are just as dangerous as demons, parasites can have good uses, some people want to live with spirits inside them, and some humans really just are not worth the effort to clean them up—they will happily go right back into a mess as soon as you have worked on them. There is also a natural order in the universe and every being, no matter what it is, has a balance and a part to play. An exorcist has to be very careful to not get a sense of spiritual righteousness when it comes to these beings.

Opting out—the loneliness of the path

Clearing parasites from people is one thing, but dealing with complex intelligent beings is a whole other ball game and before you go into the fray, you have to take care of your business—you can have no family tied to you in this work. This is one of the reasons why exorcists tend to be celibate priests (no family), or over a certain age when family has grown and gone.

When you realise that this is the path you are starting to walk down there are very specific things that need to be done before you go too far into the work. At a deep inner and spiritual level you have to be willing to give yourself wholly to the service of Divinity, to give up and let go of everything that is in your life and accept the full implications of what Divinity is.

This is either done through ceremony and pledge in religious orders, or through magical vision in magical work. The magical vision consists of going to the edge of the Abyss (one of the main inner areas of work for a western exorcist) and asking to be placed in judgement. In this vision you are placed before the power that you would meet in death where you confront your imbalances, your debts, and let go of all that you are connected to. It must be done in life so that no being can use any imbalance or outstanding issue against you or your family.

If you have children (best let them grow up first if they live with you), then you must be willing to acknowledge that these beings are of themselves—you were only their care-taker, and their souls are not held in any way by you. You, in effect, hand over their protection to Divinity and break connection at a deep level with them. This way, if a demon gets a hold of you and looks for an umbilical cord to something that you are protecting, it cannot find anything to threaten you with, and it cannot attack them as it cannot see them. It doesn't mean you are never going to see your kids again, it means that you truly understand that we are all alone in a soul sense, and every one of us is responsible for ourselves.

While in this vision you also have to look clearly at what you have done and what has been done to you. It will give you understanding of how you conduct yourself and what imbalance of the scales of justice need rectifying. You have to be willing to accept full and immediate rebalancing of the scales (get it all out of the way so that you can work—its like cold turkeying off chocolate while being pre menstrual…it's a real stretch). So if you did something really terrible to someone and it hasn't been rebalanced within you, it would be best to deal with that before going any further. It doesn't necessarily mean that the rebalancing involves making amends to your victim (if it is impossible for one reason or another), it is within yourself—have you learned your lesson and rectified it with someone else in your life, or given back in some way?

Curiously, if you have done too much to rectify a past mistake that also causes an imbalance and will need to be redressed. You will usually find that once you have taken the step into service, the universe will put things in your path, both good and bad, to allow you opportunity to redress and rebalance things.

The other thing that you will have to let go of is your attachment to life. There is nothing wrong in not wanting to die before you are fated to die, but if you have an agenda regarding your life span, health, power etc, then you are setting yourself up for a very dangerous fall. Your fate is handed over to Divinity and you accept what that fate gives you. This vision often changes your fate and pulls you out of ancestral fate lines, family fate lines, and any current interference in your fate by other humans (curses, magic, etc).

It is a frightening and sobering vision that really puts you in a position where you cannot hide from yourself and you have to step up to your own failings and weaknesses. This way, when you walk into danger, there are no closets for demons to open and play with—you have already aired them and dismantled them. This clearing of the slate is also a profound gift that can be used throughout the rest of your life to try to maintain that balance in your life and work.

Do this vision when you feel ready, and do it at a time of day when you will be able to rest afterwards. Do not do it when you are tired or distracted and take your time with it. Do not have any other person or being in the room with you (i.e., a cat or dog). Turn off your phones, pagers, timers, clocks, etc.

The vision of Judgement

(This vision can be recorded and then played for you to follow, or you can memorise it.)

Light a candle and sit with eyes closed.

With your inner vision see the candle flame before you. As you look closely at the flame, beyond it you see darkness, like a door-way that is unlit. Pass by the flame and walk into the darkness, leaving the room behind you. You find yourself passing into a void, a place of stillness and timelessness where you stretch out in all directions. There is no time, no space, no restriction. You remember the feel of this place, its peacefulness. This is where you came from, and this is where you will return to—all life flows from this place and all life returns back to here.

You remember your intention of judgement and you step forward with that intention and find yourself stepping out on to a flat desert with two beings walking alongside you. Both are tall and have very long hair that trails behind them, wiping away their footprints. These beings walk with you, singing to you and listening to the songs in your heart as you walk. These are the companions, the brothers—the fragment angels of Sandalphon.

As you walk, one of the companions places a hand upon your chest and warns that danger is close ahead. You slow down and find yourself coming to a large crack in the earth that is bottom-less—you arrive at the threshold of the Abyss.

Standing on the edge of the Abyss, you look to the other side, but it is obscured by mist. You look up and again the view is cov-ered by mists. You look down and you see many ledges with beings upon them, looking up at you, and the deeper you look down, the more and more faces, ledges, and beings you see.

The companion at your elbow nudges you, urging you not to get drawn down into the faces, and you look back up. Across the Abyss, a being walks through the mist to the edge on the other side and stands looking at you. It asks you what you are seeking, and you reply that you wish for judgement in life so that you can walk in service.

The being nods and puts his head back. The loudest sound you have ever heard comes from this being and you cover your ears to try and protect yourself. The ground rumbles, and the sound is joined by many other sounds that vibrate through you.

Out of the depths of the Abyss rises an angelic being that is so big that he can only be seen in bits. A hand is placed before you for you to step upon and the companions urge you to do so. The hand takes you high up into the mist, until it joins with another hand that is coming down out of the mist to meet you. You step onto that hand, which takes you up higher to another hand, which you step onto. Hand by hand, you ascend the stairway up through the Abyss.

At last, a hand holds you up before a being that you can feel but cannot see. Your body reacts in fear to the power of this place and you breathe carefully to calm everything and be still.

The presence before you asks what you are seeking and why. You must answer that you seek judgement in life, and say why. The presence will then ask you: What things in life have you left unbalanced? What debts are unpaid? What wrongs have you not righted? What wrongs have been done to you? What help have you given? What help have you received? What deaths have you caused? What lives have you saved?

Then you must tend to your family details. Any children that you have, your connection with them must be given to the Divine (the non-polarised universal power, not a specified deity) and you will be shown your life as a solitary being. You were born alone, and you die alone—all relationships are temporary and are not connected to you as a soul.

It is then that you must ask for the scales to be balanced and state that you are willing to have any imbalances weighed in during this lifetime—you submit to justice and the balancing in fate while in this life.

The presence will then place a sword over you and it will come down whereever it needs to and do whatever it needs to. The results of the judgment of the sword will play out through your lifetime.

The presence withdraws and the hand lowers you down to the edge of the Abyss where the companions are waiting for you. They walk with you across the desert away from the Abyss and they listen as you tell them what happened to you. They may offer you advice and guidance, and it would be wise to listen.

An area of mist appears ahead of you and the companions hang back, indicating that you must walk into the mist alone. Stepping through the mist, you find yourself back in the room where you first started and when you are ready and seated, you open your eyes.

* * *

The vision of judgement is not one to be approached lightly as it does work and it cannot be reversed. But for those who fear such a vision I would say to them that it is better to face yourself and your mistakes with your eyes open and in life, than to hide from your imbalances and go into death with such a burden. How much better it is to put your soul affairs in order while you have a chance, and learn from the rebalances that play out through your life.

When I did that vision, the rebalances started immediately and I was very surprised at how the rebalances came, and in which areas of my life they played out. It also gave me a deeper insight into how fate works, how energy moves around, and for how much we truly are responsible. After a few months of planks of wood swinging through the inner worlds and smacking me on the back of the head, I got the message that I make a lot of mistakes. Hmph.

Once you have been through that experience, it would be wise to keep an awareness of the need for balance and to try to use the experience to keep that balance. The easiest way is the hardest and is the way that was drilled into us in convent school: do unto others as you would have done unto you.

Caring for body and soul—the shopping list

When you are put into a position where you are in the fray with heavy nasty beings on a regular basis, the body, mind, and soul need a little bit more care and attention than usual. The basic body rules are simple: keep clean, keep life and home simple, and don't take drugs (even Ibuprophen will cause problems sometimes). Most drugs, even prescription ones, can open wide the endocrine system for attack, and a simple pint of beer can bring devastation if consumed at the wrong time.

Coffee can act as a block to certain powers (hence edgy exorcists seen clinging to a triple shot latte at all hours of the day and night!), meat will shut you out of deeper realms (many exorcists seen gazing longingly at meat in the supermarket), and any food or substance intolerance will get worse if you are working to any higher level of power.

There are many exorcists who do eat meat, but that does block them from working deeply in the Abyss, which is an area that Christian exorcists don't work in anyway. It all comes down to where you want to be able to work and what you want to be able to see. I opted for veggie as it opens all the inner worlds for me, and I can get in to obscure places and connect with most beings, which is a skill that comes in mighty handy sometimes.

Tobacco can act as a 'smoke screen' sometimes and can be used as a tool when working or when needing to discuss a situation— just be careful that you don't develop a habit!

The body and spirit will become more vulnerable to 'inner dirt,' so there are certain clean ups that are needed on a regular basis—ritual salt baths and cleansing of house/home become regular routines, as does learning to work with candles to silence a busy space.

Make sure that your living space is very balanced and uncluttered—don't leave piles for things to hide in. Once you become able to see into many worlds, don't forget that you will also become 'seen.' The deeper the Abyss you work in, the more visible you become to unsavoury beings that would ride you, eat you, or work through you. Using your common sense, keeping a clean mind and body, keeping a clean home and work space will all contribute towards staying safe. And above all…if a being says 'trust me,' fall about laughing and then run like hell.

Protection

Too much protection can become a hindrance to work as an exorcist needs to develop sensitivity to certain beings and frequencies, and a tough skin can only be developed by regular knocks. A heavy protection or amulets can make an exorcist weak and should only be used when absolutely necessary. There will be times to use these tools, but never ever become reliant on such things unless you have a death wish!

Most protection comes from the beings that you work with and from your body's ability to react to inner work. If you learn how to work with different orders of beings, they will help with the things that you cannot do just as you help them. Guardians can sometimes come in handy but they tend to have a very needle-point focus—they usually, in reality, guard against one thing.

There is also a whole area of work that can be developed regarding armour and tools which becomes very protective and is discussed in a later chapter.

When you are ill, injured or going into a very dangerous situation then using a temporary talisman (see below) or stole can come in very useful. It is used just for the job in hand, and then goes back into its box—only use such tools when you really need them.

When you use a talisman or stole, put it on after you are clean and ready for work, but before you go into the room where the person or problem is. When you come to take it off, it is the very last thing that is taken off and only done so after you have left the situation or the person has left the building. You take it off just before you get into a ritual bath. If it should break while in the middle of working, which sometimes happens, then you put it in a pocket or even in your shoe—it must stay on your body at all times while you are working.

Preparing the body for work and clearing up after

If you have a heavy job coming up, make sure you keep yourself away from things that would normally be irritants as the effect will become much more pronounced in the run up to a job. Magic is curious: the effects of the work start before the work starts, often days before, so the body must be in preparation well ahead of time. Things that would normally cause a minor irritation to the system can leave you wide open for illness and injury. For example, I am intolerant of dairy but I occasionally pig out on a little milk chocolate which normally just upsets my body a little. I once pigged out three days before a major job and I ended up with a really nasty infection; a lesson well learned.

Such sensitivity will come right out and appears to weaken the whole system. A minor intolerance can expose the body to outside forces that affect it and the result can be illness or injury. I have injured myself in the same way by working while slightly ill with no protection and I ended up with a dislocated shoulder. (Trust me, if you can think of a stupid thing, I have done it and got the badge.)

It took a while to dawn on me that there are some interesting dynamics having to do with magical inner work and the body. If the body is fighting fit and the mind is balanced, then it is astounding what a person can achieve. If, however, there are any imbalances in mind or body, minor injuries, minor illnesses, allergic reactions etc, they open a door that lets lots of things through which can affect the body.

Normally when you get an inner impact, its physical affect disperses quickly. If however you have an existing weakness, the physical impact can dig right in and manifest fully as a nasty injury. It can also lower your immune defences a little, which will allow latent bacteria or viruses to multiply, thus making you ill.

So, moral of story: keep well and fit, and don't binge out on milk chocolate if you have a heavy job coming up.

Once you have finished your work, the first thing you should do is take a ritual bath (see below) and throw all your clothing that you wore into the washing machine with a little salt thrown in for good measure. When you have finished with your bath, light a candle and look at the flame. 'See' any residue left upon you or around you by looking into the flame and feeling what is within and around you. Project that residue into the flame by 'seeing' the feel of it and hold it there. When you have it all there, blow out the candle and send the residue into the void. It is a difficult and strange technique but it is very effective for removing things; it just takes practice.

Drink coffee, eat grounding food, and do something moronic like watch a film that has nothing to do with exorcists. Do not drink alcohol or take any drugs at all, not even Ibuprophen. Any of these things will open doors that you really do not want open. If you have a headache, use paracetamol/tylanol.

Put your tools away carefully after cleaning them over incense smoke—frankincense, sage, osha root, wormwood (don't breathe it in)—any of those resins or herbs will clean any residue out of your tools.

The following few days after working should be rest time with no inner connections what so ever. This gives the body time to reel the spirit in from the work. The work can often continue for hours or sometimes days after—the body has to slowly assimilate what has happened and readjust itself accordingly. This is a time of great vulnerability when the body needs to be protected.

Belongings

As an exorcist, you will find that the deeper you get into the work, the more complicated the simple things in life can become. If you are visible to all beings in all worlds, then at some point some of those beings are going to want to hang out with you which might not be such a good idea. It is like being a priest or priestess and having icons, deities, etc, around your house—at some point they will spring to life and want to be looked after. So if you have an object that has a face or a creature/human/bird-like appearance there is a chance at some point that some being will try to move in and hang out with you. Sometimes it's not such a big deal but sometimes it can become a problem, so keep an eye on what is around you.

Keep your home simple so that when you have worked, you can relax in a clean and quiet environment. Don't bring your work home. If someone needs help, do not bring him to your home—your home must be your haven. I made the mistake a long time ago of working at home sometimes—and it is a mistake I sorely regret. Once that path to your door has been trodden, it has big landing lights on it and every being in the neighbourhood will be at your door. The old rule, if you can see them, they can see you, and if you work at home, all the lights will go on and everyone will see you.

If you want to work in this field, just do some basic organising—get a tool bag and keep it clear. Sort your tools out and maintain them properly. Keep yourself clean and healthy, keep your home quiet and simple and learn how to shield yourself properly without over-protecting yourself. Know when and how to protect yourself and, most important of all, know when to walk away from something. There will be times when there are jobs that are just too much, too big, or are self-inflicted.

There are situations, usually around sex/magic/drugs where demonic beings enter a person and begin a symbiotic relationship with the host. Before you get to taking out such a being, the host has to be able to walk away from whatever payoff the demonic being was giving her. Otherwise what happens is you break your back taking a 'heavy' out of someone, just for her to return to old behaviour and invite it back in again. It's like the typical immature magician stuff—summon a demon 'because you can,' and then get stuck with it.

The following ritual cleansing techniques are old fashioned, clunky, and a little strange in places but they work like a dream. I am of the opinion that if it works without strings attached, then it is a tool that could or should be used. Its background is that it came out of the Catholic Church and was altered many years ago to work in a non-Christian background.

Most exorcists will have a mixed bag of tools and rituals from a variety of backgrounds that can be used, which is handy because as the world shrinks, we are facing more and more problems that are often unfamiliar to our culture. And if one doesn't work in the face of a raging demon, then a girl definitely needs options! I haven't put many options up, just odd ones that are not so easily found. For the others, you can find them yourself through training, the internet, or the more usual way: when the job appears, you often also fall over the remedy.

The consecration of salt and water

Use the first two fingers of blessing to point at what you are working on and where you see + it means make the sign of an equal armed cross over whatever you are working on.

Recite over a bowl of salt while pointing first two fingers:

"I exorcise thee, creature of the earth, by the living gods+ the holy gods+ the omnipotent gods+ that thou mayest be purified of all evil influence in the name of Adonai, lord of all angels and men." (Use the flat of the hand over the salt.) "Creature of the earth, adore thy creator. In the name of God the father+ and God the mother+ I consecrate thee to the service of the gods and goddesses."

Recite over a bowl of water or a bath of water while pointing first two fingers:

"I exorcise thee, creature of the water, by the living gods+ the holy gods+ the omnipotent gods+ that thou mayest be purified of all evil influence in the name of Elohim Savoth, lord of all angels and men." (Flat of the hand.) "Creature of the water, adore thy creator. In the name of God the father+ and God the mother+ I consecrate thee to the service of the gods and goddesses."

Pouring the water and salt together, recite the following as you pour the salt into the water:

"Lord God, father of the heavens above; great Goddess, mother of the earth below my feet, grant that this salt will make for health of the body and this water for health of the soul." (Pour salt into the water.) "Grant that there may be banished from whence they are used all powers of adversity; every artifice of evil shall be banished into the outer darkness in thy holy names. Amen."

Once the salt and water are poured together, the mix is ready to cleanse and purify anything it touches. For a ritual bath, consecrate the whole of the bath water, consecrate a dish of salt and then pour in the salt while doing the recitation of pouring.

Cleansing of a space in a case of possession

First go around the space with frankincense incense, making sure you go into each corner. Then, with the consecrated salt and water, go into each room, sprinkling the water into each direction, including up and down while reciting:

"In the names which are above every other name, and in the power of the almighty, and of the mother and of the holy spirits, I exorcise all influences and seeds of evil from this room, I exorcise all demons, parasites, ghosts, bound angels, thought-forms, curses, spells, and bindings from this room, I cast upon them the spell chains and I cast them into the outer darkness where they shall trouble not these servants of god. Amen, Amen Selah."

That cleansing ritual can also be recited over a consecrated bath to add strength to the cleansing if the person has been badly attacked.

Creating a talisman

There are a variety of ways to create talismans that would protect you as you work.

The first option would be angelic: if you are working within the realm of demonic beings, then you are also working in the realm of angelic beings so it would make sense to work with them for protection.

Angelic talisman

The simplest, easiest, and most affective way to work angelically is to obtain a blank pendant or dog tag on a chain. Choose which angelic being to work with carefully—don't just go by book listings, look carefully at their actions and origins. Go in vision and meet the beings to connect with them and see if they will actually work with you. Usually you will come across them in your work and it will become apparent that they want to work with you (unless you are stupid like me and it takes a brick over the head for it to dawn you).

Once you know who you are working with, then look up the script of the language that your angel worked through. Most angels that work with people in the western world tend to be responsive to Hebrew, Aramaic, Greek, Latin, or Arabic. I have come across people working with angelic beings through Norse culture and language, but I have no personal experience in such work and when I have a very large nasty demon trying to eat me, I want to know at that point in time that when I call for help, that the help can understand me and work with me.

Engrave the name of the angel (in the appropriate script) onto the blank disk, and then place it by a candle (or go out in nature). Rather than go to the angelic being in vision, bring the being into your world by calling upon him through the void. This involves going into an opened-eyed vision to the threshold of the void and standing with one foot in the void and one foot in the human realm. Call the name of the angel until you feel its presence, or see it with your inner vision. Once the angel is on your side of the candle, hold out the talisman and ask him to protect you and guide you through it. Place your hand over the disk so that the power can flow through your hand.

You will feel when it is finished and the contact pulls away. Put the disk on a chain (if it is not already) and place it in a box where it will not be touched or messed with.

Directional talisman

Another way of working for protection is to draw upon lines of an inner priesthood that has experience in magical inner work—usually it will be a line of inner contact that you have worked with before. Working with the inner contacts of a particular line, you light a candle and make visionary contact with that line. Then you approach the candle with the talisman and hold it up to the flame, while in vision work with the inner contact to put into the talisman whatever is needed for your protection and guidance while you work. Then treat it the same way as an angelic talisman. Engrave the mark of that priesthood upon it before you work with it to empower it and put it away somewhere safe once it is finished.

Just be aware that if you work in this way, you will be working with a particular lineage of inner contacts and will have to field all the baggage that can go with that. If you are working with a line that is relatively clear, then that is good. If you are working with a very ancient line, then it will have its limitations on its workable knowledge. Ancient Egyptian Setian priests might be able to help you work with demons, but they might not have the needed expertise to untangle a being that has dug in to a space using the electromagnetic field of a house power circuit.

If you work with lines of priesthoods, it is best not to dedicate yourself to one for ever, but to learn how to communicate with all of them and have them be willing to communicate with you. That way, you can get the best of all worlds while working without the burdens that dedicated lines can bring. On the other hand, deep connection with a line can bring great strength and knowledge with it, so it's six of one and half a dozen of the other. I've done both and had good and bad from both.

I carry the apostolic succession as a bishop through the Independent Catholic Church and it has been invaluable to my work. It as given me access to deep pockets of knowledge, but I have also had to do mountains of work to clean up the line. I also carry an initiation that came down from Dion Fortune which at times has been a true pain in the ass. These days I work more with beings than with inner human contacts—angels and demons are much easier to work with than human consciousness!

If you use a stole, the methods are the same but the angelic name or contact mark is painted at the point where the stole is draped around the neck (C7 vertebrae, the knobbly one, is about where one of the access points into a human is), and on both ends of the stole.

Shielding

When there is no real need for a talisman, the best protection is internal mental shielding which is very simple but can be pretty hard to do, so it takes practice. Shielding consists of focussing the mind on something simple when you are not engaging a being. So as you clear the space, prepare to work, arrive at your work area, etc, if you are fully shielded, the demonic being does not see you coming.

This is where eastern training of mantras comes in, or the Belfast method, which is composed of repeating a nursery rhyme in your head over and over (courtesy of a very interesting wee priestess in Belfast) which works like a dream. I see a pattern and I loop my thoughts around and around the pattern so that when the being knows I am near (which it does), it gets drawn into the pattern in my head and gets frozen. It's like crashing a computer, which I have lots of experience in!

Whatever you use, it must be mindless, simple, and repetitive with absolute discipline. You cannot let your thoughts drift as the being will follow your line of thought and that can endanger people and yourself.

Another very important and often overlooked dynamic in the work and life of an exorcist is the understanding of wants and needs, and how potentially dangerous they can be. If you approach this line of work with a bag of wants and needs, you leave open the possibility of beings viewing those wants and needs and using them to manipulate you. An important step forward in the work is to look deeper beyond the surface expression of our lives that drive a sense of need, and to move towards a sense of stillness of being—to be in a space whereby a need is recognised but is not a driving force nor a truly relevant dynamic. This puts the exorcist in a position of solidity and power. You cannot be bribed and you cannot be tempted—a hostile consciousness cannot threaten you if it cannot find need within you.

***

In Summary, one of the most important things to remember in this work is that there is no good or evil. Truly there is only consciousness—and what is important is ensuring you understand what effect a particular consciousness has on you and the people or land around you. The second thing is to understand and be aware of what belongs where and why—everything has a place where it is balanced and in harmony with those around it. Demons have a home too!

Going into this work with the idea of slaying evil and saving good is going to get you in a mess really quickly. The deeper you go into this work, the more the boundaries between good and evil fade and become irrelevant. It is what is good or bad in context—a fungus is not evil, but if it invades your inner ear, it can feel like the devil incarnate in your brain. It's all relative.

Take the same approach with your body. If something is supposed to be bad for your body, be aware it might not be in certain circumstances. It is all dependant on where you are, who you are, and what you are doing. Learn to listen to your body and let it tell you how it is doing, and be thankful to it for keeping you in one piece. Learn to find coping mechanisms for your body that allow it to roll with the punches, and listen to its signals—the body is often the first one to notice that you have been attacked or invaded, and it will try to tell you. Just as you look at a potential possession with a cold eye, learn to observe your own body in the same way—it will help you stay alive.

Chapter Two
The tool kit

Before you set off to put the world to rights and put all the universal ducks in a row, you need to make, develop, and learn how to use specific magical tools that you will need for the job. The tools in this tool kit are a mixed bag of things that you would possibly or most probably need if you were up against a demonic possession or an aggressive angel. Ghosts, parasites, etc, don't normally need much in the way of tools to get rid of them, but the best tool kit is packed for all possibilities.

You will need a deck of cards specifically designed to focus on looking at a possession situation, and that can identify what beings are involved. This saves a massive amount of wasted time while you stand in front of a frothing teen asking the being who or what it is—you can just look with a shielded deck and see that the spotty youth is possessed by the discarnate spirit of Sid Vicious, a strange and wondrous being that is coaxed out of its host by a pint of lager and lime.

You will need certain resins and herbs—frankincense, osha root, wormwood, and rue—along with charcoal and a holder. (Some beings hate certain smells, I have heard of certain demons running screaming from Gloria Vanderbilt perfume....) You will also need certain sounds, things to draw beings out (demon traps), binding cloths to trap something, a marker pen to draw sigils, two stoles, tobacco, large bag of salt, A three-foot mirror, total change of clothes, ritual sword, frankincense oil, clove oil, pimento berry oil, large block of chocolate and a strong black coffee.

If it is a natural possession then the above will be all the tools you need. If the possession is the result of magic, then you will need to know the family of 'beings' that are involved in that stream of magic. For example, most possessions in the U.K. that are the result of magic tend to stem from western magic, so you would need to know about the Semitic, Roman, and Egyptian streams of beings/angels/deities/being.

In the U.S.A. the story is similar but with a heavy dose of African and Caribbean magic thrown in. That is when you need to know your limits. With regards to African magic, I know very little about it. I have come up against it a few times (Ugandan and then Ivory Coast stuff) and have witnessed the moment of possession of someone by a terrible demonic being that was sent as a result of Ugandan magic. It was not something I ever want to go through again.

What I have had to do in such circumstances is try to get in someone who knows what she is doing, or who can guide you. There will be times when you have to walk away and the ability to do that is one of the most important tools of all.

So the last tool to mention before we go into detail is a good library—you need to know the background and history of what you are up against. When you are dealing with parasites and ghosts, pfft—that's easy, its like doing housework. Intelligent powerful beings are different and you need to know your adversary.

Because of the 'new age,' there are tons of useless books out there on angels and magic, etc, and getting a good reference book on certain orders of beings is nearly impossible—you will have to compile your own. My advice, after tearing lumps of my hair out on a regular basis, is to stick with academic books, archaeology, religion, and history. That filters the bullshit and although the writers often don't understand what it is they are talking about, their ability to describe, collate, and translate information, texts, and images becomes invaluable. Learn your angels—the first most important rule.

The most useless source of all is the Solomon stuff—lots of demon stuff and angel stuff that the author/s copied from older text without understanding, and was then re-introduced to the world by the Golden Dawn and then Crowley. The lesser (and greater) key of Solomon is a virtual dead end and still to this day has people running around like headless chickens drawing that sigil and uttering this name without much useful stuff happening at all. It has to be understood in the context of the Renaissance and what was driving people at the time. If you approach such books in that way, rather than books of 'truth,' then you might find the odd snippet, seal, and pattern useful.

It is much more useful to look at Jewish texts, some Mandean artefacts, early Egyptian myths, objects and seals, early heretic gospels, Etruscan, early Roman and Greek mythology, Luristanian, Mesopotamian, and Babylonian texts, myths, and objects. From fragments of these sources you will start to see coherent patterns emerge and find bits of useful information hidden among the texts. Adding all of that to your knowledge of western ritual, visionary magic, and Christian patterning, you will start to gain good background knowledge of the kinds of beings that traverse our worlds and how they operate.

An example of how this can work is as follows (and bear in mind that I learn by the baseball bat around the head method): I was trying to get a demonic being out of a space and every time I got rid of it, another one would come back, often different but from the same order of being. I put said being back in the Abyss where it belonged and sealed up its access point out to humanity, but more kept coming. They were drawn by magic that had happened in the property and the property was sitting on land that was a natural entrance to the otherworlds. So the first task was to stop that magic happening at that spot, but that would take time for any portholes to slowly heal up.

In the meantime I had to be able to 'catch' and contain the demonic beings that were seeping through and creating havoc. Nothing that I tried worked—they got through every level of magical barrier I could think of. So I spent some time researching how things were done in the past. It led me down a very interesting road (which is a whole book in itself) regarding the relationship between demons, humans, and civilisation. I stretched back and found the most interesting patterns emerging as protections around 3000 BC to about 1500 BC after which they faded off and were replaced by more structured and complex methods.

I then looked at the methods I had found from an inner point of view and was shown some really interesting applications that spanned many octaves of consciousness, possession, and balance. So I tried it...and it worked like a dream. Phew.

What I had seen while I was researching was a repeated simple pattern that was being used first in a protective sense around names, entrances, and images. Then it developed over the span of about 1000 years to become a more complex instrument that would trap and hold beings—it was the simple, intricate inter-weaving swirls and knots that we commonly see in Celtic and Scythian art. It was also used in early Egyptian, Mesopotamian, and Semitic seals.

When I looked from an inner point of view, I was shown how a certain class of demonic (and angelic) being was attracted to shiny things and patterns—they could not resist its draw. The glitter caught their attention and their consciousness started to follow the lines of pattern and would get trapped going around and around a pattern that had no end.

Later I was shown how that same pattern could contain and sustain power, a bit like a motor. Inside yourself the pattern of existence can be used consciously to create an energy field, like the earth's magnetic field, to repel as well as attract a stream of consciousness.

The more I looked at ancient texts, artifacts, seals, and structures, the more I saw this use of patterning as a form of protection. It was eventually developed into demon bowls which used an incantation or text written in a swirl where the angelic name that trapped the being was at the end of the swirl which was painted on the inside of the bowl. The bowl would be placed upside down on the ground, land, or area where the demon was rising from.

The outside of the bowl had complex patterns upon it to also trap and seal in anything within it. Very clever!

So it could be used in two ways, one to specifically trap and contain the being, and the other way to distract beings and protect a place or thing.

So back to the porthole that was spitting out annoying demons. I narrowed the area of access of the demons in the building down to one corner, which was the most I could achieve. And in that narrow area I placed and hung objects and hangings with complex bright knot work, swirls and loops, making sure there were no depictions of animals or beings in the knot work (which is just begging for trouble). I used a gold ink pen to brighten the patterns and I placed a candle there that was bright.

The demon problem stopped immediately. It was like turning off a light switch. Now, I haven't got rid of those demons, they are just very very busy amusing themselves to this day while I work on developing enough of a relationship with the larger land beings there to slowly heal the porthole up. Once it begins to heal up, I will take the demons and put them back where they belong and that should be the end of it.

So how do you make and use these tools? Herbs/resins/incense/substances

Smells are very important in this work. They can flatten out minor stuff and prepare your body, a working space, and a tool for action. They can also help clear residue out of a host once a being has left. Certain types of beings are not able to tolerate certain smells or sounds, hence the use of incense in temples and sacred spaces. Other smells and sounds attract certain beings, so you have to be careful about what you use and why (wind chimes attract ghosts for example).

Frankincense cleans a space and tunes it nicely; rue and vervain will clear more nature-based intrusions if they are weak, or can cause an area to become uncomfortable for certain types of beings. St John's Wort is not liked by the types of beings that mess with people's minds or emotions.

Wormwood is good to use if you need to talk with the dead in their own realm, it quietens their influence in the physical space so that you can connect with them. It can also be mixed in very small doses into tobacco and smoked. Tobacco is useful to use if you need to talk to a person in the midst of work and not have your communications garbled. It 'clears' the air so that truth can be heard.

Pimento berry is very cleansing and protective during an exorcism and osha root is very good at clearing spaces, and can also be used as part of a protective talisman if a bit of root is attached in a pouch to the talisman around a person's neck.

Resins are best used on a piece of charcoal (the sort designed for incense burning), and oils can be used in tiny drips on the body and around a space.

After a hard working, eat chocolate and drink coffee to ground yourself (they are both power substances that affect the brain at a deep level). And if you need to smokescreen and talk, then use tobacco. You can make it a stronger tool by grinding osha root or a bit or wormwood and adding it into the smoke mix.

Cards (see Chapter 13)

A specifically designed tarot deck and layout can be really useful for identifying what being is doing what to whom and can quickly identify when there is mental illness involved. Don't become too reliant upon the deck—use it along with your common sense, your observations, and the symptomatic presentation. It is not beyond the realms of possibility that a demonic being can reach out to interfere with your readings and perceptions.

Do not for one minute (note the wagging finger here), when dealing with powerful demons, think that their influence is limited to the person that they are possessing—that is a dangerous and stupid mistake. A powerful demon will only be using its host as a plaything and a set of physical senses—once out in the surface world, they can reach through thoughts, magic, dreams, electricity, and life in general to mess with you and to try to stop you from doing your job. They can be physically and psychically dangerous and will stop at nothing to halt you in your tracks.

The host is their access point out into the world and that is the ground zero where you work. But they can reach you once they have made some sort of connection with you—even a phone call asking for help from the host is enough in such circumstances to make a connection. Thankfully these beings are not overly common. Once you have identified that you are dealing with such a power, you have to go into shield mode and stay there day and night until the job is done.

When you first get a call, use the deck to see what it is that you are dealing with. Keep the deck in a box or bag that has salt in it and smoke it often over frankincense. You can also use the deck to figure out what angelic or other type of being would be helpful to call upon for a specific job. You can look at the outcome both short term and long term—this is very important if using divination to look at the results of a job. A certain clearing method might be good in the short term, but counter-productive for a variety of reasons in the long term. So make sure that what you do will have lasting effects.

Binding cloth/braid and demon traps

These tools are used when there is a need to contain a being or beings under circumstances where the exorcist is unable for one reason or another to work directly in the Abyss in vision at that time. They are also used to contain the power of a magical tool so that it is not seen by demons until the moment it comes into use.

They were, apparently, used by Solomon to trap demons and make them do his bidding, which is the most stupid thing I have ever heard. If he was supposed to be wise, he had a blind spot with that one! It is most likely a myth, as far as the historical King Solomon is concerned, but it most certainly was and is a practice still used in some cultures to this day, and is not advisable. It is like saying that you can use meth as a power tool and not get affected.

Binding cloths or braids are strips of fabric or thick wool braids that are of bright colour and are woven and knotted together. They can be used in a variety of ways one of which is to 'lock' something, i.e., wrapping up a magical tool in a sealing cloth and then tying it with a binding thread to make sure nothing gets in or out. They can also be used to cover over and tie up demon traps.

The second is to 'trap' a being into the weave as you braid it up while working in vision to pull it in. This is an old method that was used a lot in SE Europe many years ago: the being would slowly be enticed by song to draw close to the singer who would be weaving. The being then becomes absorbed by the pattern of the weaving and is slowly pulled into the weave and then trapped. When that being is wanted for action, the knots or weaves would be unwoven.

Back to modern day…. If you have an object that needs heavy protection, or its power needs to be heavily contained, then you would use a cloth to wrap it in and a braid to tie it with. The cloth is most affective if you use raw silk (its shiny and has an interesting weave), upon it you would use either the primitive but affective swirls, or angelic script, Greek, Latin or paleo Hebrew script (works better than later Hebrew for some bizarre reason). It all really depends on what you are trapping or protecting, where it has come from and what beings are involved.

If you are sealing in the power of a magical instrument, then a script that is connected to the power/line of the implement is best used. If you are trapping a demon that has been accessed via ritual magic, then use the script most associated with that line of magic. If you have no idea what the hell it is or if it is a more natural indigenous demonic being, then use the swirls in as many complex intricate ways as you can.

Paint the text or pattern on the cloth, wrap whatever you have used to trap the being in the cloth with the swirls facing inward, and then bind it with the braid. Finally, put the whole thing in another cloth or a box that has the swirls on the outside and a key that has knots or a knotted rope around it. That should keep the bugger in for a good while until you are ready to take the being in vision and put it back where it belongs.

Clothing/robes

When you do any type of magical clearing or exorcism, you can guarantee that there is going to be a lot of psychic sludge/dirt involved in the building, on the people, and on yourself. The first step is to get sensitive to this type of inner dirt if you are not already. Then you will learn to feel such sludge on your body, your clothing, and tools.

If you want to get a small example of the feeling, go around charity/thrift shops and junk shops. Handle all sorts of things, try clothes on, etc, and then see how your hands and body 'feels.' Then wash your hands in a mix of salt, soap, and water. You will feel the difference immediately. Then take a ritual salt bath so that you are clean, and put on thrift/used clothing that has not been washed and see how they feel. Sit with them on for a little while— see how they affect your emotions and your thoughts. If you are very sensitive, you will feel that the clothing is grimy or greasy.

Building up that level of sensitivity is very important in this type of work. You need to be able to feel sludge straight away and be able to identify where or who it is coming from.

From a working clothing point of view, have a couple of outfits that you use for the work and when you wash them, always throw a little salt in the machine with them. Make sure that the clothing you choose has no images of people or creatures on them—you might find the odd spirit will decide that it can jump into your clothing and it can be freaky to have the image of Jim Morrison that is on your T shirt speaking to you in the middle of the night.

This is one of the uses of robes, but then such use is a minefield of drama and ego—it is often best just to have a couple of pairs of jeans and sweaters that you can use. When you have finished your work, strip off and put the clothing in a plastic bag or bin liner and tie it up. Put on fresh clothing to go home. Never go home in the clothes that you have worked in—you could end up sludging everything around you. Once you have ritually bathed, put on yet another set of fresh clothing and throw all the others in the machine.

If you do opt to use robes, then I would suggest just a simple white cassock to go over your clothing. I have seen some people use very glam intricate robes with all sorts of magical and spiritual symbols on them which is really asking for trouble. The more complexity within the clothing, the more likely it is that something will get attracted to the patterns or faces and decide to hop aboard for a ride.

Magical implements

The only magical implement I have used in an exorcism is a ritually consecrated sword with a sharp blade. This is not a good idea if you have a short fuse and a bad temper....

The sword is not used as a sword per say, but as a being in its own right playing its own part. The ritual sword of an exorcist usually has an angelic power flowing through it and its job is to bring that presence to the table. The sword would be unbound and placed in the room (out of arms reach of the host), usually behind the exorcist or to one side or held point down in its cruciform shape. It is an inner tool that can be drawn upon, it is not pointed at anyone and is not used to threaten anyone at any time.

It creates a situation where a bag of power is released in the room for the exorcist to work with or draw upon. It also protects you as you work, holding back certain inner powers so that they cannot interfere with you.

To create a ritual sword of this type, there are two main ways; one is to connect with a raw angelic power without its human framework i.e. not using any names or images, just its function or power. The second is to work with named and identified beings. Both have their ups and downs and limitations. Because you often do not know what you are going to be up against in the role of the exorcist, then I have personally found it better to work with a form of angelic power that is identified purely by its function.

I have used specified angelic beings before, but usually more in a guardian or short-term protective role.

To choose the power of angelic being that you want to work with you have to think very carefully about what powers you are going to be up against and ensure that what you draw upon is going to match that. There are angelic powers of justice, judgement, balance, death, destruction, fire, air, etc, and sometimes a working couple can forge within the sword to give you a powerful working combination—just make sure that they do actually get on and work well in harmony.

To create that form of a sword, you need a blade with no markings upon it and a plain hilt. After the usual preparations, go with the sword into the void and call upon the angel/s that you wish to work with. As they appear in the void, in vision, step into them with the blade and tell them what you are trying to achieve.

The first layer of the sword is put in at this level as they work through your imagination and hands—you will witness them changing and putting things into the sword and they may also tell you about how it works. They will often blow into your mouth, or put things into your body for you to mediate into the sword. When they have finished, you back out of that angel, going back into the void where you stay for a moment in silence. While you are in the void in vision, you place the sword to you mouth or hands and you mediate whatever was put into you into the sword by a 'laying on' of hands or by breathing down the blade.

Finally, you step back out of the void, open your eyes, and raise the sword to the flame or altar and outwardly ask that the angel of (name of whatever you are working with) to complete and seal in the power of the sword to make it whole. You then leave the sword by the flame to be worked on while you go out and leave the room. You will feel when it is finished and you can go back in to blow out the candle.

If you chose to work with a specific named angel, then the inner method is more or less the same but when it is finished, you would engrave the name of the angel is its original script on the blade. So if it is a Hebrew name, then you would use Hebrew script.

There is a version of the work where you would go in vision to the Abyss and connect with the angelic consciousness there, but I would not really recommend it. The further into the inner worlds you go, the less grounded the contact will be in the sword. If you want an inner consciousness to work with you through a physical object, then it is better to bring them as close as possible to your world.

A most extreme version of that is to bring the angelic being out of the void and into your realm and have the angel work on the sword through your body. That can be very powerful indeed, but it can also have a massive physical impact on your body.

When you have finished your sword, make a sheath for it that is covered in patterning that will stop things getting into it and also down its power when needed. Sometimes they need to be 'on' with you at home, and sometimes you will need them to be quiet. At that time, wrap them or sheath them but be aware that their vigilance is not working when they are bound up.

When you first start to work with the sword, use your deck to see exactly what you have put into the sword as opposed to what you wanted in the sword, and use the deck to track how it would assist you in certain situations.

Sigils and seals

Signs and sigils are used for all sorts of things from binding cloths to stoles, altar cloths, door seals, etc. The sigil of an angelic being is a doorway that its power can connect through—it is a fragment of that being that you can use as if the angelic being was working with you. Learn a small vocabulary of angelic sigils and what they do—there are plenty of references out in the world to John Dee's angelic script and the angelic sigils. Just don't fall into the badly researched new age 'expert' book trap.

When you are faced by a very serious possession and nothing you have tried works, the drawing upon the forehead, heart, and hands of the victim who is possessed will often either severely weaken the hold the demon has upon the person, or it will get it out all together. This is an extreme method that uses force and although it works, it is better to be more in control and able to put the being back where it came from.

If you are ready for it, and you are quick in vision and are very focussed, you can pull out the being while drawing the sigil upon the person. You need to be able to do two things at once in difficult circumstances.

The sigils are very useful to employ immediately after the demonic being is pulled out, to seal up the person and protect them.

It would also be a very good idea to have already-consecrated water and salt handy with you as a part of your tool kit, and have plenty of extra salt to consecrate if you need it. The water cleans and the salt absorbs—use them separated in bowls around the room where you are working. Also have some combined and ready to use on someone if they need it.

Stoles for use on the host would also be a very good thing to have in your bag of tricks. Have a consecrated stole with angelic sigils on the ends and the back neck piece, and magically create it as a silencer—the angelic being connected to the stole needs to be one that will protect the human rather than battle the demon. Putting the stole around the neck of an out of control rabid host should quieten things down so that work can begin.

Summary

The most important thing that you could have in your tool box is common sense and grounding. Know your beings, know your inner sigils and be able to be calm and focussed in the centre of chaos. The other skill to really develop is a good bullshit meter, and the ability to not lose your temper in the face of ignorance and stupidity. I once got called out in the middle of the night to attend to a possessed Christian teen. I drove for 2 hours at 4am and when I got there I found a distressed teen who just didn't want to go to boot camp because she had been found smoking weed.

Be ready to work without your tool kit. Don't get dependant on anything in this work—you need to be able to work with nothing if confronted with a surprise situation. If anything, salt would be the only thing I would really want handy in an unexpected situation and it is something that can be easily obtained. I used to waitress in a greasy spoon and used the salt pots many times to 'clear' something out of the café when a heavily parasited customer left. I found covert ways of doing things while wiping down tables, washing dishes, and slapping food down in front of someone while conducting a rite of cleansing over the crawling customers—they just thought I had a salt fetish.

Chapter Three
Working with Beings

There are many different types of beings that you might encounter in your work as an exorcist and you should never assume that because a being is not a demon or parasite that it is not harmful or dangerous: that could be a very stupid mistake (one that I have made often).

It is back to the understanding that life is not simple and straightforward with good on one side and bad on the other. Anything can be bad for you if it doesn't follow your agenda—a good dose of Ebola virus will focus your mind on beings that are not inherently bad within themselves but are bad for you. I'm sure that if you were infected, and laid on a bed with blood squishing out of your eyeballs, you would feel like the greatest of all demons was eating you alive.

Also be prepared for encountering consciousness that is completely off your radar. Don't be too ready to give a being a tag or name—by doing that you might actually miss what the being is and therefore not be able to get rid of it or work with it. Living human spirits can possess other living humans, angels can possess humans, the list of weird and wonderful permutations of invaders is breathtaking. (Hey, do you have any ancient Sumerian bone eating spirit in you?...want some?)

While you digest the fact that anything and everything can invade just about anything and everything, be aware that there is a really stupid idiosyncrasy that humans have—they melt at cute faces. In the world of an exorcist, nothing is cute, nothing is harmless, and you take nothing for granted—children are not born sweet, puppies shit everywhere, and yes your mother-in-law is an alien. If something has big soft gentle eyes, that is good: it means the target is easier to hit when you have to poke them out. If you are easily taken in by fluff, spin, or sob stories, then don't be an exorcist straight away—go work for central government and be a therapist for members of parliament; that will be all the preparation that you need.

The other thing to remember is that the wide variety of beings that you could potentially take out of someone can also be potential co-workers. You will work with a variety of beings in your job and you must not have prejudices regarding certain beings—you just need lots of common sense and strict boundaries. You will make mistakes, they will be hard and painful, but you will learn a lot from them and you will learn about the beings from direct experience, not some poky 17th century magician's version of dungeons and dragons.

The first set of beings we will look at have had the worst and longest history of being misunderstood, abused, ridiculed, and deballed. Angels have had to suffer the indignity of their image being dressed up in spangled frocks and Birkenstocks, and made to tend people's cabbages...Findhorn has a lot to answer for!

Angels

The first thing to remember about angels is that they were not invented by Judaism. Most if not all western ritual magic today relies heavily on the names, hierarchies, and systems developed by Semitic peoples—but angels did exist before that!

The next thing to understand is that angels are not constructs of humanity, were not invented by anyone, and they have no sense of humour (I know, I tried...). They are thresholds between non-existence and existence. They are messengers, doorways, weavers, destroyers—they manifest the action of Divinity, and they ensure the manifestation of Universal patterns.

They only appear to us as vaguely human sometimes because otherwise they would scare the shit out of us. But if you can step beyond that, they appear as fire, as wind, as sand, as stars, and their deeper forms are platonic solids and geometric shapes. A mathematician who does deep magic might see them as mathematical script and a nature worker might see them as the elements or particles in full force.

For the work of an exorcist, all the many different manifestations have a place and a use, and none should be discounted. There will be times to work with angels in their Semitic expressions, other times to work with them by function and others still to work with them in their raw form. It depends on what you are doing, why, and where.

So before we look at angels are helpers, co-workers or guides, let's look at the negative aspect of a possession that involves an angel. If an angel is doing damage to a person, then it has to be ascertained whether it is supposed to be doing that or not. Usually if an angelic being is just doing its job, then you and said victim will know nothing about it and it will just happen.

Bound angels and ritual attacks

If an angel is attempting to destroy someone and you pick up on it, then chances are it has been bound or chained into service by ritual magic and is being operated by someone. The most common presentation of such an angel is usually in a form of an angel of air or fire. Sometimes you will come across a 'named' one, i.e., Samael (a favourite with magicians who have no ethics, a bad temper, and a mental age of six) in which case you have to deal with them in context of the culture that the name came from.

Some angels have been bound in service for centuries by the use of ritual magic, usually Kabbalistic, and because they are beings of operation, some humans figured out how to capture and operate them for their own will. One very interesting thing I discovered while working on a bound angel was that its presentation (part eagle, part lion, and loads of impressive wings, talons, eyes, and weapons) was a direct result of the binding. As soon as I managed to unbind it (after nearly killing myself in the process), it completely transformed into a different being. It told me that its presentation was the effect of the magic and clued the magician as to what its capabilities were in a visual language that humans could understand. Interesting, huh?

This mentality of binding and subduing is the basis behind the magic expressed in the greater and lesser key of Solomon—also known as magic for retards. Do you go around kidnapping government workers, bankers, shop keepers, delivery men, and 'bend' them to your will? No. If you need something you ask them or employ them.

Slavery went out of fashion quite a while ago. So why do it in the inner realms? The need to capture angels or demons and bend them to your will shows a distinct lack of intelligence, maturity, and a huge inferiority complex. It also shows intense ignorance about how to work magically with angels and demons.

But surprisingly it still happens and is a technique that is handed down through magical lines along with the bound angels and demons.

Here is a practical example:

Not too long ago, I started to get dangerously ill. Nothing was helping, and I and others went into the inner worlds to see what was happening. I had an angel chained to my ass with orders to destroy me. (I have tended to piss off a few prominent Kabbalists. It's a particular skill that I have.)

So I worked in ritual and vision, and asked the angel if its orders of death came from God. He said no (thankfully angels don't lie, they are very open about who, what, and where, and they are also very Aspergers). I asked the angel who had sent him and he willingly told me all that I needed to know. I pointed out to the angel that death can only be the will of God and not the will of man. The angel agreed but said that he had been commanded, and because he was magically bound in service, he had to do as he was told. The angel then showed me the terrible energetic burden he carried from the suffering he had caused by being bound in service, and that the binding had been there for a long time. I asked him if he would still destroy me if I managed to find a way to release him. The angel said that if he was released, I would not be destroyed unless God willed it.

I looked and saw a chain attached to the angel's leg and as I looked closer, it appeared as a braid of words and sounds that felt like metal when you touched them. Before I could decide what to do, I had a deep instinct to eat the words that bound the angel. It took a while and when the binding was gone, the angel marked me, (Hey dudes, got a spell eater here.... Look out for this one if you get stuck....) and was gone.

For weeks I had a terribly inflamed intestines/colon, nausea, etc, but the deathly cold and weakness was gone, and besides my insides processing the magic, I felt great.

That was a whole revelation to me and set me off in a line of research that I am still digesting (ha) regarding the binding of angels and demons in religion and magic. I was horrified to see how much it was and still is practiced in certain quarters, and explains a lot about why angels really don't like a lot of humans.

The binding of angels to attack usually happens in relation to curses rather than possession but it is something that has to be taken into consideration when you are first making an assessment of a host.

Angelic beings will appear as humanoid beings with many wings, or as wheels of fire, or as geometric shapes, or they may appear as a platonic solid suspended above the head or buried deep in the body of the victim. Most tribal societies don't work with these beings in a cursing/attacking sense. It tends to be more in a community that uses ritual magic or the mystical arms of the monotheistic religions. One major exception to the rule is Tibetan magic which is a category all of its own.

But in the strict cases of possession, you are much more likely to work with an angel as a helper rather than as a problem. From this point on, most angels will be talked about in plural as angels tend to be like money problems—one divides into many and is endless.

Working in vision with angels

The ways to work with angels are many and vary from ritual, to simple calling, or to visionary working. It all depends on what you need and why. Visionary work with angels is the least well known method but can be very effective, although it can knock the shit out of your body if you are not careful.

When you work in vision, you are using the imagination as an interface so that your spirit can work in the inner worlds and interact with beings that have no outer body expression that you can work with. It is not psychology or wishful thinking—that is the therapy domain and has no use in the work of an exorcist.

When you work in vision, the mind passes through the imagination into an inner arena and the inner contacts and beings can use the content and structure of your imagination to find a common vocabulary that you can both use to communicate. So when you 'see' something in vision, it is not often literally what you are seeing, but it is the signature or vocabulary of what that being actually is—an angel of air will appear with wings and eyes to tell you it's an angel and can see a lot. When it no longer has to do that, because you have gotten used to the feel of it, it will appear as a tornado or as a geometric shape.

The more you get used to working in vision, the less you will eventually see and the more you will feel as your brain gets used to interpreting things beyond its comprehension. Because various branches/races within humanity have a wide variety of things in common, the visions of major beings like angels are all held in common—they are seen in very similar ways all over the world. That is because we all have certain things in our imaginations in common, so our interpretations of certain powers can be very similar.

One thing to be aware of when you are working with angels in vision: it's bloody hard work! The vision, although playing out through your imagination, is actually a real energetic contact which impacts the whole body. Be prepared to be wiped out by working in vision with angels—it's like carrying lumps of stone uphill while having toddlers crying at your ankles and your mother nagging you on the phone all at once. You can end up bruised, aching, and irritable while sporting a smacking headache. And the cure is coffee, lots of it.

Sandalphon

The Sandalphon are a great lot to work with and they have somewhat of a sense of humour. Maybe they have to, as they were commissioned to be companions to humans and one must have a great sense of humour to be able to take humanity seriously.

The Sandalphon work as close companions when you are operating in service in the human realm. As an exorcist, even if you are working up and down the Abyss, you are still operating within the human realm as you are approaching the various levels from a human starting point—from the 'humanity ledge' which is our world.

If you are going deep down into the Abyss, then just the fact that you appear as human is like painting a large juicy target on your head. The Sandalphon can help by disguising you and walking beside you.

Many years ago I had a dream of a being walking beside me through a desert, his legs vanishing into the earth up to his knees and his hair trailing behind him on the ground. He told me about the golden city, about death and the holy of holies, and he disguised me by blowing sand over me until I looked like a stone. I asked him who he was and he said:

"I am he upon whom you lay between the stars and the underworld, I am the rock upon which you stand, the grains of sand beneath your feet, I am around and within you, I am completion."

Well that was all good and profound but I still didn't have a bloody clue who or what he was. He began to turn up whenever I was working in the desert by the Abyss and then two of them began working with me. Over the years they have saved my ass more times than I can count and taught me a great deal, but it took me a few years to get the information out of them that identified them as Sandalphon.

Then, me being the great intelligence that I am, I assumed they were called Sandalphon because they were always in the desert (sand...clever, huh?). It was only fairly recently that I came across the Greek word 'Synadelfos' which means co-worker, and the penny finally dropped. I guess I am beginning to understand why angels sort of look at me in despair sometimes when I am working.

Practicalities of the Sandalphon

They will walk along side you in the desert if you call upon them as you emerge out of the void towards the Abyss. They will assist in holding a being with you (not for you) and if you have to go deep into the Abyss, they will disguise you as an earth type being (sand, rock). They will teach you how to inwardly bind a being up and put it into storage, and similarly how to release beings that have been bound in the desert. Just be careful that if you get the urge to release something that you know what it is and why it is there.

As you walk across the desert towards the Abyss, you will see many beings, usually angels, bound up like cocoons and placed at the edge of the desert. These are beings that do not have a shelf life like the beings of the Abyss—they are immortals and have been bound to stop them expressing themselves in life and death. They will be released when the time is right and when their power is needed out in the universe. Until that time they stay cocooned and sleeping (so don't get the urge to free them...).

The one thing the Sandalphon will not do is to go 'up' the Abyss. They have a stone-like density to them, which enables them to go deep into the Abyss, but that density prohibits them from going up to less formed areas within the Abyss.

The Barakiel

The Barakiel are an interesting lot and are taken up with protection and justice for innocent victims, accompanying new life as it falls into generation, striking things/lightening, electricity, etc, and they will work with you if there is a heavy possession of an innocent.

There are two main ways to work with them: bring them to you without vision or go to them in vision. If you bring them to you, it can be very effective but you often end up with a flurry of dead cows in the neighbourhood (lightening strikes). If the possession is serious though, it might be necessary to just bite the lightening so to speak and get on with it.

If the possession is subtle, then you can go to them in vision either for them to come back and work with you, or you can take the victim there in vision for them to work on the soul. It can be very dangerous for a variety of reasons, so they are very much a last resort in some cases, but they are effective. If there is cursing of an innocent, then they can be very good.

The way that they work in such circumstances is that they will strip the deepest part of the possession or curse from a person, so that you as exorcist have a popped boil to work with. They won't do the whole thing, but they will do what is beyond you to do and they will also set in motion a chain of fate, in the event of a curse, to rebalance the scales.

If you call them to you, do it on sacred ground. The reason for this is that they are a very powerful consciousness and are not regularly worked with, so the path for them is steep, i.e. the energy filters are not well used, so they can cause damage. If you are on sacred ground, that filters them a little. I work in a church when I have to call them in.

Stand in both the void and the outside world, and inwardly call on them to assist you. If you cannot work in a church, then open your working space properly, using the east for an altar and a flame. Set up a sacred space with the directions so that there is an inner vessel to hold them.

If you are going to them, the vision to get to them is below.

The best way to work with these beings is to go to them if you are in a dangerous situation as an exorcist and ask them to work with you or to work upon you to strengthen you. The way they affect the body is through electricity. They work through the brain and nerves, which is precisely the area, along with the endocrine system, that gets burned out with magical attacks, fielding demons, and clashing with angels. They champion people on the front line as long as you don't step off the fence—the minute you cast judgement on a being, or attack, or lash out, they will strike you.

When you work with them, their action is twofold: to uphold your body in the face of demonic attack, and to rebalance fate in a lightening strike. When you take on the role of exorcist, you wipe your slate clean and get to work. If you muddy your slate, particularly while working with them, the rebalance of that slate is quick, sharp, and dangerous. Slap a demon while you are in a bad temper and a bolt of lightening slaps you. You can just see the wagging finger in the sky....

Sometimes they will also give you work to do. You crawl to them on your hands and knees, exhausted from battling a demon and you ask for their help. They will give you help and then sometimes also a job that needs a human touch—down time is not in the angelic language.

The following vision can be used to go to them for help, training, upholding, or putting back together if you have had a very nasty time. But they will only help if you are innocent—they will not help if you are being attacked by a demon that you yourself summoned. They will also not help if you are working as exorcist and your host brought the demonic influence into themselves by their actions with violence, sex, drugs, etc. The whole fluffy bunny expression 'they had a bad childhood' as an excuse for bad behaviour does not wash with these beings.

The vision of the Barakiel

Sit quietly before a candle and close you eyes. See the landscape around you with your inner vision and look up to the sky. Notice clouds gathering as if a storm is coming in. Lightening begins to strike all around you and you remember your intention to go to the Barakiel. You call out to them in vision and a bolt of lightening strikes the ground close to you and time freezes. The lightening bolt stays, like a ladder, going up into the clouds.

You climb onto the lightening and step up and up into the clouds until you are at the top of the lightening strike and out in the stars. All around is you is darkness and bright stars, and you reach out to touch them. You hand feels something that you cannot see and you realise that there is a structure before you that is clothed in night and stars.

Stepping off the lightening, you find yourself walking along a tunnel of stars until you come to an entrance into complete darkness. You are reminded of the Abyss and the need to trust the powers that are all around you. You step out into the darkness and find yourself stepping into a cave that vanishes deep into something. You are drawn to walk down the dark passageway where you come to wall of fire.

You know you must walk through it and as you step into it, you find yourself unable to move forward. Things are burned from you, magic, illnesses, rage, fire magic connections, all lifted from you, and you realise you are stood in a filter. Stepping out, you feel very different and you begin to understand how much you carry around with you.

As you walk on you see a wall of water before you and you know it is another filter. You step in and find yourself being washed of emotions that you have hung onto, hate, pain, sorrow are all washed from you and as you stand there, you begin to see how the emotions are a body expression but are not part of your soul. You begin to detach and look at your emotive structure as a human, and how that structure allows your soul to express itself in life.

Stepping forward you walk further into the passage and see a wall of falling sand that you must walk through—yet another filter to prepare you for meeting the Barakiel. The sand pours over you and abrades you. It rubs your skin and stings, but in some places it fills holes, gives ballast, and strengthens your bones. You feel the strength that substance can give you, and you begin to understand why the soul searches for physical expression, for life.

As you step out of the sand a sharp and powerful wind blows all around you, filling your lungs and screaming in your head. You find yourself trapped in a tornado which pulls words out of you, and shows you the power of those words. Your breath takes on form as you struggle to breathe and the form stands before you—the Word that is God and that is humanity stands before you as you begin to see the power of recitation.

The wind pushes you forward and you fall out of the tornado. Looking back you see that four angels stood in the passageway—the thresholds of the elements that make up humanity. They have prepared your body, mind, and soul for the meeting with the Barakiel in vision—to meet such beings in vision without preparation is to dance with death. A hand is placed upon your shoulder and you turn to see an angelic guardian waiting to take you into the hall of the Barakiel.

You are led down the passageway into a large circular hall with thirteen beings stood in a circle. You are placed in the middle and one of them speaks to you. They ask you who you are, why you have come and what do you want. You must answer with what comes to you first, not what you decide to say.

From your answer they will decide if they are going to help you or not. Commune with the beings, and be willing to do whatever they ask you to do.

When you have finished and you are ready to go. The floor beneath you vanishes and you find yourself falling away from the hall and falling through stars. One of the Barakiel falls with you in the form of a shooting star and you fall together towards the earth.

You fall through a storm with lightening and you see the Barakiel all around you in their conversation with the land as the lightening bounces back and forth.

You fall towards the room where you first started and if you are going to work with the Barakiel, they fall in with you. When you are ready, open your eyes and begin your work or blow out the candle.

***

If you are going to use the Barakiel vision with a victim, take their spirit into your arms and carry it with you as you do the vision—do not speak it out to the person. It is best though, if you need the Barakiel with you when you are working, to do the vision away from the victim. Once the Barakiel are with you in your world, they will stay with you as you go to work on the victim/host.

Sigils/signs/names

Another way that you can work with angelic beings is through sigils and names. If you have a demonic being that is of a particular line that responds to Semitic structures, then sometimes just draping the host with a stole embossed with the name of a specific angel and breathing the name of the angel into the human can be enough for the being to start to move out.

Drawing sigils upon the host is also another way of forcing a being out if needs be. The names or sigils of angels can also be used to seal a space that you are working in, or to lock beings out of a space or person once they have been cleaned.

The sigils for angels come from a variety of sources: some can be found in the work of Dr John Dee, some are in and around various ancient sites and will remain obscure until an angel shows you it—then the markings on stones and old icons you have seen suddenly begin to make sense. For example: the Barakiel can be connected to humans via the use of a lightening Z with a small star at the side of it (Z∗). The Barakiel showed me this to use, alongside a figure of 8 that lies horizontally through the abdomen of a human and would pass in and out of the body like an energy circuit.

Those two images are shown together on Pictish stones carved in Scotland, which I found very interesting. Very possibly a coincidence, seeing as the images themselves are common enough. But I found it really interesting to find them together in exactly the way I was working with them.

If the angelic being you are working with is operating through a Semitic filter, i.e. it has a Hebrew name and operates through that personality, then you can use the name of the angel written in Hebrew as a sigil. I have found by sheer luck (with me it is never intelligent deduction) that for some reason Proto-Hebrew script is a lot more successful than more modern versions of the alphabet.

The name or sigil can be used to seal, protect, heal, or banish. Just be careful how you use them—as with all magic, intent is the major fuel and if you are a natural mediator of power, and you draw an angelic name on someone with intent, you are potentially pulling a lot of power through into someone. That doesn't mean don't experiment—just experiment on yourself rather than someone else, so that you can learn directly from the experience without getting into trouble for blowing up the cat or the neighbour's first born child.

The options of which angels to work with can be endless as there are so many of them in their various forms. Like homeopathic remedies, you will find that there are certain families of angels that work with certain types of people of certain blood lines and cultures. I accumulated my 'family' of angelic beings just by luck, chance, stupidity, and inner ability.

I would suggest that you work with a very small amount of beings and get to know how to work well with them. From there your experience will expand along with your introductions to other angelic beings. The ones that have been most prominent for me have been the Sandalphon, the Barakiel, the Irin, Samael, a nameless angel of air, a nameless angel of fire, Gabriel (in its non-fluffy form…as an angel of death), Uriel, Metatron, and a very large dude that I know is angelic but I have absolutely no idea who/what/where or why it is. It/he turned up one day and announced that he was 'stationed' to work with me. The poor being looked like he had been put on potty emptying duty and did not seem overly thrilled with his job.

Summary

Only use angelic beings when heavy magic, demonic influence, or major power shifts are happening. They are not needed for hauntings, parasite possessions (unless really big), and faery infestations. These beings are one of a number of tools and helpers that you can work with, and learning a healthy respect for them will take you a long way.

Most cultures will tell you that you could not possibly work with them because you are not a priest/prophet/messiah/god. Total bullshit, that is just a human power grab, which is a by-product of religion. But at the same time, they are not soft fluffy helpers hanging around to help at the drop of a hat, and who are here solely for our convenience. Be wary of reading up on angels by way of new age websites—they are all copied from one another and are full of inaccuracies, fantasy, and wishful thinking. Look to Hebrew text, biblical and Koranic text, Egyptian history, Mesopotamian images and histories, and early church carvings. They will all tell you much more about angels than anything else, and don't forget the beings themselves—they can also tell you, you just need to ask.

Chapter 4
Beings you may encounter

Before an exorcist begins the tenuous task of convincing large obnoxious demons to 'move it along,' it's a really good idea that he knows what it is he is dealing with, where it has come from, and where it needs to go. We have covered the tools and helpers needed to conduct an exorcism, so now comes the first juicy bit...what is it that you are taking out?

The juiciest of all are the demons, so we will start there as I was always a dessert first child. As I have said before in this book, demons are not evil, they can just seem that way to us when they cross into our realm. What they are is conditional which is what makes them so dangerous, unpredictable, and appealing when they come into our lives.

Demons
There are many types of demons and the closer to our realm they are, the closer to our consciousness they are, which makes it easier for them to attach to us. There are many 17th century theoretical texts about demon names and their descriptions, and those texts have very little relevance to today's current situation. Contrary to popular belief, knowing a demon's name alone does

not give you power over it, knowing its behaviour pattern, its wants and needs and where it came from (and therefore where it needs to go back to) is far more useful.

Most demons (when inhabiting humans) tend not to stick themselves to ceilings, spit fire, or talk in ancient languages—only the ones who live in Hollywood do that (when they are not stood on street corners selling star maps). They operate through the human, using the human's memory, thought pattern, and latent abilities.

Because they work 'through' the human as opposed to 'in' the human, normally suppressed emotions, behaviours, and even medical conditions will come to the fore. This is what makes a possession assessment so difficult: the symptoms of possession and of certain medical conditions are very similar, with only subtle differences. This is why it is a very good idea for an exorcist to have a solid understanding of the basic mechanisms of the human body: you must be able to recognise the signals that the body puts out when it is in distress and be able to understand what those signals are saying.

A demonic being will use the memories and emotions of a host to drive the host into a behaviour that feeds it. So if it is a demonic being that feeds off negative emotion, then the body will be driven into situations where negative emotions can express themselves. All normal conditioning that would filter a person's wish to act on an emotion is removed, so that when a victim feels hate, for example, he or she will act upon it. This is also a symptom of certain mental illnesses, which is why an exorcist has to first ensure the victim undergoes medical assessment.

If you have a possession where the being is playing through more subtle manipulative emotive patterns, then chances are it is a parasite rather than a demonic being. Demonic beings that are closer to humanity tend to operate more on the spectacular side of emotions so that they can get a good whack of energy and then express their function, like destruction, death, or torture on a grand scale.

So a demonic possession is more likely to become involved in mass murder, destruction of a group, place, or structure, or major societal/cultural interference. Deeper demonic beings are seen very rarely but when they do emerge they are huge, they work through major power structures or land/weather patterns and tend to cause massive change in our cultures.

A parasite on the other hand is usually happy to make do with unstable emotions, weird sexual acts, drugs, more personalised violent acts, etc.

Type of demonic beings

The most common type of demonic being that we see in our realm tend to be ones that are fairly close to us from an inner evolutionary point of view, and if you are working in the Abyss, they are relatively close to our 'section' of the Abyss. (For more detailed information on the Abyss see appendix 1 'Notes on the Abyss.')

These types of beings have very similar wants and needs to humans, and some of them were once human, just as some angels were once human. So when you are dealing with these types of beings, you have to keep in mind that the being will think in a way very similar to humanity—you will have to be careful not to get drawn into playing psychological chess when dealing with this type of being.

Their ability to follow a human line of thought and to be able to mimic certain cultural characteristics makes them very difficult to isolate away from the human when you are assessing the host. You have to carry out your assessment on other manifestations of the possession, and ignore the verbal and non-verbal communications. This level of being is very difficult to spot and can often appear to be a mental illness. There are ways to draw the being out which will make it far more obvious that it is not an illness, but it would be wise to always have a doctor present when dealing with this level of being.

The further down the Abyss and therefore further away from humanity the demonic beings are, the bigger and more dangerous they become. These beings tend not to inhabit single people (although sadly it can happen), but tend to work through larger collections of humans. Their agenda tends to be something that will feed them longer term, and about establishing themselves as a living force in the surface world. These beings are very dangerous, not just to individuals, but to groups and societies in general. It is not something you would tackle alone as an exorcist, but something that a focussed group would work on over a generation. The trick is to not get drawn into the agenda for good or bad—stay neutral and get a job done. The other thing I have found with some of these larger demonic beings that flow through a structure is that they are often doing an important job: aiding in the breaking down of a structure that is decaying. This is what I think the natural function of a demonic being is: to assist in an end to something corrupt.

Every being in existence has a purpose and beings only become problems when they are in the wrong place. It is also a matter of overview: if a demonic being is aiding and accelerating an unhealthy situation to facilitate its demise, then that being is doing a service. But if you are a part of that situation and you don't want it to end, then the demonic being becomes an adversary as far as you are concerned—it's all a matter of perspective.

Between the two extremes there are loads of variants that present in the outside world and men have spent generations writing heavy tomes on the names and attributes of the many thousands of demons that populate the Abyss. Really useful.... When a demon is charging at you out of a victim at the speed of light, speaking its name is going to do...what exactly? Stop it in its tracks so that it can shake hands and practice good manners?

One of the first practical lessons I learned as an exorcist was that these beings really don't give a damn if you know its name. That name is nothing to do with it—the name is a construct of humanity used to identify it. Yes, you can use the name to call it, but why the hell would you want to call it, anyhow? The whole theory that knowing the name of a demon gives you control over it is total bullcrap—and can become very dangerous bullcrap.

Hence all the confused Catholic exorcists out there who were trained to find the name of the being, and that knowledge not giving them the power to remove the being, only to engage it further and wind it up. There are a large percentage of demonic texts that were written from theory, and relying on that sort of a source in a life-or-death situation is just plain silly.

I know there is a whole body of thought that uses demonic names to call them out of the Abyss so that people can get used to banishing them—not a very bright idea. What the demons failed to tell the very bright person who thought that one up is that if you use a name, it narrows the field of action down to the attributes of that name. But the being is so much more than that, and when you banish that name, you are only sending off part of the being. When you call it by name, all of it will come by choice. When you banish by name, only the named part is affected, so it doesn't really work. That is why they are so happy to be summoned by hapless trainee wizards in their goth clothing—they get to be invited out to tea.

And when you summon such a being out to tea, by inviting it, you disengage a whole host of intertwined protections, guardians, and safety nets—it plays straight into their hands. When a human invites a demon, it releases the protective net that stops the demon rising out of the Abyss. And when you try to banish them using their name, you only banish a part of them—the rest gets to hang out and parasite off the closest victims.

This, then, illustrates the wisdom about trusting the inner worlds to do their jobs and you do yours—the complex beautiful weave that is our universe has many layers that work together in perfect imbalance. Our problems come when we interfere with that weave and then try to over-control the mop up. There are lots of checks and balances in operation, far too many to understand, but they do work and the trick is to figure out what you don't need to do.

So in all, the general types of demonic beings that tend to express in our world are:

1. Smaller human-connected ones that are trying to live a life on the 'surface' and live by means of feeding their conditionality usually through extremism of personality.

2. Medium-sized demonic beings that express in a single or small amount of humans through the build up and then execu-

tion of an act that will generate bigger amounts of power, such as mass murder, suicides, sex deaths, or other violent acts.

3. Large, deep, and ancient demonic beings that express through society, government, land mass, or large groups of people, and basically drive the lemmings over the cliff. They will manoeuvre a large amount of people to behave in an extreme way that will end in war, murder, or suicides. They are sometimes intent on creating an environment that will suitable for them to live in the human world indefinitely.

As far as all the listings of demons names and attributes go, they are interesting and sometimes mildly useful, but to put it in context the variety of demons is about the same as the variety of humans. So having the names and characteristics of a few humans is hardly going to give you a handle on how to deal with any human in any given situation. Also don't forget that those texts all speak from a Judaeo-Christian standpoint—most demons are not religious.

Where do demons come from?

This is an interesting question that opens many other questions for me. Were demonic beings around before humanity? Or are they a part of the family of beings that are the braid that is humanity in its various waves? I have no idea and that path is a long complex and difficult one to walk down if one wants to work on the inner to find an answer. I don't have time to do that, I'm too busy peeling beings off stoned teens and out of buildings.

For us in today's world I would say that the demonic beings that are in our world have been pulled, coaxed, and invited out of their world by a variety of human acts and that activity is accelerating. It might also be that there is a natural order in place and we are in a time of decay which is facilitating more beings to 'leak' through into our world.

Most of the time when people summon demonic beings, they fail miserably and are content to have witnessed a whiff of smoke or a haze which they are convinced is a 'sign' of demonic presence (it can be a sign of presence, but it can be a presence of any being of moderate power). But occasionally someone who is a natural talent will summon up a nasty and then have no idea how to get rid of them. In that circumstance the being usually inhabits one or more of the humans present and is thankful for a chance to play out in the yummy human world.

The need to know where they came from is only important when it becomes obvious that they did not get through to our world by natural means. If humans have aided them in breaking through, then humans have to put them back, in which case you need to know where to put them.

The other very sad door opener that is bringing more pissed off demons into our world is the fairly recent aggressive attempts by certain American evangelical Christian groups to cleanse the Abyss (which they see as Hell) through prayer, trance, visions, and ritual. It is rather rude to stomp into someone else's house and tell them that you don't like them or their furnishings, and then trying to evict them from their own home. It does tend to piss beings off when you do that. The direct result of this work is that doorways into certain realms of the Abyss are being opened and the traffic is two-way. If humans create a door into the Abyss, then it will be used and can only be shut and dismantled by humans.

My theory as to why their invasion of the Abyss is so effective in creating doorways is that the roots of the people doing this work are in Africa, and latent ancestral beings and knowledge comes to the fore during such work. Their methods of working look very similar on the outside to tribal ceremonies from the west coast of Africa. And that magic, however it expresses itself, is powerful and dangerous. So it doesn't matter what you call it, or what faces or deities you put to it—the method works, the ancestral skills kick in, but it doesn't have a suitable vessel to hold it. The Christian religion is not built for such work. So the old tribal methods of going into the otherworlds work, but the structural protections do not kick in as it is not in context.

Energy created from magic and religion are the two biggest door openers for such beings and they will search out the nearest host who will then be 'encouraged' to open the door wider either through more religious/magical actions, or through actions that create large energy boosts which the demon then uses to open the door wider himself. Mass murder is one of those energy-boosting actions.

And taking down the host in such situations is not enough. The being will merely walk along to the next available and compatible human to take up residence. The human hosts that do all the spitting and talking voices are the ones that are holding the demon at bay to an extent, and their inner immune system is fighting its action. The really heavily possessed ones just go about quietly doing what the demon wants.

The variety of realms and depths that these beings can come from are seemingly endless, but for our consciousness we can narrow it down to sections within the Abyss, which are essentially the back doors to those worlds. So if you have a demon in hand, or trapped, then taking it down the Abyss until you reach its recognisable section is the safest way to deal with them.

Once you have established which part of the Abyss they are from, then if you are brave (otherwise known as immensely naive, stupid, and insane) and want to be of real service, then you can go back to that area with suitable disguise and armour, and look in depth at that realm and learn what it is about. That way, you will have a very deep and useful knowledge about the demon's own world, which in turn can be useful when having to deal with a long term dangerous stream of demonic consciousness invading our world. You can also use that information to stop the traffic into our world for a very long time.

Symptoms of the various forms of demonic possession

I will go further in depth on this issue in the chapter on host assessments but here is a brief rundown on how these beings tend to manifest in humanity. Please bear in mind that a lot of the signs and symptoms listed can also indicate a mental health problem and you need to be very aware of that fact. In the chapter on assessment we will look at the various ways of distinguishing mental health from possession. One further complication is that sometimes one can trigger the other off so that you have a dual situation to handle.

It would be wise, as part of the learning process in the world of the exorcist, to familiarise yourself with the various presentations of mental illness.

The smaller demonic beings present in humans and animals first by way of mental, emotional, and personality changes, and then later physical changes as the body struggles to hold two beings in one space. The first symptom is usually withdrawal from friends and family, hearing voices, mood changes, and obsessions. Deeply religious or spiritual experiences often happen at this point as the being tries to operate the host's brain and the demon inadvertently exposes the host to lines of power/consciousness that the host would not normally have access to. Sometimes clever demons will project the story that the host is 'filled with the Holy Spirit' or any religious or spiritual equivalent in order to dismantle any defence systems the mind throws up.

The being will become very clear with its voice to the host and will begin to direct how the host eats, sleeps, who the host talks to, etc. The being also has a very definite effect on what music the host listens to. Sound is very important in the inner worlds, and each being responds in different ways to certain pitches and sounds. The demonic being will steer the host away from music or sounds that will make its possession harder to hang on to. The host will begin to gravitate to music that has harsher aggressive sounds that bolster as opposed to weaken the possession. His or her whole personality changes, often beyond recognition, and he or she often displays previously unknown skills.

At this point you can see the similarity in certain mental illnesses and also in some parasite infestations. If the possession is allowed to take a hold the mind of the host will begin to struggle against the being—sometimes that will display as aggression and attack. Just as a cat will bat its paw at a piece of hot chicken that has burned it, so the host becomes aggressive in an unconscious way to try to push out the demon. The demon will often use this and aim it outwards at other people. Someone who does not have a great deal of strength, or who is an empathic type of personality will quietly absorb the being, withdraw, and enter into a relationship with it.

After a short while, maybe a week or two, the body will start to react to the invasion. It will initially show through the digestive system (seeing as the emotive route didn't work), their digestion and appetite will change dramatically and their taste for certain types of food will change. Certain minerals burn up very quickly in the system. (I do not know why this is, only that it seems to nearly always happen. My theory is that the being needs the energy of certain substances to continue inhabiting the body.) So the host will become anaemic quickly, will often display a positive chvostiks sign (go look it up) and begin to suffer from low blood sugar. From these signs it becomes apparent that the being is affecting the metabolic function as it tries to operate the body's energy system. Sometimes they become very spotty as the skin which is the body's biggest organ, is the safest most externalised route for toxic dumping.

The body stance also begins to change and certain tremors, fits, muscle cramps and contortions happen as the body struggles against the intrusion. The facial features will often slightly distort and for exorcists with inner sight, at this point you will be able to see the being looking out of their eyes. These are all the most extreme symptoms, but most people do not get them—the possession can often go unnoticed by all but the closest relatives/friends. Often it is a subtle but dangerous shift in thinking and reasoning, and a loss of normal balanced emotions.

One of the most spectacular indications that all these symptoms are possession rather than illness is that after a basic removal, or a shutting of the being down without the host realising, all the symptoms immediately stop. It's stunning—within hours they return to being normal people. If it is mental or physical illness, such magical actions would have no affect at all. One must make sure though, if using binding or shutting methods to diagnose, that the host does not realise what you are doing—that way you do not get a placebo affect.

If left unchecked, the possession can last for years as the demonic being enjoys being in the human world. The person will often become labelled as mentally ill with violent tendencies, and the being will affect and influence all the people around the host.

The intention of the being is to have power in the human world, one way or another. It will try to express that power through relationships, workplace, religion, and will become obsessive in having followers. They are dangerous but usually in a manipulative way: they are paranoid, controlling, aggressive, and addictive. They express their need for power through sex, substances, illness, violence, and occasionally deaths.

With the medium-sized demons all the above happens but most often the human fights hard against the invasion, the very soul recognises the danger of the being and will often fight hard to stop it. There are many sad tales about desperate people walking into hospitals, police stations, and mental wards to warn people that they are going to kill. They are trying to warn humanity against the being that is within them and what it is going to do. Most of the time they are brushed off or medicated, and the medication lowers the host's ability to fend off the being, so that it digs in deeper. Not long after the cry for help the mass murder usually happens, and they kill themselves, which gives the being a large boost of energy so that it can move on. Sometimes possessed people have killed themselves in the belief that it will also kill the demon, which it doesn't.

These types of demonic beings express themselves either through individuals or small groups, or sometimes even places. They want death, sex, violence, fear, drugs, anything that expresses raw powerful emotion. The more the merrier as far as they are concerned and they will often get the host to build up to a large event. Murdering more than one person at a time that will elicit the most outpourings of emotions, which often means children. The stronger the land that the host lives upon, the more powerful the urge to kill will become as the power spots magnify the influence of the being.

The very large demonic beings usually express themselves through groups, organisations, and families. They work for the long term, slowly building a structure that will enable them to manipulate large amounts of people to behave in a way that they want. To see how they operate, just look back through history, particularly the last hundred years to see what I mean. They will often begin with one person who is very psychic, and therefore a good doorway, and build from there. These large beings are hive beings, so they infect many people, but they are the same being. It was this type of consciousness that Dion Fortune was fighting during the Second World War. She burned out her body protecting England from a large hive consciousness that the Germans were working with.

Parasites

These beings are often mistaken for demons, but do not have the same danger level that demonic consciousness has. They can have a similar impact on a human as a demonic possession, but they are easier to deal with and remove. They tend to be less intelligent but fairly crafty, and are just looking for food. They do not get into the major social-cultural consciousness thing that demonic beings do, but they tend to go hand in hand with major demonic influences.

So, for example, when you have a demonic consciousness operating through someone or a group, parasites are often in there right with them to feed off the ride and benefit from the energy bursts. This has to be taken into account when you are pulling a demon out—there will most likely be a whole host of large and small parasites hanging on in there that need removing.

Parasites, unlike demons, are very common indeed, and pervade all parts of the human world and consciousness. Some have a symbiotic relationship with their host, in which case you have to think very carefully before you remove them. Some pass down the generations in families, some infect areas and affect all who live there, some hang out around certain activities, and some are attracted by certain illnesses. The list is endless.

But an exorcist who is used to looking closely at people will learn to spot one easily so that a good assessment can be done. The inner parasites are like Candida: you have to cut off the food source and point of entry to ensure that they do not get back in. The host usually also needs some educating so that they learn the symptoms of early infection, and the behaviour patterns that attract them. I always view parasites as an inner illness rather than a possession. It is like having a bacteria or fungus in your body—they not only affect your health but also how you think and act, just as an outer illness can.

Just as there are endless types of humans, they are endless types of parasites, and there are far too many to list and discuss all of them. But there are a small amount of 'types' that are the most common in our society and these are the ones you are most likely to come up against.

Emotional parasites: These feed off strong emotions and will encourage the host the get into conflicts and dramas. It will 'ride' the host so that a lot of energy is released that it can feed from. When there is a long term infestation, the host, if younger, tends to not develop emotionally as he is not given the opportunity to learn from experience—the parasite will work to keep the host unstable so that it can feed. If the host is using any form of chemical depressant or relaxant then the being will be able to dig in deeper as such drugs lower the inner defence systems.

Sexual parasites: These beings tend to be attracted to sexual acts and feed off the excitement and then the release of energy at orgasm. They will work through the imagination of the host making the imagination more vivid, but like a drug, the host will adjust quickly and the being encourages the host to look for more and more powerful images or acts to think of or do. When such beings are taken out of a host, the host may lose their sex drive for a while as things rebalance themselves. The imagination is a major doorway into and out of the other worlds and it should be guarded carefully.

Violent parasites: these parasites encourage violent behaviour and feed off conflict. They can be strong enough to urge a person to kill but more often it encourages fighting, aggression, destruction of property, and violent, fragmented thinking.

Healer parasites: these are the creepiest...they work through healers so that when the healer puts hands upon the patient, the being plugs in and drains off the patients' deeper energy. They then send in a backwash of 'feel good' to ensure they come back. But the healing doesn't usually work (as the healer is blocked by the parasite) and within a couple of hours the victim becomes drained and exhausted.

Most parasite symptoms can mimic unbalanced human behaviour so one cannot assume whenever he sees such symptoms that it is only the parasite. Sometimes it is just the human who has such parasitical behaviour; sometimes that behaviour in an individual will encourage a parasite to move in.

The difference is that when treated, the host changes behaviour almost immediately but will still be vulnerable for a while and will need to be watched closely. Parasites are very common and seem to be a part of the natural order of life, just as fungus infections and viruses are.

In a positive way they help us to adjust our behaviour and also to develop an immune system to keep them out. Whenever it is possible with a parasite infection, if the host tries to starve it out themselves and learns to see the infestation signs, they will build immunity to it very quickly.

Many people, however, are driven by their wants and needs, and that egocentricity is an open door for these beings. The discipline not to be driven by urges is the first barrier that keeps these beings out.

There is a whole industry that has sprung up in the new age world: plastic shamanism, and it focuses mainly on taking out parasites but it approaches it in a very psychological way and absolves the patient from his or her own responsibility as far as inner cleanliness is concerned.

As with demonic beings, a sensitive exorcist will be able to see well-entrenched parasites within the host and sometimes even non-sensitive workers will feel drained and 'invaded' around a parasited person. If the victim has been infested for a while, then he will start to look slightly ill and grimy as his body becomes drained slowly of life force. It is not as severe as a demonic possession, but it does eventually become quite noticeable.

The key times in people's lives that they can become vulnerable to these beings is puberty, sexual awakening, surgery, accidents, certain illnesses (particularly ones that affect the brain, i.e., meningitis), menopause, extreme emotional incidents, and near death.

One type of parasite that has to be carefully thought about before taking action is the type of parasite that targets elderly people or those who have terminal illness. As the spirit weakens its hold on the body, parasites ease their way in and set up shop. They live in the host, feeding off the food, emotions, and generally enjoying living in a body. They will operate to keep the body alive so that they can get as much time as they can. Sometimes, aggressive ones will try to ease out the spirit of the human and completely take over. Although they do try this quite a bit, it is very rare for one to be successful.

What tends to happen is an ill, dying, or very old sick person will seem to drag on without being able to let go into death. Sometimes this is just emotional or spiritual fear, or a wish to stay alive at all costs, and it should not be assumed that it is a parasite all the time. But sometimes one does get in and will prolong the suffering of the host so that it can feed.

In those circumstances, taking the being out will often kill the host in that, without the being keeping her alive, her body finally lets go. In a coma patient, which is a very common condition that attracts parasites, she will often die within 48 hours of the parasite removal, even if she has been in a coma for a long time.

If you are taking the responsibility for taking out a parasite then you must also take on the responsibility of doing the death vision for the patient (see the chapter on death) either silently while you hold her hand, or out loud to her if she is open to that.

Ghosts and hauntings

Most of the time, when people think they are haunted, they are not. True hauntings are pretty rare, but they do happen. The sources of hauntings can get complicated and it is important to quickly ascertain what types of haunting you are dealing with.

The most common hauntings are echoes that are stored within a land space or a building. Some major events that output a lot of energy seem to lock 'recordings' of a person or people in to a building, and certain conditions trigger a replaying of that event. A very well-known one is Roman soldiers marching through the basement of a private school in York. Many people over the years, including police, have witnessed lines of soldiers marching through the basement and vanishing into the walls. They were not aware of the modern-day people watching them—it is simply a recording that plays over when the conditions are right. Those types of recordings tend to peak and then vanish when the building is torn down or remodelled. They are harmless and usually no interaction happens between witness and 'ghost.'

Another type of common haunting happens when a person who has died does not move on but his self-structure or personality is taken over by a parasite that steps into the image of the person and uses the image of the personality to create situations that will feed it. These situations are dealt with as parasites and not as dead persons. The easiest way to tell if it is a parasite or not is by its actions: if it is doing things that fall into parasite activity, i.e., getting into dreams, manipulating people, creating fear, aggression, etc, then chances are it is a parasite that has found a fragmented personality. Sometimes you get a mix, where the original ghost is still there but is driven by the parasite. These types of hauntings can become dangerous and have to be handled very carefully.

In such a combination, the parasite will give the ghost strength and skills that it shouldn't have, particularly if the ghost is of a person who died violently, was involved in violence of some sort, or was mentally ill in a dangerous way. These are difficult to get rid of and have to be approached from a variety of ways all at once, so they are not a one-person job. The updated film of the Amityville haunting made in 2005 was rather free with the original story, and they really beefed up the 'haunting.' Certain elements of the film reflected how this particular mix of parasite/ghost hauntings can play with the minds and bodies of people. It was a fairly good portrayal of how an extreme haunting of this type can present.

A real haunting that is just a dead human usually works through the dreams and thoughts of the victims, while also affecting the environment. They tend not to be too spectacular as far as 'happenings' go, but are more destructive for the victims because of the psychological damage these hauntings can cause. It is as if the person tries to latch into the victims' head. They can also attack the victim, or follow her around the house, often in an attempt to communicate.

Most real hauntings are about communication attempts, or clinging onto lives, power, money, relationships, etc. They will try to stop the living from moving on, or they want witness to their pain or suffering. With such hauntings, banishments, etc, are a complete waste of time as they slowly tend to creep back. The ghost has to be approached from a visionary point of view, usually by the living going in vision into death and talking to them on their own 'turf.' Once the person has been escorted through death, they do not come back and everything tends to settle down.

In some countries that have a raw land power that has not been deadened by thousands of years of civilisation, there are pockets of land power that create doors for beings to flow into our world and when they meet humanity it can sometimes be a total disaster. Some American hauntings, like the famous Tennessee Bell Witch for example, are not a haunting at all. These incidents are beings, akin to faery beings, that are often hostile to humanity and dislike the intrusion of civilisation—they become aggressive and will fight for their land. In such a situation I would suggest that the people just move—it cannot be resolved easily if at all and these types of hauntings are truly dangerous and have been known to kill people.

Such clashes with these beings can occasionally be negotiated, but in reality, the house is on their land or burial grounds and they want it back. Those sites are often very powerful and hold burials that can date back a couple of thousand years or more as the native people will have recognised such an entrance to the underworld. Sometimes the attacking being is a guardian and is just doing their job. They will watch the humans, learn their 'language' or mode of appearance and communication, and then mirror it back to the victims.

This presents as a haunting by a ghost, but is anything but. I have tried quite a few times to work on clearing such 'hauntings' and have failed miserably each time while also getting my butt kicked well and hard. I learned to communicate to an extent with such beings, but they are often very ancient, very hostile, and very powerful. They are immune to bargaining, have no sense of humour and love to play ball with your brain. If you come up against such a haunting, I would suggest you back out quietly while telling the people to sell up.

Finally there are poltergeists, of which I know nothing at all, and have no idea how to get rid of them. My theory is that they are faery-type beings with a warped sense of humour and really good aim. I have been whacked over the head a couple of time by these little bastards and they only stopped when I lost it and adopted my 'teaching obnoxious children' voice. They resumed breaking windows and throwing stones as soon as I left. Obviously the faery realm has bratty children, just as the human realm does.

The more you do the work of an exorcist, the more beings and situations you will come across that you have never seen, read about, or experienced before. The variety is endless, tiring, and bloody annoying sometimes. Just when you think you have got it sussed, you come across something that knocks you on your ass and you have no idea what the hell it is or how to get rid of it.

When you come across something new, take notes, and observe before you get to work. Learn as much as you can about it so that others can benefit from your black eye and frazzled brain. The more you can watch and listen to a being in action, the more you will learn about it and be able to know how to get rid of it and where it has come from. If you cannot figure out what it is and where it has come from, you can always ask it. I have done that a couple of times and got straight useful answers which surprised the shit out of me. Old rule: if you don't know—ask!!

Chapter 5
Assessing a potential possession

When you come to assess the possibility of a possession, erring on the side of sensible caution is a really good idea—that way you don't get wiped up the wall unexpectedly, or mistake an illness for a demon and make someone's paranoia just a little bit more intense.

The first and most important golden rule to keep repeating to yourself over and over is: *make sure that what is presenting to you is not just an illness*. A possession or infestation has many similar symptoms to an illness, but there also are things that are not similar. If the victim is presenting possession-type symptoms then your assessment must include consultation with a doctor who is also an esotericist.

Many people have asked me if I ask the victim permission to work on them. If the family have asked me in, then that is good enough for me. Do keep in mind that if you ask a victim, there is a really good chance that your answer is coming from the being itself and not the victim. If there is someone out in the community that is doing really bad things and it becomes obvious that it is a possession or infestation, then I will take the being out whether the host likes it or not. My concern is for the people around them. I am not going to stand by and watch a being operate through a human that makes them attack people—I will take the bugger out regardless of what anyone thinks. I only get involved like that though if it is a being that is trying to get the host to kill, rape, etc.

In the end it comes down to personal ethics. Make sure your ethics are about what is spiritually balanced as opposed to the societal ethics which can change like the wind and are often based more upon culture and social engineering rather than what is actually right and wrong—murder and rape are wrong, being odd isn't.

first contact

The first contact starts the minute you answer the phone when someone has called for help. If it is a demonic possession, then the being is aware of you the minute you speak into the phone, even if you are talking to a family member or friend of the host. Do not underestimate these beings: they are not governed by the host body, that is just like a base for them. That inner awareness of you from first contact also means that anything you say to the family is potentially also information going to the being. You do not want to give the being too much information that it can then use to attack you, or that will warn it of your methods so it can retaliate.

Mercifully, 99% of the time, when you are called out, it is for parasites, ghosts, curses, and false alarms. Probably 70% of calls that you get are false alarms and are more about illness, depression, bad drains (strange house smells), paranoia, over-active imagination, attention-seeking, and puberty (i.e. my son won't do as he is told, I think he is possessed).

But for your own safety you always have to work from the assumption that until otherwise proven, you could be dealing with a demonic possession. If you approach your preparation (not your host) that way, you are prepared and ready for the worst and hopefully you will find nothing. It is much better to go ready for battle and not have to use it than it is to go not prepared for anything and find that you have a really nasty demonic being in front of you, sharpening its claws, ready for dinner.

So when you first answer the phone call, the minute you speak, you are working. You have to be able to gain as much information as possible while giving out as little information as possible. This is nearly impossible, as most people are frightened by exorcists/the whole idea of possession, and they want to know as much about it and you as possible. I have had people asking me my family history, religious training, schooling, relationship details, everything. You have to be able to not answer a lot of these questions, as they potentially give the being ammunition and a way 'in' to you.

That gives you little option but to give them a minimum base background of what they really do need to know and tell them that you cannot tell them anything else until after the work. That doesn't really make them feel any safer but you do have to protect yourself. They also need to protect their family member so you need to be able to give them basic information that tells them that you know what you are doing, and how you are going to do it, and where you are coming from.

To do this you need to be clear with yourself about what needs to be said. First off, it really helps if you are part of a religious organisation under whose umbrella you can operate. You do need to have a good understanding of religion and have a solid spiritual/magical foundation to operate from anyhow, and some religious or magical lines do carry consecrations that link you to lines of past priests and priestesses that you can draw upon while you are working.

To want to get to this stage of work you must have developed through a spiritual or magical tradition anyhow, so I am assuming most people reading this are adept initiates, and/or religious/spiritual priests or priestesses. The fact that you have a position within a spiritual or magical organisation is a good indication to someone that you have training and experience (and the fact that you blew up your cat in a magical experiment the week before is just a minor detail.)

The other strand of information that people will need and want to know is what you are going to do. While you cannot really go into detail with such information, it is valuable to point out that the methods are very 'hands off,' calm, quiet, and don't involve anything painful or scary. Real exorcism is actually quite boring to observe: people don't usually tend to spit porridge and shout really interesting insults while you are exorcising them.

What will be one very early indication of either a possession or a bad infestation is that when you question the family or victim over the phone they will very quickly become defensive, sometimes hostile, and quite secretive. They will often feel confused as to why they are feeling this way and will sometimes offer an apology. Another manifestation of this is they will find it hard to speak, or get easily confused and forgetful. It is common in these circumstances to hear someone saying 'I'm not normally this scattered, I don't know what has come over me.' Although the family member is not possessed, they can be mildly affected by the being as it tries to control and defend its territory.

With the two bits of information regarding your spiritual/magical training, and the fact that is it very hands off and not melodramatic, that is enough to re assure friends and family of the victim without giving too much information that would jeopardise you in any way. Don't forget, if it is a true possession, whatever you tell the family is also being heard by the being. (If you weren't paranoid before, you will be now....)

What is most important for the exorcist is to be able to get as much information as possible to be able to make some pre-contact assessments. You need a basic history of the changes within the host. Ask: What are his religious beliefs? His relationships? Job? What medical assessments have been made? Inquire into his current family situation. Is he on medications? If so, what? What seems to trigger an event or make it worse? When did it start and how long has it been going on? You also need to know what area he lives in and what his living situation is.

The reason you need all this information is that you need to be able to possibly identify why the host was infested, what triggered it and what has strengthened it. You also need to know his spiritual makeup so that you will know if the host is going to be able to work with you or not. People who have a spiritual life tend to fight infestations harder and can be reached through the possession to give them instructions. If they are on medications then it is going to be harder to reach them if there is a possession. A lot of medications, like antidepressants, lower the human's ability to fight the being, so it digs in deeper and the host has no power to stop it.

After that first conversation, which usually happens over the phone, you must be on guard and prepared. That means that you are working from that point on which will affect where you go, what you do, what you eat, how you sleep, and who you talk to. The longer you do such work, the more you will learn to get a feel for what it is you are probably going to be dealing with, so the intensity of the preparation does ease somewhat. But in the early days of your work, you must be prepared for what could possibly come at you.

After first contact and before the meeting

Once you have made contact with the host or the hosts family, it is a good idea to make sure that there is not too long a gap between the contact and getting to work. Because you have to be 'on' all the time after the call, it can get very wearing on the body to keep your guard up for very long—so the quicker you can get to work, the better.

Once you are on notice, it is a bad idea to do any socialising, going out to bars or busy public places that might put a strain on your everyday outer 'skin.' You are potentially under pressure, and need to stay clean, quiet, and be able to focus in on preparing yourself. I have ignored that advice myself to my own peril and found myself totally overwhelmed after having a single glass of sherry in a café with friends. My inner defence systems were holding off a being from an upcoming job and the alcohol coupled with public exposure dropped my defences a little and I essentially got my ass bit by the being I was about to work on.

My other silly act (I'm saying other, but there is a long list of stupid acts that have my name on them) was just a couple of hours after a job I did in NY to de-possess someone. I went out with a friend for a bite to eat and forgot how vulnerable I could be after that type of work. A street person who was heavily infested spotted me (when you work, it's like a flashing light switches on over your head so you become very visible to parasites, etc) and made a beeline straight for me. He crashed into me, knocking my shoulder and one of the heavier beings that he was infested with transferred onto me. I had no defence as I was still weak from the work and I took the impact full on.

I got back to the apartment, got the thing out, and took a ritual cleansing bath. I then went into teaching that evening which was the second silly thing I did that day and nearly killed myself. I took 20 people, mostly beginners, into the underworld, and on the way back up I began to struggle under the burden of so many people who could not carry their own weight. My shoulder that had taken the impact earlier popped out literally—it dislocated under the inner pressure. To this day I have terrible pain and problems with that shoulder because I did not look after myself or the injury properly.

Which is another point to be aware of not only for yourself, but also for the host: inner impacts can cause physical manifestations of the inner injury if they are intense enough.

So the moral of the story is: keep out of public areas when you are doing this work. You are far too visible and vulnerable to be wandering around city streets in the midst of an exorcism. Don't forget, (ok, I'm nagging now,) the exorcism starts from first contact.

Don't drink or take any mind altering substances or drugs, make sure you sleep with a lit candle in the room that has been tuned in to whatever stream you are working with and have a demon trap in the room working with you. Don't connect or get into conversations with vulnerable members of your family or friends (you instantly expose them to danger through you, and it gives the demon information and connections to attack you with).

Basically you have to be clean, simple, tuned in, on guard, and isolated until well after the job is done. It usually takes a couple of days after the work is finished for it all to calm a little, and a couple of weeks to be completely clear. My friends sometimes get pissed off with me for not being chatty or falling out of contact for a few weeks or sometimes months. It is usually either because I am exhausted and laid in bed wondering why the hell I do this, or I am in the midst of dealing with something. Either way it is a lonely, hard, and bloody antisocial activity! I lucked out in that I married someone who is as mad as I am and we work together on this path.

The other preparation is to look after your body: don't fill it with junk as you are preparing to work. Eat clean and simple foods to support and help your body with the burdens it could possibly face.

If you are going to be dealing with parasites, then most of the above is less intense and less urgent, although still necessary. You will eventually learn to feel the various waves of impact coming towards you and be able to gauge just what threat it is that you are up against.

Inner guardian

It is good to build up a working relationship with an inner guardian when you start doing this work and this can be done by going to the Abyss and calling upon the keeper of the Abyss to connect you with an angelic being that will watch your back as you work. It is good to learn to work in the Abyss and get comfortable with it as it is a vision you will use often. Although there is a version of it in chapter 1 (the vision of judgement), here is a simple and straightforward version. This version is taking you to find a guardian, but learn the actual method of going to the Abyss and calling the keeper—you will use this journey a lot in your work.

Vision of the Abyss

Light a candle and still yourself. With your eyes closed, see yourself stepping through the flame and into the void, the place of no time, no movement, nothing. Spend a little time there quietening yourself and feeling yourself expand in the nothingness. When you feel still, focus on the intent to go to the Abyss and with that intent step out of the void and find yourself walking across a flat desert. You will see beings in the distance bound up as they sleep and wait. Pass by them as you focus your intent to travel to the Abyss.

In the distance you see a faint glow over the land and as you get closer you come to a large crack in the earth which seems to go down and down forever, and out of which is a faint glow of light—this is the Abyss that flows through all worlds. As you stand on the edge of the Abyss, you become aware of the beings below and above in the Abyss, and of Divinity across the Abyss hidden in the mists that cloak the other side.

Call for the keeper of the Abyss and out of the depths will rise a large being of human shape but monstrous size that stands up within the Abyss and looks down to you. Hold out your hand to him and whatever appears in your hand, you give as a gift. (If it is something that you own in life, burn it or bury it and send its power or energy to this being.)

Ask the keeper to take you to an order of beings that would be willing to work with you as a guardian while you work in service. Tell the keeper the type of work you are doing and the being will hold out his hand. Step onto the hand and the keeper will lift you up to a place higher up the Abyss than the human level to a place where there is an order of angelic beings that would be willing to work with you.

The keeper will place you on a ledge that juts out from a long dark tunnel. Out of that tunnel will come a being that will be willing to work with you. Commune with that being, tell it what you are trying to achieve, and ask it formally if it is willing to work with you. The being may ask you to offer something of service back, or it may not. When you have both come to an agreement, the keeper will lift you both down back to the edge of the Abyss and the two of you walk away from the Abyss and towards the desert.

As you walk along with this being, you notice things ahead of you that you recognise from your life and your home. One thing in particular draws you—it may be a door, a room, a window, a fireplace, or something similar that is in or near your home. You realise as you walk towards it that the being is looking into your mind to see a possible threshold that it can use to access you. You both step through it and you find yourself back in your home where you first started. The being comes back with you and tells you that the threshold you just used will now be an access point for that being to use when you call upon it.

When you are ready, blow out the candle and look at the access point. When you need to work with this being you will light a candle and focus on that access point to call it through. Don't forget, if the being asked you for service in return, then you must honor that agreement.

Cards

The next step after the first contact is to look at the problem using the modified deck and layout (see Chapter 13). Be aware that when you look after having first contact, you have to shield your readings so that the being does not know that you are looking at it, and also to ensure that you do not inadvertently connect with the being through the reading and pull part of it into your home.

The best way to shield is to work within a sacred or tuned space with a working candle, and using a spiralled cloth to lay the cards out on. Keep an awareness in your mind that there is a possibility of interference and when you ask your questions, ask for a true answer, not an interfered one. Sometimes it can be that simple, just ask the deck and the beings that work with the deck to keep out any intruders from your readings.

When you look using the cards, use all three layouts that are listed (the healing layout is in the appendix): the health reading, the identification reading, and the directional reading.

First you will look at the overall health of the person using a health layout. This layout will also give you plenty of clues as to whether the infestation is actually just an illness, or an infestation, or both. Then you will look at a directional reading to see what elements and powers flow through the being, what inner direction it is coming from, so that you have a better idea of its make up and therefore will know which angelic beings to work with to get rid of it. Then you will look using a larger advice and identification layout that will tell you where in the Abyss it comes from, what order of being it is, and also possibly how it got from its own world to ours.

Once you have looked at those details, then it would be a good idea to do a reading to look at the home and see what the energy is like in the home and if there are any beings in the house itself. For that you would use the directional reading and a tree of life layout.

Once you have got all of your readings done and you have written them down, refer back to them as you work—obscure details often come to life as the work progresses. At the end of the exorcism, burn the readings and notes—these notes will be a potential doorway for the being to get back into our world. Nothing that has information of the being should be kept. I cringed when watching the film dramatising the exorcism of Mary Rose: they used the original tapes from the exorcism as information which enabled certain fragments of being to reach out through the movie. It didn't matter that most of the movie was fiction—a fragment is all that it takes.

first contact

The first few minutes of contact are very important as that is the time in which the being weighs you up and looks for your weak points, and while the being is doing that, you are doing the same—you need to assess the host, the house, and the family. It is not unheard of for a possession to be invited in by a family member, or for a family member to be the doorway for beings to flow through. So you are basically assessing everyone in the house that is connected to the host.

The minute you walk through the door, you are looking, listening, and smelling. Smells and sounds are very important to demonic beings and some larger parasites, and there are things they cannot tolerate—a possessed person will react violently to certain frequencies and noises. A cheesy but pretty effective way to get a reaction or loosen a being is to play certain types of Tibetan chants. I have an old CD that is a ritual cleansing and invocation that hasn't been 'new aged' with extra 'Twinkie' sounds. I found one day, quite by accident, that the sounds on the CD made it very difficult for demonic beings to be around. I started to use it intentionally and it was very effective in clearing spaces, so I started to listen carefully to the tones and to identify at which point the frequencies pissed the invading beings off.

Since then, I have the CD in my tool kit and use it sometimes to clear spaces and to occasionally clear people. I work in vision with the music, reaching through the chants to connect with spirits that work with that music, and I have them guide me to take things out of the host or the building.

Smells are also very important. The human body often reacts to possession by making certain noises and giving off certain smells—rotten eggs/sulphur smell is the most common as the body struggles to expel the intruder. Some hosts develop a musty scent and most heavily infested hosts will have stopped washing and will be a little ripe to say the least.

Sometimes the host will develop little noises that she makes, clicking with her fingers, or tapping repeatedly without realising—she becomes very uncomfortable around total silence.

When you are brought to the host, look around the room where she is, and notice what adjustments has she made for herself: is she bothered by light, heat, cold? Has she surrounded herself with objects, noise, etc. How is she dressing, has her dress code changed? Is she trying to cover her head (like with a hoodie), or cover her hands? Has she started self mutilating? Look at her eyes, skin, hair, her mannerisms and hand movements. Listen to her voice and watch her feet.

What you are looking for are signs that:

1. The body is struggling. Is her face pale or spotty? Does she have rashes? Is her hair dull? Is she constipated? (The body will often go on hold when under attack.)

2. The mind is struggling: does she avoid eye contact? Does she fidget? Is she cutting herself?

3. The personality is struggling: has she changed dress habits? Music tastes? Sleeping patterns?

All of the above can appear with mental health issues that have nothing to do with possession, so do tread carefully and make sure that you are considering all possibilities at every step. It is very useful to have a doctor or psychologist with you at first contact.

If the host is able to communicate, then sit and talk with her. Let her tell you in her own words what is going on. What does she feel is happening to her? When did she feel it begin and how does it feel now?

In the case of a demonic possession, some hosts retain enough of themselves to be able to communicate well, and if the being is a parasite, then communication is easier and less interfered with.

Watch the person's eyes when you talk to him or her, and listen carefully to any subtext that happens—sometimes the being tries to talk to you through the host without the host realising.

While she is talking to you, put a consecrated stole around her neck and pour her a glass of consecrated water to drink, without telling her what you are doing. Just watch for any reaction or sudden sleepiness/confusion of the host.

If the person is heavily possessed and is unable to communicate rationally, then you need to elicit a reaction from the demon as opposed to the mind of the host—this is one of the factors that can determine if it is a possession or a mental illness.

If you perform obvious actions in front of the person, they may react from a place of mental illness, but if you do something that is hidden from the host, and if it still elicits a reaction, you know that a possession is at least part of the problem.

There are a number of things that you can do, including:

1. A silent ritual of cleansing spoken in your head.

2. A glass of consecrated water for her to drink (I have never used this method but have been told it works. I am a little wary, though, of things that I have not directly experienced. I have never had to use it, but I may in the future just out of curiosity.)

3. Placing of a consecrated power object near the host.

4. The draping of a consecrated or swirled stole or scarf around the neck of the host.

5. Lighting a candle and silently opening the gateways to death or the Abyss.

6. Putting a small effigy that is empowered with an angelic being or destroying deity near the host.

If the host has a demonic possession, it will cause a reaction. If it is a parasite, it may not react as much, but may react to the effigy. If it is mental illness, as long as the host doesn't see what you are doing, it should have no reaction at all.

Another way to gain a reaction is for the exorcist to wear consecrated stoles, frankincense oil, a bit of osha root, and a sacred object around her neck. Something within all that lot will probably get a reaction from the host. She might find it smelly or offensive.

At the end of the day though, the most telling way to diagnose an infestation or possession is through listening, watching, and feeling. There is a certain feel and pattern of behaviour to possessions that cannot be explained, but it is a sense that develops over time. Some beings learn not to react to things, but when talking with the host the being eventually can be drawn out and seen. That along with a reading, for me, is usually enough.

Once you are more or less certain you are dealing with a parasite or demonic being, you must get to work pretty quickly. It is best if you can work directly after the assessment so that the being does not have chance to hide or dig deeper. If you are still not sure, then it is best to err on the safe side but also have a doctor or mental health professional with you, and keep in mind the effect on the victim if she is not possessed—it should appear more to her as a blessing and healing. That way you do not traumatise the person by convincing her that she may have demons. Instead she feels a more spiritual connection to what you are doing and will hopefully take it as a spiritual act—the blessing of an ill person.

Assessment of a house

Houses or buildings can also be possessed by demonic beings, parasites, faeries, or ghosts (and many other forms of weird and wonderful beings that we just don't have names for).

Assessment of a house is a little harder as you cannot question it and you need to be in it for a while to observe any activity. The quickest and easiest way to assess a house is to do a reading using the adjusted deck, and to question the occupants.

Usually house activity will manifest in a variety of ways and the most common is that the house affects the people who live there. They often report changes in mood once they have been in the house for a few hours, nightmares and sleep disturbances, uneasy feelings, etc. If the occupants have any natural inner sight, they will report seeing fleeting shadow-like movements, noises, voices, things moving, strange smells, doors refusing to open, doors or windows opening, lights turning on and off, things falling, and things setting on fire.

The most common intruders in houses are ghosts, faery beings, land spirits, parasites, and thought forms. It is very rare to get demonic possessions in houses but it does happen. They are usually drawn to a house by natural vortexes on the land site or ancient power sites near by. They can also be drawn in by ritual activity if it is not carried out properly and by demonic images or statuary.

Images and statues can also sometimes bring in deities or spirits attached to deities that are out of place or in the wrong culture/land.

To assess a house after you have interviewed the occupants, go around the house and look for any unusual images, statues, tribal artefacts, clothing, weapons, ritual implements, etc. Many house disturbances can be traced to objects that the occupants have brought home with them.

One example is a house I was called out to in the bay area in California. The family had trouble with nightmares, personality changes in all the occupants, odd behaviour in the children, frequent fires, and fleeting shadow-type beings moving around the house.

When I arrived—after talking at length to the owner over the phone—I felt heavy aggression as soon as I walked into the house. The energy of the house was confused, aggressive, and confrontational. When I got upstairs I noticed an extensive collection of African masks, nail fetishes, and statues. As soon as I got close to them a being appeared and threatened me. Being the brave person I was, I hoofed it downstairs and asked them about the collection. (Some of the many African forms of magic are particularly powerful and aggressive, and not something to be messed with.)

I went away from the house and did a series of readings that identified something in the collection that was causing the problem. It also looked as if some of the pieces clashed with each other and it was like a mini tribal war going on in the bedrooms of this house. I suggested that the couple get rid of the artefacts and they refused, saying it had taken them years to build the collection.

I did a clearing on the rest of the house and it made little difference, which didn't surprise me. So I went back to the house and talked to the beings in the collection. They were very angry and insulted to be where they were, and they felt they were being used in a disrespectful way. They wanted to be where people would interact with them, feed them, and work with them.

Because the couple would not consider doing anything with the collection I gave up and left them to it. A month later I was called again after one of the children had been physically attacked and was becoming very ill. The child was losing weight and the doctors could not find a reason. She would wake up covered in scratches, bruises, and rashes.

I told them again that they needed to get all the ritual and magical images out of their house and to do it properly with respect. In the end they relented and I contacted a friend of mine who was a Nigerian priest. He came and identified the objects, saying that they were indeed ritual objects, curses, and spirit beings. His advice was to send the objects back to the country they had come from. Arrangements were made with people in Africa and the pieces were shipped back to Africa to be housed with someone who could deal with them properly.

The house was ritually cleaned, and the child immediately improved. All the problems stopped and never returned.

This is a very good example and warning to people not to acquire religious or ritual objects that are not from their own culture and use them as ornaments. Ritual objects, deities, and spirit statues are usually powerful living beings that need to be respected and worked with in the culture that they come from. It has become very fashionable to have a profusion of ethnic objects through a house and it often brings a whole host of problems with it.

So when you are assessing a house, look for objects, pictures, statues, etc, that might be carrying something. Sometimes, though, it can be something simple but powerful that has been worked on. That doesn't tend to happen too much in western culture but it does pop up occasionally. I was once called out to a place where someone was being magically attacked quite badly. I went around the house and couldn't see anything. So I went in vision around the house and found a very aggressive being in the wardrobe. It was bound into a Barbie doll that the owner had been given upon leaving their home on Haiti. It had been cursed and a being tied into it. I stripped the being out and the doll was then safely burned. Humans can be so nasty sometimes.

So if you don't find anything by walking around the house, then go around again in vision, just make sure your body is properly protected as you do that.

If the house is affected by a parasite then the symptoms will be simple: either everyone just gets drained from being in the house, or everyone starts arguing once they have been in the house for a few minutes. The affects of a parasite are usually just a manifestation of its eating habits and nothing more. So it will be one type of emotion that everyone gets sucked into as they spend time in the house. There will be no other symptoms as a rule.

As for ghosts—we will deal with ghosts in the chapter on death, as the methods of assessment are different from possessions and infestations.

Summary

Assessments are more or less about being observant, using your common sense, and not getting pulled into dramas. Keep an open and sensible mind, clean yourself off as soon as you have finished assessing, don't let people get carried away with drama, and always look at the possible practical sensible reasons first—

most perceived possessions are usually illness, emotional trauma, drama, bad drains, house subsidence, or drugs.

But always keep a guard up just in case. It is easy to get caught off guard and attacked through complacency. And always make sure you don't take anything home with you. Clean up, shake off, and double check yourself before you let your guard down.

Happy hunting!

Chapter 6
Working with dead people

One of the jobs of an exorcist is to deal with the spiritual remnants of a death, which can present in a number of ways. Our society as it is does not have the religious, magical, or spiritual structures to deal with the inner issues that surround death—instead it focuses on the bereaved and their recovery.

This lack of guidance for the dead, combined with the often neglected inner impact that a death causes, can lead to quite difficult and unhealthy situations. The work of an exorcist is to address these situations sensitively to ensure that the souls of the dead continue on their path, and that the energetic after-effects are cleared and rebalanced. All of this must be approached with a careful sense of understanding not only for those left behind, but for the beings and energies that the exorcist encounters. Doing an aggressive exorcism on a death/haunting situation is inappropriate and doesn't really address what is going wrong, why it happened, etc, nor does it really resolve the issue—it just moves it to one side and sweeps it under the carpet.

The work with a dying person, a coma patient, or a very recent death is addressed in my book *The Initiates Companion Book*—that is more the work of a priest or priestess. The job of an exorcist comes to the fore when the job of a priest or priestess has not been done for whatever reason.

So what causes all these things to go wrong in the death process?

Some people die in a way that they were not expecting, some die suddenly, some fight it aggressively, some don't even know that they are dead. Then there are those who do not want to be dead, or do not want to let go of that which drove them in their lives. This is a common problem in esoteric lodges when a leader dies— he refuses to let go and continues to try to run the lodge from the inner worlds. That is different from becoming an inner contact, which is a totally different process after death for a teacher or leader.

Some cultures have specific rituals and vigils that are performed for and with the newly dead person to guide them on their way and to assist those left behind in letting go. Clinging by either party will result in an unhealthy situation that could develop into a haunting. The ability to let go completely is something that some spiritual systems teach at great length and those cultures connected to such spiritual practice, have very few problems with true hauntings.

Hauntings

There are a variety of different types of hauntings, some that involve dead people, and some that involve the echoes of what a dead person has left behind and a parasite has stepped into. Another form of haunting (although in true terms it is not a haunting), is where an impression has been imprinted upon a place— certain events release a lot of power all at once and leave a 'mark' on the place, i.e. accidents, murders, etc.

There are some imprints that can be left from fear, sex, pain, birth, and are not involved in a death/haunting, but may present as a haunting. These appear as recordings that play when they are triggered, but the 'people' that appear cannot be interacted with as there is not actually a being there.

The two most common types of hauntings that an exorcist would be called out to attend to are the ghosts of recent dead, and then long term disruptive hauntings. The recently dead types of hauntings are obviously the saddest and the exorcist is often called out not to get rid of them, but to find out what they need.

Recent Deaths

When an exorcist is called out to a recent death, the family will report dreams, sightings, interactions, and the feeling that they are experiencing emotions that are not their own. A family will approach a priest or spiritual leader for advice who will sometimes in turn contact an exorcist.

When this sort of haunting is reported, it is often where the spirit is trying to communicate, or to find a way to continue some sort of interaction or relationship with the bereaved family. This type of haunting will occur if the person who died is sensitive, or has their own psychic ability, though often unrecognised. Once they have gotten over the shock of death, some people will try to communicate with the family to let them know that they still exist. This in itself is not a problem and usually fades off of its own accord as the spirit moves further away from the old life and begins to let go.

It does become a problem if the spirit of the person is trying to communicate and cannot find a way to be understood. The frustration can often be felt by members of the family, who in turn become confused, as the boundaries between their own emotions and the emotions of the spirit become entwined. The spirit will initially go to the closest members of the family to try to communicate. If that is not successful, then, like water, the spirit will find the most accessible conduit in that family group and try to connect with that person.

So the first real contact can sometimes come through a person who was not that closely connected with the dead person and that in itself can cause some emotional pain to those left behind (why did they go to this person and not me?). To ease that pain, it is important to explain to the close members of the family that maybe the spirit had been trying to communicate, but had not been able to get through for one reason or another.

In a situation like this, the first step is to sit down with the family members and let them talk openly about their experiences since the death. It is important to steer them through what they felt/feel emotionally and physically—dreams, ideas and strange sightings that catch their attention. This guides the family through recognising potential attempts for communication by the spirit. Once recognised, the family members gain more confidence in their own ability to understand spirit communication and their barriers become less 'dense,' which then opens possibilities for communication.

It is common, though, for the close family to have not felt or experienced anything and that can be very hard for them if they realise that the spirit has been trying to get through. But not everyone has the ability to pick up on subtle communion, or the emotional loss can be so great that nothing else can get 'in' so to speak.

The next step for a family situation like this is to create a bridge for the spirit to communicate and say what it needs to say. This can be done in a variety of ways, by doing the death vision and speaking to it in its own reality, by divination vocabulary or tarot (ask it what it wants to say and to speak through a reading layout), or through mediumship. Either way, giving voice to the spirit will often release a lot of tension and allow the spirit to begin the process of letting go.

That process at this stage is very important: if a spirit or those left behind try to hang on for a length of time, it becomes unhealthy and draining for the living, and spiritually degenerate for the dead. He needs to learn to let go of his former life and all those connected to it. By doing so, he releases all of his knowledge, experiences, connections, and emotions back into the world, and the soul, polished by life, moves on to its next phase of development. This release is the source of what the Western Mystery Tradition calls the Library—the combined and collected knowledge/wisdom of all those who have gone before. This can be consciously connected with in vision, and can also be absorbed practically when a master dies—his knowledge is released and can be picked up by students/apprentices. This applies to all skills, not just magical/spiritual ones.

Once the communication channels have been established, then

information, last thoughts, emotions, messages, etc, can be passed back and forth until both sides are ready to let go. This often happens naturally once all that has needed to be said has been said—the interactions slowly fade as both sides begin to move on.

As an exorcist one has to be careful, though, that you do not become a prop for someone's grief, and that you do not continue to bridge communication after it is no longer necessary. People will try to cling to the connection and it is important that they learn to let the spirit go—working alongside counsellors who understand esoteric approaches can be really helpful at this time. The family will need much longer term help to cope, but that is not the job of the exorcist and it is very important that the exorcist does not slip into that support role—blurring the boundaries of help for the living and help for the dead can become very sticky. Leave the counselling to the counsellor and do the work of the bridge until it is time to withdraw. This helps the family to disconnect emotionally and let the spirit go. While ever the exorcist is there, some families will hope for continued communication.

Long term hauntings

Well established hauntings are a more complex affair that can need a careful 'eye' and an approach that deals with both the dead spirit and the parasitical beings that can be riding them. When a spirit has been hanging around for a while, the emotive reasons for the spirit to cling to the living world provide a choice buffet of energy interactions that draw in parasitical beings of all types. These parasites then slowly take over the personality shell that once was the living human and operate through them. This also happens with land beings that can similarly use the shell for their own agendas.

The only problem with dealing with such a situation is that the personality shell that is used in such situations often still has emotive and psychic connections with the families and places left behind—there is still a fragment of the person within the haunting and that fragment must be handled with compassion and care.

Problematic hauntings that are well established tend to elicit specific emotional patterns from the people who occupy or visit the building that is haunted—the pattern of interaction will often give the exorcist major clues as to what is actually happening. Through those clues a picture emerges of an original situation whereby the spirit of a dead person needs to attend to something or the spirit feels the need to express some suppressed emotion or agenda.

Because such a situation is highly charged, it quickly becomes attractive to a variety of parasitical beings who then learn to 'operate' the personality of the deceased and drive her down a road of food supply—the original driving emotion is amplified and ridden with the need to interact, thus forming a chain of interactions with the living that would initiate emotional reactions, therefore creating 'energy food.'

A good example is a haunting whereby the ghost is aggressive, sending bad dreams, being physically aggressive, and creating extreme fear to all who occupy the building. The spirit may be someone who was murdered there, who died during a conflict, or who was extremely territorial and maybe even mentally ill. They inflict their angry emotions upon all who are sensitive enough to detect it which in turn generates an emotive reaction in the living person. Fear, anger, and confusion are all very yummy energies which attract parasitical beings for dinner.

The pattern of fear generated by the living over a period of time becomes a food source for certain types of beings who quickly realise they can use their own inner ability to 'beef up' the original haunting and therefore create stronger emotions in the living. They begin to merge with the dead spirit until they eventually become almost like a composite being. Over decades and generations the truth of the dead spirit is pushed to one side as the parasite gets bigger and stronger.

Sometimes there is a situation whereby the person who died was already heavily parasited and the being within them instigates the haunting as a way to keep its energy source going. That is a very difficult one to figure out and can only really be diagnosed, as it were, by detailed questions put to the living relatives. If there is a long history of mental illness, bizarre or abusive behaviour, or extreme sexual drives that were destructive, then there is a very good chance that the person was parasited before death.

Dealing with a parasited haunting

The first step is to figure out what is actually going on. The second step is to remove the parasite before you try to deal with the dead spirit. The removal of a parasite from a dead spirit can be real fun. If there is no body, i.e., if there has been a cremation, then the chances are that the parasite is a strong and intelligent one—weaker and dumber parasites tend to cling to flesh/shapes to express themselves through, a little like body builders and botoxed actresses. In such a case, a mild exorcism and blessing of the body, along with a clean up of the haunted space will usually get rid of the parasite, leaving the way forward to walk the dead spirit into death.

If, however, the body has been cremated, you have to work purely in the inner worlds to remove the parasite from the spirit, which can be tricky and exhausting. There are two ways this can be approached and it is best to use both: through the spirit image that exists in the inner pattern of the building, and through the death vision itself.

To attempt the first part of this method of clearing, work in the building as is—don't try to clear the space first because that will cause the spirit to become flattened to the periphery of the space which will make it much harder to deal with.

Kick everyone who is living out of the space, put on a prepared stole and sit down before a lit candle. Using inner vision, pass into the void first to disconnect yourself from your daily life and then return into the space as the priest/ess. If the haunting is a bad or aggressive one, then call upon the Sandalphon to work with you as you step out of the void. Look around the space, the parasite will have been attracted by your actions and will be curious. If it does not appear immediately, just wait. Ghosts are like horses, if you pretend not to be interested in them it drives them nuts and they just have to come over to investigate.

Once they are in your range, the parasite will be more visible than the spirit (the two will often be overlaid, or the spirit looking out of the eyes of the parasite, which is the reverse of a living infestation whereby the parasite looks out of the eyes of the living). Treat it from this point like an ordinary parasite: grab it, wrap it, and dump it back where it belongs (underworld, Abyss, etc).

The spirit then needs immediate attention to take it into the death vision before another parasite can move in. Once the spirit has been walked into death, you will need to clean and clear the space. Use consecrated salt and water to clear the room, then burn frankincense to clean it (see chapter one, use of salt and water to clear a room). You might have to do the death vision a couple of times over the next few days just to make sure that the spirit has indeed gone into death and that there is no pattern left behind.

Before you start the death vision, put on a stole if you don't already have one on and, if you have an attending priest or priestess with you, have them guard you while you work. To do this they need to be sat opposite you and hold the space in vision by being still, silent, and vigilant. If any beings appear in the inner space of the room while you are working, they must banish them or ask them to leave. If you work with a ritual sword, then have it at your back as you work to protect you.

Death Vision

Light a candle, sit down, and close your eyes. See the flame with your inner vision and as you look at the flame, see the flame fall down into the earth and you are drawn to follow it. You and the flame fall down and down, deep into the underworld, leaving the surface world behind.

As you fall through the darkness, the flame falls ahead of you and you follow it as you fall together through the underworld. You land in a cave, landing on soft sand as the flame waits beside you. In the cave is a river that flows through the darkness and you call out through the darkness for the boatman.

A light appears on the river in the darkness and a slow boat appears with an old man rowing it. A small lamp holds a flame at the head of the boat and he rows towards you. Once he pulls over to you, put your hand in your pocket and pull out a coin which you give to him. He helps you into the boat and he rows off down the river, which passes through dark tunnels that run deep in the underworld.

Sunlight appears ahead and the boat emerges out in a landscape with mountains to your left and a desert to your right. He pulls over on the right hand side of the river bank and waits for you to get out.

As you get out you become aware of people walking towards the river from the desert and of people sat beside the river. Many seem confused and shocked; some are not sure what has happened to them or where they are. Stand among them and call the name of the dead person that you seek. Keep calling until he walks towards you or identifies himself somehow.

Once you have him, look him over to ensure that no parasites are attached to him, and if they are, remove them and put them in the river. Once he is clean, turn him to face the river and show him a bridge that spans it. The bridge is usually guarded by two angels with swords.

Walk him to the bridge and tell him that he must cross the bridge and walk into death. If he resists, you must explain to him that there is nowhere else for him to go and that he really needs to step forward onto this new path. If he still will not move, ask the help of the angelic beings. If they come to help, do not be surprised if they change their appearance—they are dressing in a way that the dead person expects them to look, and may appear as a relative or religious figure. The angelic beings choose the image that is the most likely to have a positive affect on the dead person.

Once he has crossed the bridge, walk him to the mountains and talk to him about letting go of his life, his belongings, relationships, and connections. You need to help him understand that his previous life has now gone and that world no longer exists for him. This total letting go allows the spirit to free itself and prepare for the next experience. If he does not let go, he will carry issues, fears, and connections with him into his next life, which is nearly always an unhealthy thing for the soul.

As you approach the mountain, look for a pathway up the side of it that you can both walk. The mountain is composed of his prejudices that are deeply embedded, often religious, so as you

climb the mountain with him he will often hear religious recitation or lots of discussion—it is the spirit's structure it has created
through that life to cope with energy and impact.

The higher you climb, the quieter the voices will become until
you reach the top and it is silent. Angelic beings will be waiting at
the top and they will ask the dead person to lie down and rest. He
will lie down and the angelic beings begin to sing him to sleep and
stroke him. The soul and spirit become disconnected at this point
and the soul takes rest and renewal before tumbling back into life.

At this point your job is now done but you cannot go back
down the way you came—energetically that would too exhausting
and would put too heavy a strain on you. Look beyond the angelic beings and you will see a deep mist. Walk towards the mist and
step into it with the intention of stepping into the void.

Stepping through the mist you find yourself in nothing and a
silence settles around you. This is the void, the place where all
power comes from and returns to. Be still in this place until you
are ready to move on. When you are ready, think about the place
where you started the vision, and think of the flame. With that
intention step forward and you will pass out of the void and find
yourself stepping through the flame back into the room where you
first started.

When you are ready, put out the candle flame.

***

Once you have cleared the space, go in vision and look around
the room in detail for any inner doorway or access point that
might be allowing beings into the space. From there, go around
the house in vision and check each room individually. Make sure
there is nothing in the house itself that would attract beings from
an inner point of view and once you have done that, do the same
out of vision—go into each room and check each room carefully.
It would be wise to suggest to the house occupants that they get
some protective or spiritual images in the house to dissuade any
return of the parasite.

House structure

Check the house structure for obvious things that would make a haunting easier. The most obvious one is a well inside or under the house—it is like having a tunnel to the underworld right in the house. If there is such a thing in the structure, then it needs to be properly capped both physically and ritually—a swirled and protected seal with the seal on the underside as well as the outer side needs to be firmly in place.

Also look at where the house is situated: is it on or near a power site? Is it near or on a burial ground? Is it near power substations, toxic dumps, caves, large granite outcrops, slaughter houses, etc. All of these types of locations can create an energy pattern that allows all sorts of nasties to gather and, although the dead spirit has been moved on, the situation that allowed it to happen in the first place is still there and can happen again.

If the house is badly situated and the occupants cannot move (most cannot), then you have to work with them to help balance and protect the space in the best way possible. First it is important to ascertain what affect the location has on its occupants. For example, did they have regular bad dreams even before the haunting (being accessing them)? Do they get sick and tired very easily (poor energy flow or land parasites)? Is there a lot of conflict in the house (too much fire energy)?

Feng shui can be useful in such circumstances and I once had an amazing but odd book from China which was very helpful but I cannot for the life of me remember what it was called. It was different to most FS books and its methods worked well. But I know next to nothing of the subject so it would be best to talk to a specialist.

The other option is to identify the worst areas and use demon traps, swirls, hole stones, water traps (bowls of water changed every day) sacred images, and a lit candle to mitigate the inner aspect. It would also be worth looking into the use of copper tubing at key points outside around the house if there is a weird energy flow.

If the house is on granite, that can be powerful good as well as powerful bad. The granite often holds very large powerful and protective beings that can be tapped into and worked with. Go in vision to the rock and talk to the consciousness of the land, learn ways to be in harmony with such a powerful substance.

Once you have done your work on the haunting, let the dust settle for a few days and then go back to the house. It might be a good idea to do a blessing in the house, using a lit candle and a bowl of water. A simple one can be used and adapted for most religions. It is very important that any blessing brought upon the house is within the realm of the religious sensibilities of the occupants. Their connection with Divinity is a major point in this work—do not cross beyond their religious lines. This is why it is important for an exorcist to have a good working knowledge of most major religions.

Burial sites

Some ancient burial sites can become very badly haunted and some are guarded by large beings that can in themselves cause all sorts of problems that can present as a haunting. In such a case there is not a lot you can do—the house is trespassing and the occupants are in the wrong by being there. In that sort of scenario, the most you can do is advise people how to live in such a difficult energetic place (diet, protections, etc) and see if the people are able to spiritually interact with the site (i.e., become guardians themselves by tending to the dead, singing to the ancestral spirits, honouring their burials, etc).

Other than that the best advice you can give them is to move house.

The other thing that can happen on such a site is that an ancestral collective being tries to move in to the living and the recent dead—a sort of possession of both the living and the dead. All the anger of the ancestral burials can manifest and sometimes become violent, war-like, and vicious. They can be very powerful, often hurting people and property, and sometimes trying to take the most vulnerable occupants into death.

This has to be treated like a demonic possession of the house and the occupants—it is a dangerous and difficult situation to attend to. It is a collective of ancestral spirits (which are a combination of land beings and once-human spirit fragments) that can also have a demonic overtone to it which makes it difficult to manage or get rid of.

I worked on such a situation once that was on a burial site by the Trail of Tears in the U.S.A. The focus of the collective being was a small lake by the burial site out of which beings would come and suck people's energy until they almost died. It would attack them with fury, often marking them in their sleep and all the houses of the area were badly haunted. I worked on dismantling the being in the lake and then communing with the ancestral spirits that wanted revenge. I managed to eventually calm the situation down but I paid a very heavy price: my thyroid went into freefall (the endocrine system is the impact taker in such work) and I was very ill for a long time after. In hindsight I was arrogant in thinking that I could handle it alone and it was in fact a job that needed a group of people working over a period of time.

The western areas around the great lakes is a major burial site, as is Tennessee, and I got my ass whooped in both areas. So take the time to step back in such a situation and properly assess it using readings, vision, and historical research.

Don't be a hero—it's not worth it and you will just end up fried.

Working with and on such burial sites is possible, it's just long, hard work, and needs constant attention. The occupants themselves must take a major chunk of the responsibility for the work and keep up daily interactions and protections. Don't allow them to sit back and let you do all the work. They live there—it's your job to guide them and only do what they cannot.

Summary

Most hauntings are not really hauntings and the ones that are tend to be minor. You will possibly, once or twice, come across major hauntings (unless you are unlucky like me and get swamped with the buggers) and they will be a major test of your abilities, common sense (of which I have little), and body strength. Don't overstretch yourself and know when to back out quietly.

Chapter 7
How to conduct an exorcism

The removal of demonic beings

Once you have identified the being that is possessing the victim, gathered your tools, and set a date, the exorcism begins. From that point on you must keep vigil, keep clear, and preserve your energies—you are going to need them! Once you have made your assessment, you will have a fairly clear idea of what it is you are dealing with, which in turn will dictate how you approach the exorcism itself. The one-size-fits-all exorcisms of the Vatican usually just bore the shit out of demons, and the fundamentalist method of beating the victim with a baseball bat (with a crucifix on it, of course) isn't of much more use really. The methods you use should be purely dictated by what type of being it is.

Demonic exorcism
Let's start with the yummiest of all exorcisms: the removal of a demonic being. Luckily, these are rare and you may never come across a fully blown intelligent and powerful demon, but if you are sure that it is a demonic being, then you must conduct the exorcism as if it were the most powerful type; that way you don't get caught with your pants down, so to speak.

In a way, the full-on demonic possessions with all the attendant intelligent rage, manipulation, sexual energy, violence, and bizarre behaviour is easier than the more subtle ones: at least you know exactly what you are dealing with, and such a spectacular display (like over confidence in humans), can often mask a little fear and insecurity in the being itself (there again, it might just be a really powerful show off...and not have any Achilles heel to speak of).

A lot of demonic possessions are reasonably mild in comparison to what they can be, but you have to be aware that very dangerous demonic beings can masquerade as lesser beings to ensure their survival and not be interfered with too much: these are the truly dangerous intelligent and manipulative ones. Some demonic possessions are not frothing, screaming, violent presentations. They can often appear as illnesses with emotional problems and other little weird presentations (see chapter on beings you may encounter). If you have a presentation like that and suspect minor demonic interference or possession, there is a possibility that you will be lulled into thinking that a minor exorcism will suffice. I can tell you from bitter experience that such assumptions can catch you out in a major way.

From those experiences I have learned that if you truly suspect demonic beings, no matter how seemingly weak, approach and exorcise as if it was the biggest, nastiest demonic being you can think of: that way all bases are covered and no one is harmed or left still possessed. A full-on demonic exorcism will not harm the host; it will just take a lot more energy from the exorcist.

If you really think it is not demonic, but some other type of being, then those methods will be discussed in the next chapter.

Preparing the space

To prepare the room for the exorcism, you need everyone out of that room except any priest/ess you are working with and have the possessed person as far away from that room as possible but still in the house; have at least one person, maybe a family member with them. Before you go into the room to prepare it, place a consecrated and sigil-marked stole around the neck of the possessed and tell the person sitting with them to make sure it stays on—it will dull the possession a little bit for a short while and will give you time to prepare. The sigil upon the stole depends solely upon the deities and beings that you work with. If you are Christian, then the cruciform is needed at the two ends and at the back of the neck. If you work with angelic beings, then the sigils for those beings should be in the same place. If you don't really work with beings in that way, then tight golden swirls that inter-connect will work—you just need to make sure the stole is con-secrated.

Once you have done that, put on your own stole before you do anything else, and make sure that you are wearing a talisman that is designed only to protect you from death or possession.

Go and begin the clearing of the room you are about to work in. Take out all images that are not sacred to their religion: remove all masks, dolls, photos, toys, stuffed animals, etc—any-thing that has a form or face that can become influenced or pos-sessed. It is not unknown for a demon to leave a human and take up residence in soft toy. Anything that has a recognisable shape that can be identified with as a life form is suspect and can be possessed.

Remove all mirrors from the room, but have one with you that is about two- or three-feet tall that is yours and place it propped against a chair or something similar facing the chair that the pos-sessed will sit or lie in. Place a chair behind the possessed person's chair which will be for you to sit in. If you use a ritual sword, it should go behind your chair, unsheathed, point down.

You will need a large bowl of consecrated salt, a bowl of con-secrated water, and a bowl to mix the two together in. At this point, double check the room for images and also for containers that the being might try to slip into. Put a line of salt across the corner of the floor in each cross quarter, draw the curtains and hang/stick a swirl cloth on the back of the door. Put a small bowl of consecrated salt under the chair that the possessed will sit in and a small bowl of consecrated salt and water under your chair.

Now you need to 'clear the air.' Light your charcoal and burn frankincense. If you have any Osha root, burn that first (Osha root is a rare but very powerful root that can clear a space like a good fart).

You need to ensure that the working space is completely clear before the possessed person comes in and to do that you must go around the room with consecrated salt and water to do a room clearing. (See chapter 1 for method of consecrating salt and water.)

Room clearing

First go around the space with frankincense incense, making sure you go into each corner. Then, with the salt and water, go into each room, sprinkling the water in each direction, including up and down while reciting:

"In the names which are above every other name, and in the power of the almighty, and of the mother and of the holy spirits, I exorcise all influences and seeds of evil from this room. I exorcise all demons, parasites, ghosts, curses, spells, and bindings from this room. I exorcise all thought forms, magical spirits, and bound angels from this room. I cast upon them the spell chains and I cast them into the outer darkness of the Abyss where they shall trouble not these servants of god. Amen, Amen Selah."

It's simple and to the point, no fuss, and no drama. Too many clearing and exorcism texts are padded to the hilt with drama, repetition, and sucking up to deities. It's not necessary. Simple works just as well when you are focussed with intent. At this point, go in vision into the void and stay there even though you are walking around: it will prepare you for work and will make you hard to get a hold of spiritually—it's like smearing yourself with butter before a wrestling match.

Once the room is prepared, then bring the victim in and sit her in the chair provided for her. Do not get into conversations with her or the being within her. Polite conversation is not needed and getting into a verbal pissing contest with the demon is defiantly not productive, even if it is the Vatican's most treasured approach.

Beginning the exorcism

Once the victim is seated, have a priest/ess stood beside the attending family member (who should also be wearing a stole) and if there is a doctor in attendance, have him or her off to one side. No one should be stood directly in front of the victim: such positioning will put a person at real risk of possession (demon thinks, 'ack, this is too much like hard work, hmm, I will go...there!'). The eyes are the danger point so direct eye contact is not a good idea: most possessions are initiated by eye contact with an infested person or being. (Ever wondered why so many serious demonic possessions dealt with by Catholic priests end up with the priest himself getting possessed or attacked? They face the victim head on and challenge the being directly. Bright, huh?)

Once everyone is in place, then sit behind the victim and get straight to work. Exorcisms have a series of phases or stages that should be rigorously adhered to. Don't cut corners and don't stop halfway through because you think it has worked quickly: just because the bomb stops ticking doesn't mean it's not going to go off.

Exorcism phase one: the visionary stage

The first stage of the exorcism consists of going to the depths of the possession and pulling out the roots, so to speak. This involves pulling out the deepest part of the being, or asking it to leave (depends on how bad tempered you are that day). That depth of work is conducted in vision only, with total outer silence.

The heaviest possessions need a lot of angelic work and you will need to have the angelic beings working through you (which is why you need to be fit and healthy). You should already be in the void from an inner point of view so close your eyes and see yourself there immediately. Call upon the Angel of Air to come to work with you and be aware of a very large angelic being that appears in a whirlwind with many eyes, swords, and long hair. Step into the being, and smaller versions of the being will come up to you to give you weapons and dress you in armour. See the armour go on and be aware if there are any weak points in it: it is really, really important to make sure you have good angelic armour on with no cracks or missing bits. Just because it is in vision doesn't mean it's all in your imagination: I cannot say this enough times—be very careful. I was once working deep in the Abyss and a demonic being grabbed my foot. The armour that I had on was in layers and the foot came off like a sock. The being grabbed my foot and I had to fight along with angelic beings to get loose. I sustained quite a nasty leg injury that took a good long time to heal.

Once you are armoured, step out of the void into the room in vision with the angelic being all around you like a suit. Also call for the Sandalphon to assist you so that, as you step out of the void, they are there ready and waiting to go to work.

With the angelic being around you, look at the victim and you will immediately see the demonic being in and around them. It might try to attack you, so be ready for it. It is important that you work with focus and speed without distraction. If the victim tries to get up or do anything, it is the job of the priest/ess to sit them back down or gently restrain them. Your job is to stay in vision and be a bridge for the angelic beings to work through.

Quickly grab the demonic being and ask it if it is willing to leave with you of its own accord. Only give it one chance—usually they take it willingly. If it does not, using the power of the angelic being around you, cut the umbilical cord that connects it to the victim and immediately bind it with ropes given to you by the Sandalphon. Sometimes this phase can be straight forward; sometimes it is an all out battle. Do not assume because you are working in vision that it is not really real. If you get hit in vision by a demon, you will sustain a physical injury. I know—I have loads of battle wounds and scars from such interactions (black eyes were the most common ones I got).

Once you have the demonic being under control, see yourself and the Sandalphon walking off with the being through the void and out into the desert of the Abyss. If the demonic being is of angelic content, then it might need to be bound in the desert and left there with a guardian. The Sandalphon will advise you if that is the case. If it is substance-based demonic, which most are (conditional beings) then it belongs in the Abyss.

Taking beings into the Abyss

With your eyes closed, see yourself holding the being along with the Sandalphon, step through the flame with focus on the intent to go to the Abyss, and with that intent step out through the flame, finding yourself walking across a flat desert. You will see beings in the distance bound up as they sleep and wait. Pass by them as you focus your intent to travel to the Abyss.

In the distance you see a faint glow over the land and as you get closer you will come to a large crack in the earth which seems to go down and down forever, and out of which is a faint glow of light. This is the Abyss that flows through all worlds. As you stand on the edge of the Abyss, you become aware of the beings below and above in the Abyss, and of Divinity across the Abyss hidden in the mists that cloak the other side.

Because the demonic beings tend to come from great depths in the Abyss, the Sandalphon may cloth you in sand and dust until you look like rock.

You call for the keeper of the Abyss and out of the depths rises a large being of human shape but monstrous size that stands up within the Abyss and looks down to you. He will hold out his hand for you to step onto. All of you, angelic beings, you and the demon will be taken down the Abyss by the keeper to the area where the demon comes from.

He will hold his hand out at a ledge that goes back into a tunnel that will lead to the area that the demon comes from. Go down the tunnel until it opens out into an area where others of that type of being are. Once they are in their own realm, they tend to be less of a threat to you (though not always) but have your guard up. Ask one of the angelic beings to hold the demon while you and a Sandalphon look into the back of the area for a crack or opening (that leads into the physical world) that would have enabled the demon to pass into our world. If you find the crack, seal it up using part of the Sandalphon or 'filler' that he gives you.

Once it is filled, release the demon and leave the area. Once you are out of the tunnel and on the ledge, call the keeper who will be near by and have him take you back to the desert.

Once you are back at the desert, ask the Sandalphon to take off the dust/sand cover that was on you and walk towards the mist before you. Step through the mist into the void and drop your amour, step out of the angelic being that has been hosting you and centre yourself in the void before stepping out of the void back into the room where you are working.

* * *

That is the first layer of work done to loosen any possession: heavy possessions happen in layers and all layers must be attended to for the exorcism to be successful.

Step Two: clearing of the victim's 'inner landscape' and removal of inner imprints.

The second step looks into the inner landscape of the victim. The inner landscape is an inner filter that facilitates the soul to express itself in the physical realm. Things that appear or happen in the inner landscape often give a very strong indication of the physical health and spiritual well being of the human. When a human becomes infested with parasites or possessed by a demonic type being, it will often appear in the inner landscape. This appearance enables the being to affect the landscape, making the human more accepting to the possession and making the landscape itself more comfortable for the being.

The being will then begin to assimilate itself into the landscape in an attempt to become 'part' of the human so that it can affect, control, and feed off the interactions of the human in everyday life. If left in there long enough the being and the human become a composite being and it can become very difficult to separate the two. This often expresses itself outwardly by the human's reluctance to have the being removed: they become a part of each other.

To work in the inner landscape, it is another job that is best approached through vision. It has less danger involved in it than the Abyss work, but it can be very draining.

Working in the Inner Landscape

For this vision, it is best to have physical contact with the victim. Stand behind him with your hands upon his head and shut your eyes. Go into the void and be still for a moment, and ask any attendant beings for the tools and protection to do your job. When you are working in the inner landscape, the tools that you use appear as ordinary everyday cleaning/fixing tools like a vacuum cleaner, weed whacker, shears, a sack, etc.

Step from the void back into the room and see yourself passing into the body of the victim and travelling up his spine into his brain. Once in the deepest part of their brain, focus your intent on finding the inner landscape and a door will appear in the brain. Go through the doors and you will find yourself in a landscape.

Look around: take note of the health of the land, the nature growth or lack of, the weather, any waterways, mountains, meadows, etc. There should be no beings or unnatural shapes/objects in the landscape, nor should there be any people except for the human himself. If the human appears younger than he really is, it can be a sign of what age the possession really began: he becomes frozen in time. This can also happen if a major trauma happened in the past and he is stuck at that time in development.

If the human appears, look to see if he has any umbilical cords attached to him, or something stuck to him. If you find that, then you might be in for an easy job. Just disconnect, take up what is attached to him and stick it in your sack ready for dumping.

Just don't allow the being to deflect your attention onto a smaller being so that you think that is the only intruder.

Look around carefully, look for platonic solids (angelic beings that shouldn't be there), thought forms or constructs, parasites, demonic beings, etc. They can appear in an endless variety of forms that can be very confusing. If something doesn't look or feel right, then it is probably because it doesn't belong there and needs binding and removing.

Gather up anything weird that you find and stick it in your sack. Once you have finished, gather up your sack and go through the void from the landscape (this is why it is important to have a daily meditation in the void so that you can access it any where, any time) and out into the desert: hand the sack to the keeper of the Abyss.

Go back to the landscape and look around one more time. If you have removed something you should see the weather start to pick up and flowers start to appear—this is the soul beginning to re assert itself in the landscape.

Once you have finished, go back out of the doors and close them behind you. Place your hands upon the door and call for two guardians (angelic) to pass through you into the door. This is where you have to bridge a few worlds at once: be aware of yourself in the victim's inner brain, also in the void, and also in the physical realm. That way, when you mediate the angelic power through you, you won't end up looking like my cooking: crispy and lightly blackened....

By not specifying which angelic being should come through, you allow for whatever is needful from that type of consciousness to pass through you and into the victim. The guardians will appear in or around the door: take note of what they look like, that will give you an idea of what they are. That, in turn, will tell you a lot about how the infestation got in originally. (The need dictates the cure.)

Once all is done, step back into the void and let your tools go before coming back into yourself. Don't forget to drop your tools: they are, in reality, certain levels of energy used for specific actions (hence they appear to you as tools) and are not designed to be carried around—they can get really heavy.

Once you have finished, open your eyes and take your hands off the victim. Immediately rub your hands with the consecrated salt and bathe your hands in the consecrated water. This cleans you and breaks the contact. You might also want to rub a little consecrated salt upon your forehead/third eye area.

At this point do not get into discussion about what you found, did, or saw. You must move silently on without engaging the victim: the battle is not over yet.

Step Three: the Verbal Exorcism of Substance

Once the deepest levels of the being have been removed, then other layers have to be attended to—exorcism is like peeling an onion. The next step is to exorcise the remnants from the physical body of the host, to ensure that no doorways, connections, or echoes remain with the victim. So you started at the being itself, then you removed the being's inner imprint that was left on the human landscape, and now you take out any physical manifestation that might have taken root in the human.

I do this the good old fashioned way by a verbal exorcism over the body of the victim: it strips out any physical imprint, residue, etc, that has been left in the body. If not taken out the imprint will affect the health one way or another, and can possibly lead to cancerous conditions.

A version that was used in the Catholic Church, and was also used in an adjusted form in the early Golden Dawn, is effective and straightforward. This part of the exorcism uses the power of recitation and the exorcist does not engage from any inner point of view—it is totally exoteric in its action, which allows inner contacts to work through the exorcist without hindrance.

Before you start the recitation, rub your hands in the salt and wash them with the water. Do the same to your forehead/third eye, and to the back of your neck (c7 vertebrae) which is a major access point and should be covered by a consecrated stole.

Recitation

The recitation itself is simple, to the point, and is almost the same that is used for the consecration of salt and the clearing of a room. That is also an important thing to remember: the tools of an exorcist should be paired down, simple, effective, and to the point. They do not need to be changed, dressed up, made more impressive or be in any strange language—it is preferable to understand what you are saying. There are texts that work regardless of whether you understand them or not, and they can be used effectively. But I am always wary of using something that I do not understand. Some magical texts for recitations have conditions attached to them and I like to know what I am getting myself into.

Stand to the side of the victim and point at their head with your first two fingers (+ means make the sign of an equal armed cross with your first two fingers held together):

"I exorcise thee creature of the earth by the living God + the holy God + the omnipotent God + that thou mayest be purified of all demonic influence, in the name of Adonai, lord of all angels and men."

"And In the name which is above every other name, in the power of the Almighty, and of the Mother, and of the holy spirits, I exorcise all influences and seeds of evil from this body; I exorcise all demons and their remnants from this body; I exorcise all spiritual parasites and ghosts from this body; I exorcise all earth beings, faery beings, and thought forms from this body; I exorcise and release all chained and bound angels from this body; I exorcise all curses, spells, and bindings from this body. I cast upon all of them the spell chains and I cast them into the outer darkness where they shall trouble not this servant of God."

Lay your hand upon his head:

"Creature of the earth adore thy creator, in the name of God the father + and God the mother + I bless thee and cleanse thee, releasing thee from all bonds, that thou may go and live in peace. Amen, Selah."

At the point where you say "bless thee," mark his forehead with consecrated oil either in the four-directional cross, or the cruciform if he is Christian, the name of Allah if they are Muslim, etc, or with the triangle which is the trinity of Mother, Father, and Spirit.

When you use the word 'God' it is not in a specific religious context—i.e., doesn't mean a Christian, pagan, or any other specified religion. It refers to Divinity itself.

The first part of the recitation calls upon an angelic threshold of Divinity to intercede, then it calls upon the windows of Divinity itself to intercede.

Phase 4: mop up

Consecrated bath

Have someone run a bath for the victim. Light a candle in the bathroom and tune it to the centre of all the directions: the Void. Consecrate the water, add consecrated salt to the bath, hold out your hand over the bath while saying:

"Lord God, father of the heavens above, Great Goddess Mother of the Earth below my feet, grant that this salt will make for health of the body, and this water for health of the soul. Grant that they may be banished from whence they are used, every power of adversity and every artifice of evil shall be banished into the outer darkness in thy holy names. Amen."

Have a clean set of clothes laid out for the victim and ask him to leave his old clothes outside the bathroom door. Have them taken away by your attending priest/ess in a bag/sack and pour consecrated salt over them before putting them in a washing machine. They may need burning if the possession was a strong one—the resonance of the being can stay in the clothing.

This is where you and all attending helpers stop and have a strong coffee while the victim takes a bath: the quick coffee helps to break any connections and has a mild protective quality to it. It is also a good idea to eat some chocolate or something sweet-ish: you will have used up a lot of energy and the brain will need some replenishment.

Once you have taken a quick break, then the room needs attending to while the victim bathes. Burn plenty of frankincense and go around each corner with it, and also 'smoke' each other, washing your faces and hands in the smoke.

Then, using consecrated water and salt, cleanse the room and put out all candles. Wash the mirror that was used with consecrated salt and water and then wrap it in a swirl cloth. (The mirror will need to be put out in nature for a while just in case any residue was caught in it. If it feels weird when you bring it back in, do a recitation clearing on it.)

Once the room is still, light a new clean candle and tune it to the power of Divinity above and below, with the flame in the middle. Take a plain pendant and go around the four directions with it and ask the powers of each direction to put into the pendant whatever will be needful to protect the victim in the short term, to allow him to recover and strengthen his own boundaries.

As soon as the victim comes out of the bathroom, put the pendant on him and tell him that he must not take it off for any reason, for any length of time, not even to shower. It should stay on for at least a month. It will probably break when it is finished working.

Have someone take him away from the room, (but still in the house) and feed him. After that, he should sleep a little while with a priest watching over him for any inner activity. Make sure a candle is burning in the room with him while he sleeps and there should be a safety candle burning in his bedroom every night for a week or two. A living flame pushes away much interference. It doesn't push everything out, but it is a good filter nevertheless. It is also a good idea to put a bowl of consecrated water under the bed each night and pour it away each morning for at least a week, to mop up any psychic resonance.

Building aftercare

Once the room has been cleared spiritually and physically, tell the owners to completely rearrange the room, even redecorate it if they can: this flattens out any residue that can hover in the building. The same goes for the victim's bedroom.

Before you leave the house after finishing the exorcism, go around each room and cleanse them with salt and water. Don't forget, if a room was once made up of two rooms, you must work on them as if they were still separate.

The room where the work was done should have a candle burning in it night and day for a month, and no images should be put up in that room during that time. Any images or statues that were around at the time of the possession should be cleansed, and if the family is of any particular religion, then a round of prayer should happen each day in the house.

An alternative is to ensure that sacred music or recitation is played for a couple of hours each day. The sounds resonate in a way that makes return for a being very difficult: it makes the inner pattern of the building 'slippy' to beings trying to get a way into the house. I still do this in my house on a regular basis and it works like a dream.

Aftercare of the exorcist

Once you leave the building, change your clothes and put them in a sack with consecrated salt before you go home. As soon as you get home, take a consecrated bath (same method that you used for the victim) and put on clean clothing. Although you will feel full of energy, that is a false feeling that you have to be careful with. You are still full of the strength given to you to do your job but it will fade off soon: with it goes your complete energy tide and you will go down like a ton of bricks.

Eat a good meal, keep a lit candle going night and day in your home and always have a candle going where you sleep for a while. Drink coffee and do nothing magical at all for a week at least: you need to rest and recover. You will feel the impact the day after and if you manifest any injuries, have them treated both magically and physically: homeopathy, cranial osteopathy, acupuncture, herbs, and flower essences all work in their own way, see which works best for you. But also attend to it allopathically—if you feel like you have fractured something, get it x-rayed. It is very possible to break something during an exorcism—I have had dislocated joints, fractured ribs, black eyes, burns, cuts, and all manner of rashes when doing this work, even when the injury is sustained in vision.

After doing a full demonic exorcism, you will need to rest for many days to recover. Although most of the work is done in vision, the body takes a massive impact from the energy that flows through such actions and it will need recovery time.

Retrospect

It is very important to your own learning and the learning of others that you keep diaries of your experiences; what happened, what worked, what didn't, etc, so that you can pass on your experiences to help others. Just be careful what you write in your summary regarding the actual being: do not write descriptions that may create a doorway for it to return.

It also helps to give an assessment a few days after to see how you feel after the event. It will help you self-analyse, which is very important. You need to be very body- and mind-aware to ensure that nothing got a chance to sneak in and fly under your radar. If you start to feel depressed, angry, or really weird, you might have a deeper impact than you realised, or you might have picked up a hitchhiker that needs to be removed. If you have strange reactions like that a few days after, get another consecrated bath and if that doesn't fix it, go see a colleague for further investigation. It will show up in a reading if looked at through tarot or similar methods.

If the demonic possession was particularly powerful and nasty, you will need to have all alarm bells on full alert for a long time after. Their pattern in establishing themselves can be complex and easily missed, so be very vigilant and careful.

Chapter 8
The Exorcism of non-demonic beings

There are lots of beings, from all different realms—including our own—that intrude, possess, drain, and interfere with us in a variety of ways. The most spectacular are the demonic beings that were dealt with in Chapter 7, and the most common ones are the various forms of parasites which are easily dealt with. In between those two extremes are yummies like humans possessed by Deities, living humans trying to move in (usually someone involved in magic), dead people trying to move in or grab a hold of you, elemental or land beings, faery beings, and ancestors. Let's look at some of the more efficient removal methods that can be practically applied.

Parasites
Before you attempt to remove a parasite, you need to know what type it is, what it feeds off, and if possible, how it got in. (See the chapter on 'Beings you may encounter.') Once you have figured that out, it will have bearing on how you approach its removal. There are a few different methods, including visionary work, Shamanic journeys, ritual, and herbal—it all really depends on how big, intelligent, and dug in it is. It is also worth trying to

figure out if the parasite is attached to an outer parasite, i.e. an inner parasite that uses intestinal/skin/blood parasites as a vehicle. If that is the case, then usually just dealing with the outer parasite and then giving the victim a ritual bath will suffice.

The more intelligent the parasite, the more dug in it is going to be, and the deeper the exorcist has to dig to get it out. An intelligent and well established parasite—particularly one that feeds off violence and fear—is going to be dangerous and should be treated exactly as a demon. In this scenario, use the exorcism methods in Chapter Seven but don't give it a chance to choose to go—parasites that are of that type and intelligence can use that few seconds to dig much deeper and become almost impossible to reach. (However bizarre it may seem, demons are actually more honest than parasites.)

Most parasites can be removed by using a combination of hands on/vision/ritual. The room does not need all the major preparation that a demonic exorcism does, but it is hard energy work (the buggers are heavy energetically).

Gaining an inner bag of skills

To deal with all these different types of beings, you need a good inner skill bag (to go with your outer tool bag). There are many places that one can find a 'skill bag,' and it really depends on what sort of powers you work with and what sort of problems you are sent to deal with. The two following visions are just some of many that can be used—once you have looked at them, you will be able to figure out the mechanism of the inner work and re-form the visions to work in your own spiritual field.

Neither of the visions are from known spiritual traditions—they are visions that have been found through deep inner work and are passed on to those willing to work with them. If you are a Christian, Jewish, or Muslim exorcist, the second vision will work best for you—the inner contacts within that vision are connected to the streams of inner consciousness that the later monotheistic religions manifested from.

The first vision is of the deep Underworld and of an ancient Goddess who is still very active in our world in a variety of forms, and who passed on her threads to newer Goddesses who are her daughters. It is suitable for exorcists who work within the Pagan/nature magic/shamanic, etc, fields of spirituality.

This vision will work for parasites that are of the Underworld, or are of a heavier, earthbound nature type—these parasites are very old, very clever, and feed off sex, death, and war. This Goddess is also one who is very interesting to work with in the field of medicine, healing, etc. She is not a fluffy Goddess, though—she is a deep power that can rain destruction down on nations. So tred really carefully and take loads of chocolate!

Vision of the Ancient Goddess of the Underworld

Light a candle and close your eyes. Look at the candle flame and feel your inner self become still and silent. After a few moments see the flame with your inner vision and as you watch it, the flame falls down into the earth and you follow.

You fall down deep into the earth, falling through roots, rocks, earth, and caves, falling down and down in the darkness, leaving the earthly world behind. As you fall, you hear voices, whispers, and find that you are falling through generations. All the ancestors of the land are around you as you fall, watching you, calling out to you as you pass by.

You fall into a pool of water, and as you climb out you see columns around the pool—tall, ancient, and intricately carved columns designed to look like giant trees. Climbing out of the pool, you walk among the columns, looking through the dim light to see what is beyond. You realise you are in a massive under-ground space, and the floor beneath you is tiled with carved stones that look like faces and strange beings. In the distance you see flames and you walk towards them. As you get closer you see that it is an opening in the ground that fire is coming out of and its light reveals the space around you. The roof is so high it van-ishes into the darkness, and the cave is so expansive that you can-not see the walls in any direction.

It is then that you see the feet: a little ahead of you is a giant pair of feet seemingly made of a polished black stone. They reflect the firelight and you are drawn to these giant carvings to look closer.

As you get closer, you see that they are attached to a colossal statue that is seated before the fire: the statue is of a Goddess who is part lioness and part human. Her black skin glows in the firelight and her eyes watch you intensely, like a child watching an ant.

The eyes move and you realise that what is before you is not a statue—it is the great Goddess herself, deep in the Underworld. She is seated upon a throne of volcanic rock and between her feet is a pair of giant golden doors that seem to lead to a chamber under her throne.

Put your hand in your pocket and take out whatever you find there. Place it at her feet as a gift. (If it is something that you own in real life, then you must give it to her by throwing it in a river, lake, sea, or burying it.) Take note of what you give her—it might not make sense at the time, but in years to come it might make a whole lot of sense.

The doors open as you look and priests come out to stand before you. They ask you who you are and what you want. Tell them who you are, what you do, and that you need specific skills to work with. The priests will look into you to see what you need and to see if you are capable of wielding the skills, and if you have honor to use them wisely.

If they see what they need, they will either hand you tools or put skills/tools into you. The Goddess then reaches down and picks you up in her paw. She looks deeply into you until she has reached the depths of your soul. She will challenge you to vows, usually to do with working with the tools, intentions, and service.

When she has finished, she will lift you high as she stands up. You will be lifted higher and higher until you reach the surface world. You will emerge out of a spring or pool of water and she will place you carefully on the earth before vanishing back deep into the Underworld. Bathe in the spring and drink from it. It will give you strength and understanding. From the spring, step into the void and be in the silence: be aware of what was given to you and the responsibility that goes with it. When you are settled with what you hold, step out of the void back into the room where you first started. When you are ready, open your eyes and blow out the candle.

***

This second vision is an odd thing to drop into the middle of a book like this but it is a very important vision and needs to be worked with to keep the bridge working—it links to an ancient well of wisdom that is quickly falling into the void. The skills that these adepts pass on are of a power far beyond the everyday workings of an exorcist—they are deep inner skills of service to humanity and Divinity. They are the foundation adepts of the magic and mysticism that came out of the near east and gave birth to Sumer, Parsa, Canaan, and Egypt.

If you feel you don't want to engage with a vision of this depth, you can get skills by going into the void and calling upon a deity or contact that you work with to teach you or transfer skills into you.

The vision of the Hall of Elders

Light a candle and close your eyes. Go into the void and be in stillness with no time, no movement. When you are ready, you step out with the intent to go to the desert of the Abyss. Stepping out on to the desert, you walk towards the glow of the Abyss, observing the many beings that are bound in time, held in the desert until the allotted time of their release. Many of these are bound angels of destruction, held until the end of time.

Walking towards the glow of the Abyss you notice something out of the corner of your eye. To the right of you, on the threshold of the Abyss, is a partially collapsed step pyramid that seems to be crumbing into the Abyss itself. Moving closer, you see a child with golden hair sitting on a stone at the foot of the pyramid, and he is watching you with interest.

He greets you as you reach the pyramid and puts out a hand to touch you. As you both touch, you feel his ancient power and he feels your intent. He points to a stone stairway carved up the front of the step pyramid which seems to crumble near to the top. He tells you to climb the stairs, and you ask him to where? He tells you to just climb and you will find out.

Climbing the large stone blocks you begin to feel strange. You smell very old smells from your childhood, you recognise smells from a time you cannot remember, you hear snatches of things that evoke a lost feeling with you and these feelings unnerve you as you climb. Half way up, some stones are missing and the gap is almost too large for you to continue. You stop and look down at the child who waves you on with irritation.

There is nowhere for you to step, but a deep urge within you forces you to put your foot out and with surprise you feel a step beneath your foot even though you cannot see anything. The step is actually a flat path and the minute your foot touches it, your inner vision kicks in and you see an entrance to the pyramid before you and the path leading up to the doors. At the same time, you see the collapsed stones, broken stairs, and the two visions merge.

You walk to the doors and put your hands upon them. The door moves under your hand and you realise the door is a being: an angelic keeper of the doors to the Mysteries. The door keeper challenges you by appearing before you as a being with many eyes that look into all aspects of you. The keeper sees your failings, your ignorance, and your prejudices, and it sees your compassion, wisdom, and love. The keeper weighs the two in its hands and shows you the level of balance or imbalance in your life.

The keeper then tells you how going into the Hall beyond will affect the imbalances, and the rebalancing actions it will initiate in your life. At that point you have to choose whether or not you are willing to accept the gift of those rebalancing actions/lessons into your life. If you are not willing (and lessons can be hard...truly hard) then you must return to the void at this point. If you are willing, then say so, and the doors will swing open to reveal a dark tunnel beyond.

In the shadows faces emerge out from the walls and you see terrifying demons painted on the walls all around you as you pass through the semi darkness towards the chamber up ahead. After what seems like hours, you come to a second set of doors and you can hear talking beyond. A faint light illuminates the door and you notice many different esoteric and religious symbols upon the door. When you see one that relates to you, touch it, and the doors swing open revealing the hall beyond.

The hall is circular and as you step into it the brightness of the place almost blinds you. In the brightness, around the edges of the hall stand a variety of elders, male and female, who watch you with interest. They are the ancient priests and priestesses at the very edge of the Abyss: they are slowly passing out of our world forever and are poised upon the threshold of merging deep into the inner worlds beyond human reach.

As you look closer around the hall you will see many magical symbols and sigils carved and painted upon the walls and they seem to breathe with their own life and power. You are drawn to one and touch it: you instantly feel a communication open in your brain and the sigil begins to converse with you. You begin to understand that the sigil or symbol is actually a very ancient elder who has stretched beyond the ability to take human form and what is left is the essence of their wisdom and knowledge. They readily communicate with you and begin to merge into you, downloading everything they can of their acquired wisdom into you. You will not be able to fully understand or absorb a lot of what is given to you, but you feel the urgency within the elder to pour the knowledge into every available vessel in the hope that some of it will survive.

One of the human elders comes and places a hand upon your shoulder and begins to explain to you that they are the last of their line and they are preparing to leave the pattern of the human world and will soon be beyond reach. They want to pass on their knowledge to those who would be willing to hold it, develop it, and use it in service to humanity, Divinity, and the sacred land. You begin to understand the importance of what is happening and how much responsibility goes with the tools and skills you are being offered.

The elder touches your forehead and your chest, another elder comes and touches your throat and the top of your head, another touches your abdomen and hands, another touches your genitals and ribs, another touches your feet and hair. You feel line upon line of magic, knowledge, wisdom, and energy flow through every part of your body. You know that a lot of it will not take root, but that some will, and the power that stays will be a learning tool for you for the rest of your life, whatever your path may be, and that one day you will need to pass it on, to keep it alive.

When you feel you are about to burst, the elders step back and the sigil you were initially drawn to hovers over you and then burns itself deep into your body. The action of communion with the sigil takes you very deep into the light of being and you fall and fall through light, spinning through all the worlds as you tumble through creation and power.

The spinning slowly halts and you find yourself in the stillness of the void, surrounded by nothing, out of time and out of life. The powers within you settle themselves and the sigil burns bright from within you. In this place of nothing, you feel all the potential, all the knowledge, all the lines of magic flow through you and you watch in detachment as your spirit struggles to adapt and adjust. When you feel settled and still, step out of the void and back into the room where you first started. When you are ready, blow out the candle.

* * *

That vision is a very powerful and deep working that bridges the worker to the skills of the ancients who have gone before us. Not only do you acquire tools for your job, but you also take on the mantle of the ancient line of priests/esses, connecting with them and ensuring that their work, memory, and eons of learning continues in a form that works for us today.

Back to kicking parasite ass…

If you do not need to go in with all guns blaring, i.e. a demonic-level exorcism, then you can work at a more chilled level which is more like delousing someone. Still keep your guard up, though—some parasites can be very quick and have sharp teeth.

The way I work in such circumstances is rather similar to a shamanic approach: get tools/contacts, go into body, and take out parasites. Sometimes, though, it is not that simple and we have to look in various levels to make sure that all parts of the human are cleared.

Basic mode of operation

If you are presented with a parasited person, the main thing you have to think about is your ability to clear your mind and work without emotion: parasites will try to hop to you if they think their tenure is coming to an end. The only special thing to attend to in the working room is a well tuned candle and some consecrated salt and water. Have the room tuned before the person comes in.

Lay the person down on the floor or a bed and sit beside them. Go in vision into the void and be still while on alert. When you come out, as you cross the threshold, ask for the Sandalphon to work with you and they will appear beside you as you come out of the void. Only use them if you really need to. Try to work yourself—it strengthens you against this order of being, which is everywhere and will be something that, as an exorcist, you need to become immune to.

Once you are out of the void and stood in vision before the infected person, look into their body. Parasites, especially the not-too-bright ones, appear as beings inside the body, often with tentacles or tendrils, and they tend to gravitate to the CNS, the brain, the spine, the thymus, and the genitals—these are all the areas that generate food for them. If you see them, slowly detach them and put them in a sack. If you get a biggy, take it to the Abyss. You can also put them down into the Underworld, or take them into the void.

Some people use an age-old method which includes putting them in to rocks, passing animals, or trees. I don't like that—it's like dumping your trash into your neighbour's garden, and there is also a very good chance that the being will get out and into some other poor, unsuspecting victim. Try to put these beings in a place where they won't come back and where other humans are not going to find them. "Oh look mummy what I found in this rock...it's a fluffy funny rabbit with big teeth...."

Once you have cleared the beings out of the body, go back and look for eggs—they seed themselves, and they tend to drop their eggs in the brain and down the spine. Take them all out and dump them over the Abyss—they will go to where they belong and where they are not considered parasitical.

When you have finished that vision go back into the void and be still. Be aware of what is within you and feel silently around yourself, make sure nothing latched on to you. If it has, you will either feel it immediately in your emotions or body (agitation) or it will emerge slowly over the next few days (changes in mood, sudden hunger, immune response, etc).

Do a consecrated salt bath for the victim and then get one yourself. Once you are both clean, go into her landscape (tell her what you are going to do so that her system doesn't get shocked) and check her landscape...very carefully. If it is just out of balance, that is for the person herself to fix, not you. But if the parasite has lodged deeply into her landscape you might need to get it out. If it has survived the visionary work and the bath, then it is a strong one (hence the waiting till after the bath to go into the landscape).

One last thing to try before you do a landscape clearing is to use the exorcism of substance (that you use over the salt) on the person herself—exorcise all types of beings out of her (as in a demonic exorcism). Once you have done that, if it is still showing in the landscape, you will need to remove it. You will also need to find out what its physical manifestation is—if it is that embedded in the landscape, then it has manifested outwardly, which means illness. Unfortunately, the most common manifestation is cancer; the good news is that it is seen in the landscape for a long while before it really gets a hold on the body. In these circumstances, seeing it in the landscape is a very good early warning system.

The other way it can manifest is non-cancerous growths, mental illness, immune malfunctions, and calcifications.

The reason you leave the landscape option till last is that every time you do something in someone's landscape, you interfere with her path in some way. If the possession is demonic, then that overrides any effect of interference. Similarly if it is a dangerous parasite that is causing a serious illness, then the benefits outweigh the risk.

All other reasons are usually not a good enough reason to plough in and alter someone's learning curve. You have to find ways to assist, advise, and strengthen your victim so that her own inner immune system learns to deal with it.

If you find something in the landscape, take it to the Abyss, clean the landscape up, and then re-check her body for any beginnings of disease. Once you have finished the vision, throw her in a ritual bath again and get her clean. I would then seriously advice her to go get a full health screening done.

She will be vulnerable for a while and may need a talisman for a few weeks until she gets her strength up. Don't let her try to lean on such protection, though—she must get to grips with how the parasite got in and what her inner immune weakness is, and fix it!

If someone keeps getting re-infected, there is a good chance she is not adjusting the behaviour that draws parasites in the first place. If that happens, it is not your responsibility to clean her up: wiping grown up ass is not an exorcist's job.

So now the common stuff is out of the way...here come the interesting ones....

Possession by Deity

It is extremely rare to find someone possessed by a deity, but I have come across it and it is a weird one. Usually the victim is an idiot and had magically invited the deity into himself. ("...I wish to join with the Goddess and become one with her"...goddess says, "use a body?? Hell yeah"....) In this section, I am not talking about people invoking/mediating a deity, nor the short term possession of a spirit/deity that is so common in Voodoo and related traditions. The possession situation is very specific: human connects with deity; deity moves into human and sets up shop; deity refuses polite eviction notice.

When this has happened, the victim is almost always a practitioner in some magical tradition, invited the deity in and did not realise what it entailed, how it would affect him and that it would actually happen. Most of the time, when people do things like invite other beings into themselves, they really do not have a full grasp on what it is they are actually doing. Usually it doesn't work, and they don't really believe it will happen anyhow. But occasionally you get the mix of an idiot who is a natural medium/mediator who happened to ask a deity/demon/whatever who was, at that time, pretty desperate to get into a human body for one reason or another.

Most of the time so-called deity possessions are either parasites just having fun with people, or it is intentionally faked, or it is a drama queen/king in full pagan throws of playacting. But rarely, it does truly happen, and it can have a devastating affect on the host.

A good thing to remember at this point: a deity is not Divinity. It is a filter for Divinity to pass through, but it is also a fragment of nature/humanity and is more often than not moulded by human interaction. This all means that you could have a bloody awkward powerful temperamental being running around in a human body enjoying itself at other's expense. The fact that the person invited it in makes it harder to then get it out again—deities tend not to gatecrash humans unless it is very urgent, and then usually just to communicate with someone.

The affect and presentation of symptoms depends somewhat on the deity involved and the strength of the host. Over all, though, carrying a deity around in ones body does tend to have certain common symptoms: the human will start to burn out really quickly. He will exhibit power, knowledge, and personality changes but his body will buckle under the weight of the power. The way the body reacts will give you a clue to the type of deity it is, unless it has already announced itself with great fanfare (which they tend to do—most deities are not shrinking violets and don't hide their light under any bushel). What you will not get is possession by a deity, which, in its projected picture to humanity, has no form at all, or no human form. It has to know how to operate a meat suit and it can only do that if it has been used to a humanised window. So, for example, if someone comes and declares that he is possessed by the Christian God the Father/Muslim Allah, then you need to give him the number of the local mental hospital with a polite smile.

If he claims to be possessed by Ganesha, or Bast, or any other part-animal, part-human, then tread a little more carefully, but it is also most unlikely, as it very difficult for the deity to translate the animal side of its nature into a human. If it should happen, the possession will not last long, just a few minutes, and will make him very ill.

The dangerous ones are deities with full human form, who take an active role in humanity, or have done until recently, and something somewhere has opened up a power porthole for them to use. It is also something that can happen where there is major change coming and they are involved in that change.

If you are presented with a true deity possession, the human and the deity will be vocal and aware in the body. The host will be aware of what is going on and deity will usually be right to the point about why it is there. If the reason for the possession is reasonable and something you can help with, then the best way forward is to get the job done and the deity will go. You will have to mop up the mess left in the human, which will be physical. The body reacts to such an intrusion as if it were an infection, so the host usually develops a very serious infection with a high fever very soon after the possession is over. He will need rest, homeopathic medicine for the fever, and possible antibiotics if it has triggered an overgrowth of normally-occurring bacteria.

If there is no apparent reason for the deity possession, and it does not leave when asked, then you are going to have to trick it out. It cannot be forced out like a demon or spirit—you could end up killing the host if you get into a battle with a deity. A deity that wants a meat suit usually wants to have a wider presence out in humanity and you can give the deity a way to do that without wearing someone else. One way to do it is to get or make a painting or statue of that deity and have the host place their hands upon it. As a priest/priestess go in vision into the void and come back out in to the room—you will immediately see the deity in the person. Show him the image and place a hand upon the image and a hand upon the host. Ask the deity to pass through you and into the image so that it can have a place out in the world without harming anyone. Once the deity has passed in, you withdraw and come out of vision.

If the host was a magical worker/priest/ess/new age idiot, then there is some responsibility upon them to carry the mess that they made. If they invited the deity in, then all you can do is to transfer the deity into the image. Now the host has to commit to tending the image, and bringing the deity through that image by working with it and bringing others to work with it. Usually, under these circumstances, the deity becomes so disappointed with the level of care and interaction that they literally get bored half senseless and leave.

Examples of living images that work well in today's world are the orthodox icons in churches and chapels, Hindu Deity statues/images, etc—they are correctly tended, prayed to, talked to, loved, and interacted with. That is usually what deities are after when they try to come through, so keep that in mind.

There are cultures that purposely bring deities through into humans, and then worship them as a living God/Goddess, but because it has become such a token gesture, more often than not, the deity withdraws quickly and what is left is a figurehead.

If a deity will not go and does not pass into an image, then the host is basically stuck with it until it is ready to leave. He could turn it to his advantage and learn a lot from the deity; these beings are bridges throughout many worlds and are also a bridge to Divinity—therefore there is much to be learned from them that would be useful in our world. It can be approached by an attitude of an unexpected sojourn at virtual online god-college.

If you wish, as an exorcist, to verify that it truly is a deity possession, which is probably necessary if the person is running around making claims and trying to benefit from it, then there are things that will make it obvious. Firstly is deeper knowledge of the deity, its culture, and its language. The person will know obscure oddities, old versions of language, or will understand you if you talk to him in that language. He will be suddenly unable to digest certain foods and will crave others. He will come alive strongly at odd hours of the day and night, will be able to suddenly mediate large amounts of power and will have very impressive nature tricks depending on his areas of speciality (i.e., affect lightening, bring on storms, rain, sun, etc).

So if some 5-ft, 5-inch guy with a perchance for Nordic jewellery comes to you and tells you he is possessed by Thor, the first thing to think about is that Thor is a major ego. He would probably choose a more impressive meat suit (there are tall powerful men out there). Second, do the runic test (ask him to translate a line of early runic text). Third, light a fire and sit and talk with him, and watch what the weather does as you touch on power subjects. It will happen naturally, no need for commanding the wind or anything. If you have a deity walking around in a human, nature is going to react—it's that simple.

ɦuman 'walƙ ins' anδ pusɦ ins

Most 'walk ins' that happen to humans are parasites that get in when the person is in a coma and their front line defence system is shot through. So it's just a matter of taking the parasite out.

There is a weirder and rarer type of possession that sadly does happen and can be very destructive for the host. This type of possession is where a living human is invaded by the spirit of another living human who takes over the host to try to live through her. This can happen for a variety of reasons: jealousy in a relationship, magical control of a group, a wish for a better body, etc, and it is always conducted by someone who is an adept at magical arts, has no ethics, but has very bad intent—this is the description of the old fashioned use of the word 'sorcerer.'

The effect on the victim is that she is manipulated and her thoughts/actions/physical appearance/wants and needs take on the flavour and character of the sorcerer to the detriment of the victim—she becomes contaminated to a point where it can affect her mental and physical health. The fallout around her also can be terrible as the sorcerer has free rein to affect, interfere, and interact with the people around the victim. It can be used to 'get at' a person who is close to the victim but is not accessible to the sorcerer. This has the added injury of turning one person against another in an unnatural way—the victim, driven by the sorcerer, turns and attacks the person who is the real intended target for harm.

It can also be used in a really creepy way so that the sorcerer can sexually interact with a person via the victim/host. Another usage of this possession method is to take over the leader of a magical lodge, or magical teacher and control/manipulate her: very nasty and very destructive.

The first step to deal with such a disgusting situation is to get the host/victim to feel what it feels like, be aware of the possession and when it is active, to basically gain a full awareness of the extent of the possession and what it is affecting within her. She needs to be able to feel what is really her and what is not. Once that has been achieved, the possession is already half out—it becomes a battle of will.

The second thing that needs attending to is that everything that connects her to the sorcerer needs to be destroyed, regardless of what it is and what its value is. This situation very rarely happens where there is no connection. Once everything has been gotten rid of, then you need to make sure that the sorcerer has nothing that belongs to the victim: everything that was once owned by a person has a trail of her energy in it which is like a key to her 'house.'

If the sorcerer owns something that once belonged to the victim then its inner pattern and energy pattern needs to be retrieved. This is great fun—adrenaline sports for occultists!!

This must not be the owner of the object unless she is really, really good at shielding herself. If she were heavily connected to the sorcerer, then even good shielding will still leave an energy marker in the sorcerer's territory, so it must be done by the exorcist.

In vision, the exorcist must go and retrieve the object, take the energy imprint out of it, and take it into the void. To do this, first the exorcist must go into the void and drop all parts of him that is connected to everyday life. This is the greatest tool an exorcist can have: to become blank. Then, stepping out of the void and working with the Sandalphon to shield and blend with the rocks/earth, go to the territory/house of the sorcerer.

As you go around the house (going down the chimney if there is one is a good access point, as is going up through the drains), look for the energy signature of the victim, it is like looking for a scent. Once you find the object/s, take the energy out of it and hold it within yourself. Cover the whole building and gardens, look for unusual hiding places and for magical filters on altars to hide things. Once you know you have gotten every part of energy fragments out of the building, then you must leave and go into the void—let the energy fragments flow into the void and dissipate.

Once the sorcerer has lost his 'lines' of energy communication, it will make it a little harder for him to connect with the victim. It would be a good idea at that point to make a talisman for the victim to block out that particular person for a while until she gets strong again. The victim will need to keep an awareness of the intrusion as it will probably be attempted again, so that when it begins again she is ready for it and can strongly reject it. It is the insidious nature of such intrusion that makes it successful—if the host is unwilling and reacts immediately, then it is more often than not unsuccessful.

If it becomes intense and repeated, then it is possible that the sorcerer has bound angelic beings to operate on his behalf to facilitate the intrusion. If that is the case, then the beings will need to be unchained and set free before you try to push the intrusion out.

The other thing that could be driving such a situation is if the sorcerer has a massive parasite feeding off of him and helping the sorcerer with his work in return. An example of how this can escalate is where the sorcerer builds up a working partnership with a powerful parasite which ends up with the sorcerer having to find victims for the parasite so that the parasite does not destroy the sorcerer—that is a common result in such a situation.

There are ethical considerations under such circumstances: if you detach and get rid of the parasite that was invited in, you are interfering with someone's learning path. But if it is destroying lots of people, then you have a responsibility as an exorcist to intervene. So it is a tricky one and you have to tread carefully with each presentation of such situations.

Usually though, with situations that involve sorcerers, disengagement/disconnection is the best option rather than conflict which just feeds it.

Chapter 9
Dealing with curses

The details in this chapter cover methods for dismantling and removing curses built within the Western Esoteric structures. There are as many forms of cursing as there are human cultures and each form has its specifics when it comes to removal and survival. Some types of curses and attacks are a lot more dangerous than others and you need to be aware of your limitations as an exorcist. Do not get the idea that because you have been a successful exorcist that you can remove anything and everything. This particularly applies to curses and magical attacks. Know what it is that you know and don't engage something that you know nothing about—that is just downright dangerous.

Every exorcist, me included, have a limited bag of tools and skills that they have learned. Those tools and skills are the product of personal experience, and will not work in every circumstance. Always be ready to learn and make mistakes. Don't ever be too proud to admit you are in over your head, and don't think you are invincible. If you approach your work in this way, you will survive and learn a thing or two.

There are major differences in the way an exorcist would approach the presentation of a curse and the presentation of a magical attack in a victim. The reason for this difference in approach is that a curse is 'bound' action—once set in motion, it runs its course unless removed. Once it has been created, the creator usually leaves it to do its job (unless you get an anal retentive perfectionist who is constantly updating his work), so the exorcist has space to consider the structure of the curse before attempting to remove or modify it.

A magical attack, however, can be on ongoing thing that is energised regularly and added to almost continuously. Because of the constant input of energy to the attack, it gives the exorcist little elbow room to step back and consider how it is being constructed and executed—removal or blockage becomes a priority if the attack is affecting the life force of the victim. Dealing with magical attacks is dealt with in the next chapter.

Curses: general background

The methods of cursing someone are endless and so in reflection of that, the methods of removal are also endless. It all depends on how it is done, why, where, when, and by whom. Curses are cast against people for all and any reason and the way that curses can manifest span a whole range of effects from illness, accident, tangling, loss of ability, death, sterility, homelessness, and madness. The people who construct powerful curses can be anything from haphazard magical workers with natural ability and some skill (their methods work and even they don't quite know how they have done it), to magical adepts who are very clear, knowledgeable, and specific in how they construct curses.

In the western magical and pagan world, the lesser, more usual curses that rear their heads are events that can normally be overcome by the victim without help—like all burdens, the body can get used to them and adjust until the effects are no longer felt and the curse becomes obsolete. Sometimes they are binding curses to stop people communicating information, usually to silence them if they leave a magical order. The curse is placed upon them at the beginning during an initiation or oath taking, or contract signing; they become magically bound to silence and if they break that silence, then the curse is triggered. Some smaller curses can be removed within the magical tradition it was made in and that is all part of the victim's learning curve—if you step into that world, you must learn to operate safely and ethically within that tradition.

There is a branch of western magic that is very self-serving and very selfish as part of its *modus operandi* and cursing is a part of that structure. For me, personally, as an exorcist, if someone is within that magical line and gets attacked, well, it's a good lesson for them to tackle.

Many of the magical lines that are passed from generation to generation through initiation are tainted by curse behaviour and the new initiate 'inherits' some of the curse pattern which must be addressed and dismantled. More often than not, though, such dismantlement does not happen and the curse behaviour becomes a seductive way for the initiate to manipulate the world to her advantage, and so the dance goes on.

The actions that interest me as an exorcist are curses that are heavily crafted, powerfully fuelled, and directed at someone who is just living his life. It always disappoints me when I see that kind of infantile use of magic (my children and I have been on the receiving end of such behaviour), and see the long term suffering that it causes.

The action of a serious curse should warrant the same level of attention that a demonic possession does—a serious curse can cause major accidents, serious illness, death, extreme poverty, and suffering. It should also be approached with the same care and attention to safety that you would apply to a demonic possession. The danger to the exorcist when tackling such a curse is similar to poking a demon; most cleverly constructed curses have trip wires that can blow up in your face and do some real nasty damage (I have a few 'inner' and outer scars from that)...so you have to consider each step carefully as you dismantle.

It is also important to know whether the curse was put on by someone who is magically alone, i.e., she is not involving groups of people or lines of initiates. If the sorcerer is alone, then you are just dealing one-to-one with dismantling, energy disconnection, and fate untangling. If she is operating from within a group or when it is put on by an adept who is in a line, lodge, or heads a working group, then it is a real nasty mess that can take years to carefully peel away. Usually the groups that such people operate from are unaware of the curse activity and are therefore innocent, but energetically they are nearly always drawn upon and therefore energetically implicated. Care must be taken in the dismantling work to protect such people.

Inner details and implications of curses

The strongest and most important implication of being cursed is the effect a curse has on a person's fate pattern. When a person is cursed properly, their fate is changed forever and cannot be restored to a pre-curse position. To add to that, some curses cannot be lifted completely, they can only be modified, so it not only alters the fate of the cursed person, it forever affects all of the people closely connected to him as its affects slowly unwind over the years.

By altering the fate of a person by cursing, the curser ties her own fate to the victim and the dance begins. When this is done, it is either because the person doing the cursing does not know the deeper implications, or because the person cursing wants her fate entwined with the victim for some perverse reason. Either way their fates walk the same path, and it can take years or even lives to get everything completely untangled.

The way that some magicians avoid this, along with the 'karma' of a violent action, is to have a scapegoat or two (or three). The magician creates a thought form being that takes the fate/karma/kickback from the action on behalf of the magician. Another sneaky way that it is done is to operate through a variety of people energetically, so that the backwash of effect hits that group of people rather than the sorcerer. An example of this is where an adept works in stages by initially constructing the curse, then gathers a group of people together to raise energy for magic (usually under a false premise) and uses the energy of the people to fuel the curse, and then sends it out to the victim shortly after the gathering.

Because the energy lines of people have been connected to the curse, they become the 'front men' for the curse and get the fate kickback. They are also the recipients if the cursed person 'sends it back.' This is one of the many reasons why an exorcist must not 'send anything back where it came from.' You can never really be sure, when an adept is doing the cursing, where it is actually coming from and where it will return to.

Another method that is often used is to create a series of inner structures and have people build/feed the structures under a false premise (we are building a temple of love and light, or we are building temples to connect power places). This was used in the Golden Dawn in the early days. The structure that is built becomes a battery for energy that is then focussed upon the person or people who are being cursed. It is usually only used when cursing a few people at a time; it is very energy-efficient for multi-cursing.

The people who supply the energy are encouraged to connect themselves to the structures as priests/esses; which results in the people taking the responsibility for all that happens within and from that structure. Therefore all concerned once again become energetic scapegoats. It's a bit like the British Government.

If they are all part of a consecrated line of priesthood, it can have deeper and even more sinister outcomes for the participants. If the sorcerer is using chained or bound angels (that have usually been passed down magical lines) to execute the curse, the binding action on the angel creates a back up of cause and effect. Essentially, binding an angel is bad juju and once it is free, the bad juju needs to be rebalanced energetically with the creator of the binding. If the creator of the binding was also a part of or a progenitor of a line of initiates, then all the initiates are energetically responsible. The more living initiates a sorcerer has, the less the sorcerer has to shoulder as energetic burden/responsibility.

When a bound angel is involved, that is a very large amount of energetic burden, therefore it is within the initiate's interest to keep the angel bound up, which in turn allows yet another generation of sorcerers to use and abuse its power for their own ends. It also encourages yet more cursing activity to ensure that the human scapegoats and energy carriers (initiates) do not leave the fold or do not formally disengage themselves from the magical line.

When the sorcerer dies, the same happens in that the souls of the initiates still carry some of the burden of the angelic binding, so when it is released, they will all have a backwash of rebalancing. This can be avoided by the initiates either by formerly withdrawing from the line and going to the Abyss and asking for judgement (they must not just leave; they have to address the issue for rebalancing). Another method is to unbind the angel and tell it what has been happening. The angel has the ability to focus the energy backwash back where it belongs and protect the innocent.

Assessment

The first thing an exorcist needs to do is establish what sort of curse it is, what powers are being used and why is being done. It is important to know the reason behind the action: you need to ascertain whether or not you are dealing with a vengeful person, a manipulating person, or a mentally ill person. If the adept is mentally ill, then real care about trip wires must be taken. Most mentally ill magicians who curse will be highly paranoid and controlling, therefore they will think out all possible scenarios of dismantling and create defences/guardians to block it. If they are vengeful but not nuts, then they will not go to so much trouble with trip wires—they will just want the person to suffer for a while. If the curse was put on as a form of manipulation, i.e., to stop a person working, marrying, leaving a magical group, for example, then the curse will more or less be specific to those actions and will not affect the rest of the lifestyle of the cursed person. Those are the easiest and the safest to take off. Even though they can have a devastating affect on the victim, no one is going to die or be permanently damaged by it. They are not too hard to dismantle once you find the lynchpin and the energy source.

Some different styles of curses, their effects, and how to deal with them

Angelic/ritual

The following outlines some of the nastier types of curse that someone is likely as an exorcist to come up against in the western culture. The removal methods can be adjusted and used in other types of curses, and the method of adjustment is discussed later.

The worst types of curses that I have come across are ones created using angelic structures mixed with ritual patterns and recitation. These are classic western magical curses produced by adepts of the traditions that come from the western mystery family of magic. The intent of the curse is recited; it is then constructed by ritual patterning (often also using a form of transubstantiation), and is driven by an angelic being which is usually bound in magical service. The whole thing is fed by an energy source, usually other people's.

The angelic beings that are bound are angels that are named and used within magical patterns (i.e. the Solomonic texts), and the use of their names gives the magician access to them through ritual (some magicians are not aware that some named angels are actually bound and the purpose that they are listed for is actually their bound purpose, not their real purpose). Some magicians will also use inner contacts/beings in vision to build the curse, and will even get into bargaining with beings in vision to deliver and implement the curse for them.

The list of beings used in such way is endless so the exorcist needs to be ready to meet anything, including demonic beings in the lifting of these types of curses. These heavier curses are often very nasty, very vicious, and frequently end in death or serious illness. Some of them cannot be lifted, but they can be modified somewhat to enable the victim to have some sort of life.

So how do you ascertain if it is this type of curse?

The victim's story will have some classic signs that will tell you if this type of action has occurred to them. A full on ritual/angel-

ic curse will be wide ranging, long lasting, and energetically devastating for the victim and his family. He will come to the exorcist with a pattern of serious accidents, assaults, and weird and
dangerous illnesses that cannot be diagnosed. Animals will attack
him or be frightened of him, people will react badly to the victim
for no apparent reason (often friends of the victim will report that
they feel aggressive, agitated, or angry when they are around the
victim for no reason—they are often confused and feel very guilty
at their reactions). Accidents will present in dangerous ways like
freak accidents, head on collisions with vehicles not seeing the
victim, freak fires, floods, building collapses, etc, and they will
not be isolated incidents—they will be a constant stream of things
happening on an almost daily basis. (Life gets mighty interesting
with the angel of death strapped to your butt.)

Such victims will report their lives falling apart in the most
bizarre ways for no good reason—i.e., suddenly fired, evicted,
attacked, shunned by everyone around them, partners turning on
them, or relationships falling apart while also suffering illness,
loss, confusion, and mental fog. Their bodies will take the impact
and become sick, aged, weak, and often gain or lose a large
amount of weight as the body struggles to survive. These affects
can also lap over to family members who will report a lesser version of the same experience.

When confronted with such a picture, it can often overwhelm
the exorcist and it is valuable to step back and try to see a bigger
picture which will give you a clue as to what the curse is about,
what beings are being used, and how.

People do not curse at such a level without, in their eyes, good
reason. So first you must move the picture of the effects to one
side and concentrate on the why. Usually the cursed person will
know why and by whom, but if he does not, work back slowly
with him to pinpoint any action that seems to trigger the curse
into action. Some curses are just all out kill, suffer, and maim
curses, in which case you just need to get it off or modify it as
quickly as possible. More usual, though, is a curse that is set to
go off when the victim does a particular thing—say, job related,
relationship related, or going to a particular place, etc. If he backs

off from a certain action, then the curse action settles back down. These are like slow boil curses—the victim gets so used to being restricted by the action of the curse that he passively retreats from his world and lives a half life. If this is happening, then look closely at the actions that trigger the curses and see what, if anything, can be modified or lifted.

Dealing with the curse itself

Before I go into the various techniques that you can use to lift and modify curses, there is an important thing that needs to be stated. When a person is ethically engaged in magical or spiritual practice and she is cursed badly in such a way as has been discussed, there is an inner dynamic that kicks in. Once she has done everything within her knowledge and power to help herself without turning it back on, engaging, or attacking the other person, then angelic beings, inner contacts, and sometimes land beings also will intervene with gifts of skills, comfort, tools, protection, warnings, and modification of the curse itself.

It is a rebalancing of the scales that happens on an inner level and I have personally experienced this myself many times, including one truly odd one where an angelic being gave me a loud clear verbal warning through a sleeping person. The message was clear and told me how a person attacking me was getting into my space, and what to do to deal with it. (You can just see the angelic eyeballs rolling, they tried the subtle hints which didn't work, so they shout it at me, like, "Did yah get that!!!" I can be dense sometimes.)

So if you are called out as an exorcist to a magical/spiritual worker who is cursed, sit with her and have her go over her situation to ascertain whether or not such a dynamic is already in place. If it is, then be very careful not to disengage it—it could be saving her life.

Once you have listened to the victim and taken notes, and gotten as much information as to the why and whom, then it is time to look on the inner and through the deck (see chapter 13). It is always best to look on the inner planes first, so that your vision is not set or interfered with by the readings.

Look at the person in a variety of ways as well-constructed curses are often cleverly hidden and cloaked. Go into vision, go into stillness for a moment, into the void, and then step back in and take a good look at the person and what is around her. Curses can appear in a number of ways, but what you are looking for is platonic solids around or within her, bindings, haziness around her, beings attached to her, threads leading away from her, sigils, text, webs, patterns, any sort of construct around her.

Once you have had a good look, take her in vision into the void with you and then look again. Once you have done that, you can begin to narrow it down. If you see any shapes or sigils, (angelic beings) you will need to find out who or what they are. One way is to take her in vision into the void and then call upon the angelic being of air to come. Once the being arrives in the void, step into it and look at the person again through the filter of the angel. If the curse is powered or linked to an angel of that element, it will really become visible. You can try the same with the angel of fire.

Those two elemental angelic expressions are the most commonly used ones in cursing, and by calling on the elemental side of the being, you are sidestepping the individual manifestations (Sariel, for example), which is helpful for a number of reasons. If you focus on a particular being, like Samael (a favourite for cursers), then a few things can happen: you can miss out on more obscure ones (i.e., your ability to pinpoint the actual being is limited by your knowledge of angelic orders), and also by facing up the actual individual angel you might trigger a trip wire and get attacked yourself.

You don't really need to know the actual angelic being used, just the line of power that it comes from, hence the using the elemental power that drives it rather than its order or name. You can then use the same elemental angelic power to remove the curse or to modify it.

When you look at the victim on the inner, you are very likely to also see parasites that are attached to the curse either intentionally or by default, and they will need removing. There are also possibilities for coming across thought forms or constructed beings that have a specific function within the curse and they will have to be approached and removed carefully as they are often booby trapped.

The other important thing that you will need to look for is power cables/umbilical cords that will lead to a power source, often an inner construct that acts as an energy store. Don't be tempted to dismantle the construct as that often has its own defence mechanism to prevent intrusion or interference, just disconnect the umbilical cord at both ends and dump them in the void.

The same goes for patterns that are around the person: carefully unwind or dismantle them and dump them, looking at all times for trip wires and beings connected to them. Some of them will appear as webs or 3D patterns around the person, but they are in fact beings, so again approach with care.

If the victim is covered in sigils tread very carefully. The sigils can be beings of a number of different orders and will attack if approached head on. In such cases, sometimes working with other sigils that interconnect with them and detach them (a little like keys in locks) can be a good way around it. This is where you need to know your sigils and magical alphabets: if the victim is covered in magical script, then sometimes adding to the script will change the word and therefore change the meaning of the script, which can obviate part of the curse. But if you come across something where you have no idea what the hell it is, sometimes calling upon an angelic being for help is useful—they love fixing things and solving puzzles...angels have Aspergers too!!

The finding-and-removing process can take time—sometimes months—as the layers can be many and deep. After each session, the victim will need a ritual bath and lots of coffee.

Other methods that can be applied for taking off the layers

These are some things that can be tried for taking off layers, pressing pause buttons, and modifying the power levels in curses. I have tried them all at various times, and sometimes all together. A thing to constantly remember is that well done curses come in layers and all layers must be attended to. By layers, I mean different power levels, different levels of manifestation, i.e., some deeply inner, and some more physical.

One physical way of taking off a layer (or downing the power of it) is an old-fashioned but very effective way that can also be very useful for highlighting what powers are playing out through the curse. The victim is given a large piece of paper and some acrylic paints. Get him to still himself and, if possible, work—while a part of him is in vision in the void. Have him paint the powers that are working through him. Start with the background power (fire/air etc), and then paint the 'feeling' of what is binding them and where. If shapes come into his vision, like cubes, pyramids, etc, then he paints them. It is best to use the paper as if it were the body so top is head, bottom is feet. Any bindings he feels on his hands, for example, would be in painted in the position of where his hands would be.

The painting should reflect powers, bindings, sigils, angelic beings, parasites, etc. It does not need to be a work of art, or even make sense, it is ensuring that the pattern of power that he perceives is transferred on to the paper. If he truly cannot do it, then the exorcist must do it, but it is more powerful if the victim does it himself. Once it is finished, then a large nail should be hammered through the middle of it, pinning the energy to the paper, maybe with a piece of wood underneath. As it is pinned, the intention to pin the power must be focussed in the thoughts of whoever is doing the pinning. Once it is pinned, then the whole thing should be covered with a swirl cloth or a cloth with a ritual emblem/sigil of entrapment upon it. Leave it outside for a few hours or overnight, and then burn it. As it is burning, you are sending the power back into the void via the flames. (Note that you send it into the void, not back to whoever sent it.)

That action will take a burden of power off the person which will make it easier to get to the bottom layers of the curse. By this time, the ritual foundation of the curse should be appearing. By taking off the angelic attachments, energy lines and then peeling the power off through the painting, what will be left is the ritual pattern that was started in the early phases of the curse construction.

This can be fragmented or removed by 'unlocking' the ritual foundation. To do this you need to know the mode of operation of the sorcerer that created the curse. So you would need to know if she is from a Thelemic branch of magic, or kabbalistic Western Mystery Tradition, Golden Dawn, etc. As most curses use fire and air that would be your starting point.

So, for example, with a Western Mystery Tradition magician curse, you would set up an altar using the four ritual implements, place the cup, sword and wand upon the shield in their directions, and light a candle in the middle. As you light the candle, tune the candle to the point in time when the curse was set and position the sword and wand in the crossed position with the cup upside down between them. Ring the whole thing with the magical cord to seal it in—you are beginning to reproduce the ritual placement pattern that was originally used to create the curse.

Build up the power with the intent to focus the pattern and merge the pattern with the original action of cursing. Once it has built to screaming pitch (a very technical term for when the power gets so strong it screams in your ears!), blow the candle out while brushing all the objects sharply off the altar and inwardly brushing them into the void, and then break the wand. This action disturbs the original pattern that was built up in the inner worlds and fragments the foundation of the curse. If you can build it up for days, and have the candle going all the time, then the effect when it is dismantled will be much stronger.

Justice

Once you have taken off as many layers as you can find and you have destabilised the foundation of the curse, then you have to help the victim deal with what is left. One way to do that is to have him place his life in the balance of the scales. This is worth doing if the curse is very serious, has death actions attached to it, and you have only managed to get certain layers off. What this working does is hand over the fate of the victim to Divinity and the angelic hierarchy. It can wipe the slate clean and put the victim under the protection of certain archangels, or it can simply ask for the scales to be balanced.

The first and most extreme option is one commonly used by exorcists to protect themselves and their families during their work: they hand over their fate to God by committing themselves to the service of Divinity and to the lineage of inner contacts. It is akin to a death-in-life scenario that an adept goes through, but with higher energies and implications. The victim is taken to the Abyss and you ask the keeper of the Abyss to take the victim before the balancer of the scales. It is written out in full as a vision in Chapter One: the Vision of Judgement.

A less extreme version of this is to do the same vision, i.e., go to the Abyss and ask the angelic being to help the victim rebalance his scales. He must be prepared to face his shortcomings, negative actions that have not been rebalanced, debts that have not been paid, etc, and deal with them. The angelic being will tell him what he has to do and what is needed for him to rebalance things. Once that is set in motion, then as long as the victim attends to his rebalancing, then angelic guardians will help keep the balance by offsetting any unwarranted negative action against the victim. So, in real terms, what that means is that if the curse continues in a strong way, the angelic guardians will step in with coping mechanisms, modifications, protections, etc, that will help to keep the balance.

Tree of life clearing of fate

This is another option for magically clearing a fate that has been sullied or altered by cursing. This one works very well if Kabbalistic magic has been used and will immediately highlight any Kabbalistic bindings that still exist, or any beings still attached to the person. The exorcist or victim can do it or better still both work together in vision if the victim is able to hold a vision and also converse with the exorcist at the same time. (That, by the way, is a very useful skill to develop: be able to hold a deep vision and converse with someone at the same time, telling him or her what you see without breaking the vision.)

Vision

Go into the void and step out with the intention of emerging at the edge of the Abyss. Call upon the Sandalphon to work with you both and stand on the edge of the Abyss. Call the keeper of the Abyss to join you and show you the path of life of the victim. The keeper will instruct the Sandalphon who will place their hands over your eyes and the eyes of the victim. As you look through their hands your vision will change and you will see the desert before you as a sort of desert runway set out in the pattern of the tree of life. You will be stood on the path of Teth with Tifereth before you. As you look down towards Malkuth you will see any interplay of powers between the spheres, any beings, bindings, patterns, etc, that litter the pathway. Anything you find, work with the Sandalphon to clear out of the way.

Once you have reached Malkuth and cleared everything, then you need to look beyond Malkuth. Beyond that point is the victim's future and if you go further beyond all the potential future patterns, you will reach the river of death. Go as far as you can towards the death river to see if there are any beings operating from a point of death back towards the Malkuth of the victim. If there is a death curse, it will show itself here. If you find anything like that, then work with the Sandalphon to dismantle it. Any beings that are bound or connected can be disconnected and put into the Abyss or can be bound up and placed in the desert—the Sandalphon will release them when it is safe to do so.

Once the whole pattern is clear, go back into the void and be still. Help the victim find that quiet place within herself, and when you are both still step back out of the void and close the vision.

***

Once you have done all that you can to strip or modify a curse, you will need to keep a close eye on the victim for a while and visit her once a week for a few weeks if possible to see how she is getting on. You will also need to touch base with her as the seasons turn to make sure that it is not timed to equinoxes and resent.

It would also be advisable to get them to put up some level of protection in the house, including protective sigils, swirl cloths, a house talisman and maybe work with a protective angelic being or a deity. Images of those beings around the house would be good, and having a vigil candle burning twenty-four hours a day for a while helps keep the space clear and tuned.

Wiccan or faery curses, Witchcraft/hearth magic

Any curses that come from practitioners of the above traditions can be worked with in those structures. So, for example, with faery curses, you are dealing with beings, so it is best to work in vision in the faery realm, treading with the usual care that you would have when dealing with faery beings. Having stuff to trade is useful: faeries will often switch sides/loyalties if it is in their interests to do so. Your working method would be similar to the visionary aspect of working in the void with the angelic beings.

Take the victim in vision into the faery realm and look at him there. Most faery curses done by humans tend not to be too harsh and are easily taken off. The dangerous ones are faery curses cast by faeries—in which case the victim is in deep doodoo unless he can identify what crime he committed that triggered such an attack and fix it by repairing whatever damage he did. In such a situation it is best to either call upon the faery queen for advice and guidance or to go to the ancient tree in the centre of the forest in the faery realm and talk to the contact there.

With Wiccan/witchcraft curses, visionary methods are not that useful in that most of the power used is fixed through ritual action and land beings. The method used to fragment the foundation of the ritual curses can be adjusted and used if the victim or exorcist can identify which ritual pattern was used. It needs to be reproduced and then ritually dismantled by reversing or breaking the pattern.

Then you can go into vision and take off any remnant, which usually tends to be parasitical. Treat as you would a normal parasite infestation and then ritually bath the victim. Because these types of curses tend to be constructed through outward action, they are generally easier to take off. You can work in vision, but what you see will not make much sense. Wax on, wax off, ritual on, ritual off.

Inherited curses

Curses that are passed down families can be slowly dismantled by using the heavy angelic methods listed above. They must be repeated at each equinox and solstice around the space of the year to untangle any link to the seasons, which is a very old method and very clever, too—each season would have its own layer of curse that would not appear until that season was reached. So an exorcist would think he has gotten the entire curse off when another layer would appear a couple of months later. When a name has been cursed, the name itself has to be cleared of bonds and tangles. This can be done by exorcising the name—write it on a piece of paper, add a drop of blood from a person of that name/family line, and then conduct the exorcism of earth/substance, and of air/recitation over it. Then burn the name.

Summary

There are many more methods of cursing and of clearing, and the exorcist must do as much research as she can. The above methods can be used in isolation or combined. They can be altered, customised, and rebuilt to suit the exorcist: they can also be combined and merged with other working methods and rituals. It's all about trial and error, imagination, and button-pushing. If you do get the entire curse off, work with the victim to ensure that it doesn't happen again, and that he is fully protected for a while.

To sum up, don't think you have failed if you cannot get all of a curse off. More often than not, one has to settle with modification or de-balling of curses rather than removal. Look to the Greek Myths for the many tales of Gods and Goddesses offering curse modifications—they had problems too!!

For the exorcist, it is important when working on curses that you don't pick any of it up yourself or end up triggering a curse upon yourself—tread carefully, slowly, and methodically...it's very much like working in a minefield.

Chapter 10
Magical attacks and how to deal with them

In the last chapter, we looked at the difference between a curse and a magical attack. A curse is created and directed, usually to encourage the recipient to conform to a boundary (most magical curses involve the protection of secret texts or rituals, partnerships, or ritual objects). A magical attack, however, is usually a torrent of magic fuelled by emotion, be it hatred, fear, anger, etc. The deeper the emotion, the nastier the magical attack. Another well of emotion that has become more frequent than it used to be (which poses interesting societal questions) is the emotion of inadequacy—there are more and more attacks within magical lodges/groups from members and leaders who assert themselves in a violent magical way to prove their power (which in itself is a very large flag that says 'small willy.'

Most of the attacks in the western world of magic/ occultism/paganism centre around issues that relate to magical lodges/groups/magical partnerships. It's all about being powerless and it's all about territory. If someone is a practicing magician and resorts to using magic to resolve some grievance, that tells us that the person has no emotive skills, no real power that can be used, and has the mental capacity of a Macburger.

I was shocked when I returned to Britain last year at the degeneration that has happened in so many of the magical communities. A substantial amount of them are heavily embroiled in magical conflicts, usually over who is the 'real one and only true,' or conflicts over who will be the 'magus' or conflicts between a lodge and someone who has spilled the secrets. Maybe it has always been there and I just didn't notice before.

The other types of magical attacks are personal, i.e. when someone has been jilted, slighted, marital disputes—the list is endless, as are the methods of attack. They can range from highly ritualised complex attacks, to beings sent after someone, to simple utterance with intent. All are annoying and some can be dangerous.

There is a saying that if you don't believe in the reality of a magical attack it cannot harm you. That is bullshit and is said by someone who does not know how magic works. Someone can be attacked and not know it, and have terrible consequence. In fact, most people who are attacked are not aware that the attack is where their problems are coming from. Then there are the people who blame everything that goes wrong for them on a magical attack—both are imbalanced and the reality is somewhere in the middle.

This is a good example of a magical attack based on east African magic: Many years ago, in my youth, I was booked on a dance tour in the U.S.A. with a couple of other dancers. I had never been to the States before and I was very excited. The other dancers on the tour with me were from Uganda. All went well for the first week but the second week, it all went quickly south.

We all shared a room and one night I was deeply asleep and dreaming happily. A voice in my dream told me to run and it was a voice I recognised as a personal guardian that I knew rather than a character in my dream. I found myself running down the street and into the house where I was staying.

In the dream I also saw a large shapeless black form speeding towards the house, its power levels beyond anything I had any experience of at that time. It came in to the house, up the stairs and into the room, and it looked quickly at the bodies on the beds. It saw the dancer next to me and dived straight for her.

I woke up screaming from terror and the dancer next to me did the same. We both sat terrified in the dark and neither of us where physically able to move. It was as if we had been pinned down. The third dancer got up and put the light on.

The following day, the dancer who had been attacked had a fever and started to act strangely. She became hostile to all around her and began to behave in a very nasty way with anyone who came into contact with her. We were, while on tour, supposed to meet with her possible future in-laws (she was Muslim and in the process of negotiating an arranged marriage) and when we did finally meet them, the dancer behaved in the most outrageous manner which put the perspective in-laws off. This was totally out of character for this girl who was usually a normal, happy young woman.

When we returned to Britain and I got on my home ground, my sight restored itself fully (it would always seem to lessen when I left the land) and I could see very clearly a demonic being within her, riding her, eating her energy, and ruling her life. I broached the subject to her and she brushed it off. I was very frustrated at being able to see something destroying her and not being able to do anything about it. These days I would have waded in and grabbed the bugger, but as a young woman, I did not have that confidence.

So her life fell apart, she couldn't get a marriage partner, she lost her job, became slightly nuts, lost her beauty—it was a terrible thing to watch. I did some discreet questioning around the ex pat Ugandan community where she and I lived, and I found out that the man she was supposed to marry had instead married another local girl whose mother practiced magic. Hmmm... He was a good catch and obviously there was a little magical three step going on. That particular community was very free in its use of magic for gain. I cut my teeth dismantling Ugandan curses in the early 80's...great fun, learned a lot.

Years later, many years later, on a return visit to that area, I drove past the house where she had lived. I saw her bent over in the garden and recognised her from the back. I got out of the car (and keep in mind she had not seen or heard of me for nearly twenty years) and without turning around, a voice that was not hers said, "Josie." The person with me looked at me and got spooked—the demon within her recognised me and spoke through her. She then turned, not aware that she had spoken and became surprised, hello, etc.

The fact that the demon was still there and knew me by name was enough for me to get my ass out of there as quickly as possible. I know that she would not have let me take it out (she didn't believe in such things) and because the demon knew me by name and remembered me made it all a little dangerous. It was obviously not interested in attacking me but I didn't want to get into conversation with it through her so I quietly withdrew from the situation. That being will stay with her until she dies and will trash her life every time she tries to pick herself up. It is not a curse, and not really a straightforward possession. It was sent in magical attack and will be kept up by someone—someone is paying for it to stay there and trash her life. There are enough feuds in that community (along with bored women with big chips on their shoulders and large grudges) to keep attacks like that going indefinitely.

Because it searched specifically for her in such a way, it will have had a marker, like hair, nails, etc, and her name. Somewhere there will be a poppet or a picture of her keeping it going.

Poppets

Poppets can be very useful in the event of magical attacks as not only do they direct attack, they can also deflect attack. Here is another story of magical attack, this time using a poppet for protection. (I'm in a storytelling mood...can't you tell?)

When I lived on the Flathead Reservation (Confederate Salish and Kootani tribes) in Montana, I was sometimes called out to tribal members who were having cursing/attack issues. One particular one was really nasty: a tribal member was in prison and was dying for no apparent reason. A sumeshan (medicine man) had said that the tribal member was being attacked by Cheyenne medicine and he would not help him.

I went to the old lodge area and asked the ancestors there for advice. They were very vocal and showed me how to protect him from the magical attack. I had to get a picture of him and something that he had worn for a long time. I went to the isthmus in the river, where the old medicine dances were done and made a man out of the earth and pebbles. In the earth man I placed the picture and the ring of his that I had been given and then I baptised the earth man in the name of the tribal member (he was a Catholic). I covered it with weeds and sticks to protect it, and then stood over it thinking about the attacks and seeing them coming to the earth man.

I then called upon the medicine spirits to send an animal to guard the earth man and a spirit bear appeared. The bear walked around and around the earth man before settling itself down to rest. As I left the river, one of the tribal contacts told me I had learned well and a gift was on the path for me. I kept my eyes peeled and about a few yards from the earth man I saw something strange in the dust. Bending over I saw it was a little bone bear with one leg broken off; it had obviously been discarded a long time ago and had probably fallen off a dancer during a medicine dance. I was very pleased with the gift and said thank you. I had a call two days later to say that the tribal member was getting better and was going to be moved out of the prison hospital the following day.

The earth man lasted long enough to take all the flak from the magical attack and the attackers eventually gave up when they realised it was no longer working. They became worried that the tribal member had gotten help and might attack them in return (which he didn't).

The bear had a nice little postscript, too. A friend of mine (who works within tribal magic) told me that the bears had all but vanished from her area and she was making a bear shield to draw them back in. Did I have anything from the mountains that would go on a bear shield? Yup I said, I have just the thing.... So the little bear went onto the shield and it joined in her magic which worked very well—bear poop started to appear in the woods by her house.

Now those are examples of magical attacks from tribal communities. As in all magical attacks, deflection is better that counter attack—redirecting or ignoring is best of all.

Redirecting

Methods of redirecting range from the use of poppets and pictures, to using elements. One way of using elements is to use a candle flame.

To redirect through a candle flame you need to have good mental focus and concentration. The exorcist (or person being attacked) lights a candle flame and 'sees' the attack in its manifestations forming in the flame. Any feelings of pain, emotions, and the problems it is causing are all imagined into the flame. The burden of the attack is placed in the flame and when you are sure that all of it is in there, you blow the candle flame out, blowing the flame and its contents into the void. This should be done a few times a day for a few days until the attack eases. It can be done for a while, but it must always be directed at the void and nowhere else.

Another very simple redirecting that works with lesser attacks, is by thought and speech. It is so simple, but can build great power when done correctly. Every hour or so the victim should stop what they are doing and sense the feeling of the attack and where it is coming from. Once they have the sense of it, then they say 'no, I don't accept it' and blow it down into the earth or out of the window. It sounds simple, almost too simple, but with straight forward attacks that are not too heavy and not powered by a group, it can work quite powerfully as it is built up. As it builds up over days, the focus becomes very strong and the blowing begins to mediate the power of air, so that elemental beings begin to join in with you. As before, ensure that it is put into the earth or the void, not at any being, not even the one who sent it.

Not sending back

I have covered this before in the chapter on cursing, but it is so important I must mention it here, too. Do not send an attack back. There are many reasons for this. First is, you don't really know who will receive your return post. Second, by taking on the responsibility of sending it back, you are not allowing other, more powerful beings to engage in the situation to create balance.

And this leads on to a deeper and more magical truth: it is all about balancing the books, keeping the tension equal between positive and negative, and not getting drawn into things that are beyond your understanding. Fate works in weird ways, as does inner magical training.

When you redirect, slough off or wash away bad things sent to you without wishing anyone harm, a greater power comes into play and a greater magical learning begins. It can sound all very moral, which in reality it is not—it is about how energy works, about job placement, and working within the complex web of inner beings as a priest/priestess.

If someone is constantly attacking you, then that bad energy is placed on your scales. If it tips your scales too far down, then they need rebalancing. If as an initiate you have submitted to justice, then the rebalancing is done for you in the way of protection and healing. It's a really slow process and very frustrating, but it does engage a lot of magical learning and maturing which is priceless. Beings do intervene to take off or divert the worst and what is left abrades you as a priest. This is not something an exorcist can do for someone else, but it is advice that can be given, and holds more power if you as an exorcist have gone through it yourself.

As an exorcist, also be aware that being magically attacked is like getting the measles or chickenpox: it really sucks while you in the depths of it, and it can be dangerous, but if you survive it without lots of drug intervention, your immune system becomes very strong.

I was magically attacked for years (still happens occasionally— I have a tendency to piss people off by saying what I think rather than what is politically correct or polite). The net result of all those attacks is that I have the hide of an elephant and most magical attacks these days are like little pinpricks with calling cards attached. I read the calling card and file it in my idiot file.

If the magical attacks are being aimed at someone who does not have the ability or strength to protect themselves, then that is a different matter. As an exorcist you will need to assess what the attack is and how best to protect the victim

𝔐ost common types of attacks an exorcist will have to deal with

The most common forms of attack an exorcist is called out to are from communities that have magic interwoven within the culture and religion, rather than magical communities themselves (magicians and witches just love a fight and they tend to get into counter attack...idiots...too much time on their hands and not enough brain cells).

If the person is really able to deal with it themselves but just wants to defer to someone else, then you have to firmly but kindly withdraw and let them deal with it. It is a common reaction to want someone else to fix things, but that does not help someone's magical development. As a very good author said to me once, if you are given lemons, make lemonade! But if the victim in the attack is a layperson then it is time to step in as an exorcist and do your job to ease someone's suffering.

If you are called out to such an attack first you need to ascertain what is caused by the attack and what is not. It becomes very easy to blame everything on the attack, and you also need to weed out what is a secondary effect of the attack and not a direct result of. Sometimes an immune system will react to an attack but the attack itself may be directed at their relationships, property, magical ability, etc.

It is important to know what are the primary effects of the attack so that you can figure out what the intention is and what powers/beings are being used. The way to diagnose the attack is, as usual, by inner vision, taking a statement of effects, and by reading with the deck. It is very important to know how the attack is being generated and by what means it is being delivered.

If beings are being used, they tend to be thought forms, parasites, lesser demons, faery beings, or elementals. When you have identified what being if any is involved, then you need to figure out if it is being bound into action against its will or if it is participating for a price.

Thought forms are easiest in that you can dismantle them, though that in itself can be a messy, time-consuming, and draining job. You need to first disconnect it from the egregore that feeds or drives it, and to do that you can either use an angelic contact to work with you, or a ritual blade to sever the umbilicus. Then the thought form itself will quickly need dismantling before it can reconnect itself.

To do that you will need to separate it from the victim and take it either into the underworld, the desert of the Abyss, or the void. Do not let the thought form plant the suggestion within you that it is a sentient being—it is not and does need to be taken apart. If you look at it in vision, you will see how it has been constructed and what energies/elements have been used to create it. Use counter elements/energies to negate it. Basically you rip it apart with your own hands or with ritual implements and put the parts, which will turn energy/thought back into recycling, hence the use of the underworld.

Once that is done, the victim will need ritual cleansing and a talisman protection fuelled to work for a couple of months to give them time to get their strength back. It would also be a good idea to check their home for objects that create access points—get rid of them and put up protective images, sigils, etc, in the home.

If they have a religious image in the home, make sure it is plugged into real power (which most are usually not) and bring the power of that deity/energy through for them so that it will engage protection within the home and family.

If the being is not a thought form but a real being, then you may need to act in the same way as a possession and disengage it from the energy source that is driving it. It may also need unbinding and setting free back in its own realm. If it is a faery being, then you may need to get into bargaining which can mean that the victim has to agree to do something for the faery in return for backing off the attack. Faeries are the original 'chancers' and are always on the look out for a better deal. Sometimes the deal can be quite simple, sometimes it can be a real stretch—this is where the power of haggling comes in!

If it is an elemental, like an earth being or fire being, then such consciousness is not too close to humanity and therefore cannot be so easily bargained with. Often they appear to us as quite stupid, which they are not. They just have a very different consciousness than we do.

Gently redirecting them away can sometimes work, as can engaging them by helping them and their kind in service, which automatically puts the victim in good graces with the being and it will back off.

In all circumstances where beings are involved, it is best to find the calmest and most peaceful way to put them back where they belong rather than attacking them and getting into a war.

When you are dealing with a minor demon that is carrying a magical attack for someone, first check to see if it is bound in service, in which case it will need unbinding. Do not do this in your own realm—take it to the edge of the Abyss and then unbind it while you have angelic beings working with you. Then you can put it straight back where it came from without chance of it hopping off to have fun at human expense.

Attacks with no beings involved

These types of attacks are the most common of all and are generated by ritual, recitation, and elements. The first job is to see the attack pattern on the inner and follow it back to the source. Then you will need to find the beacon that is being used to identify the victim, like a personal possession of theirs, i.e., a bit of hair/nails/blood, etc. You will find them like a sniffer dog—get a sense of their energy marker and look for it at the end of the trail. When you find it, take the inner energy of it out and put it in the void. Just be careful that you go through the void first before doing this, and dress up while in the void in armour or a disguise that covers your own energy marker—that way whoever is doing the attacking will not see you or will not recognise you and go after you.

Once you have gotten rid of the energy marker, then you will need to ritually cleanse the victim, take off any ritual sigils or patterns on them and clear the house of any object that might be acting as a doorway. Then you will need to make them invisible. This can be done by doing a tailor-made talisman to protect them and make them invisible to an attacker. It will need to be on them at all times and will draw upon their energies. If it keeps falling off or breaks, that means it has done all that it can and needs a replacement. It may take months until it all stops.

The other thing that can be used once the talisman is on the victim, is to make a poppet of her, direct the attack to the poppet, and place it somewhere safe in her house. She will need to make sure that the poppet stays where it is and is not disturbed. If it is broken, the attack can cascade down upon her which would be terrible. In some cases she would need to keep the poppet until her death and then have it burned ten days after the death.

The best solution of all though—particularly if the attack is not an all-out nasty—is to teach the victim how to brush it off without stopping it. Teach her how to redirect, how to do her own ritual bath, how to create her own talismans for really bad times, but in general to appeal to deities within her religion, or spirits from her land to help, advise, and strengthen her. There is nothing more frustrating to an attacker than to see the victim not only surviving the attack, but thriving. She will slowly get stronger and build a kind of immunity which is important if she lives in that sort of community. An angelic contact that can be invoked to help with learning to cope is Achaiah, an angel who helps with patience in the face of extreme difficulty. It is not a good idea to call upon angels right left and centre, but in extreme circumstances where the victim is doing her very best, these beings will step in and help to do what the victim cannot.

If the magical attack is an all-out dangerous and powerful one—that is to the death and powered by group energy, then it would be a good idea to take the victim in vision to the Abyss and call for the angel of justice to intervene and offer a balancing of the scales. The victim will be able to interact with the angel of the scales and not only will it down the attack, but it will give her a chance to develop herself spiritually.

Another possibility if the attack is a particularly bad one is to take her in vision to the edge of the Abyss or into the void and call upon specific angels to intervene and protect the victim. This will work if the attack is far more than the victim can cope with, and if it is many against one. It is particularly effective if the victim is innocent—then there are a whole host of angelic contacts you can call upon for help.

The big dudes are the Erin, who are the judges of God, and then there are the Barakiel who champion the innocent, along with Sariel, warriors of goodness. All of these angels are major beings, hive beings that can be worked with through vision or invocation to protect the innocent. Just make sure that the victim is truly innocent, because if she is not, she will suffer immediate judgment and consequence. They way it works with these beings is that they balance the scales and what is done to the attacker is also done to the victim. Any evil or major harmful thing that the victim has done to another will be held up against her and she will have to suffer the consequences in this life—calling upon these beings will shorten the balancing dynamic.

This can be a good thing in a way, if you have done wrong, then best to learn the lesson as quickly as you can and move on to learn better ways of operating. By invoking these beings that dynamic comes into play. It is not about punishment, but about bringing immediate consequence of action, so that someone has the opportunity to learn.

How this will work for the attacker is that once these beings are involved, the attacker will feel and experience the consequences of his actions almost immediately, so that he will learn what it feels like and what it actually does to another human being. If he continues his actions, he will continue to feel the effects. If his is really stupid, he will not understand what is happening and will either feel that he is being counter-attacked, or that someone else is attacking him.

An attacker with even a fragment of intelligence will make the connection and back off by realising that such action is not just, and is not the best way to rebalance the books, so to speak. If he does back off, he will be shown more productive ways to settle his disputes that will teach all involved a healthy lesson and allow everyone to move on.

Objects

If a victim is attacked by way of an object—i.e., an herb and skin/bone wrap that is buried in the garden of the victim (a Ugandan favourite)—a good way to deal with it is to disengage it and then pin it to the front door of the victim. The victim should touch it every time he passes through the door and refuse it on his territory. It teaches the victim to recognise the feel of such an attack and immunise himself to it, and it sends a very strong message to the attacker.

If it is an object that was left in the house, then it should be pinned to pin down the magic and placed in the front window for the attacker to see—same dynamic, known as fuck-off magic.

In summary, make sure you know what it is you are handling, what is driving it, and keep an eye on the situation after you have dealt with it to make sure it does not return. As an exorcist, make sure that you clean yourself properly and do not leave magical trails for the attacker to find—you may end up getting annoying crap yourself from the attacker and in this line of work, you do not have time or energy to waste on such silliness.

Chapter 11
The clearing and reconstruction of a sacred space/temple

One of the things that can cross the path of an exorcist is a situation where a sacred space, temple, or lodge has been attacked or desecrated. In this chapter I want to cover the many issues that surround the care of spaces such as structuring, re consecrating, cleansing, and maintenance.

What constitutes a sacred space?

There are many different approaches to the creation and care of a sacred space and it is important to know how a space is created so that if a problem arises, the exorcist knows the framework that the space operates through. The interface that the space is created around will be the same interface that the exorcist works on to fix it.

There are many different ways a temple/magical/sacred space can be created and knowing the method of construction tells the exorcist where the weak points are, how the power flows through it, and what beings to work with to fix issues.

Some sacred spaces are created by ritual, some by visionary techniques, and some are created simply by action. Going into a sacred space and sitting quietly will often be enough for an experienced exorcist to ascertain what construction method was used—a magical method becomes apparent simply by how the space reacts to a stranger who carries a magical line.

Once the method of construction has been understood, then any problem within that space will also make itself apparent in a variety of ways. If you know the basic background of the spiritual techniques practiced in that space, then you can 'turn on' the space to see how it is operating and what, if anything, is the problem with it.

When someone from outside a magical or spiritual tradition engages with a sacred space, any guardians will make themselves known along with any inner contacts. Through interacting with these contacts and lines of power, if there are magical attacks, intrusions, parasites, ghosts, or inner structural damage, it will come to the fore and the exorcist will have a first-hand experience of the problem. This is very important: you must never work simply from what you have been told or from descriptions of the problem—particularly if it is a magical attack, it can chameleon to look like something else to people who are not used to dealing with intrusions.

The types of intrusions are endless but the most common are: magical attacks from a rival magical group (or a hostile spiritual tradition), dead leaders trying to assert themselves, parasites, hostile inner beings brought in by sloppy protection or imbalanced rituals, thought forms that are part of the egregore and have gone feral, or actual magical structural damage to the inner temple itself.

Magical attacks by rival groups are one of the sad but regular occurrences in magical traditions. This becomes a problem when there is a fairly large or focussed group that gets a bee in its bonnet and has its roots in fundamentalism or immature righteousness. It is most common in groups that fight to be the 'real only true way,' or try to stop certain works from reaching a wider public—this in itself is often a sign of immaturity within the leadership which makes it very hard to find intelligent solutions.

The other type of attack can take the form of religious righteousness (a hostile spiritual tradition), for example, fundamentalist Christian groups 'praying' at Wiccan or magical lodges. When done in the right way, this can be an effective way of throwing a spanner in the works and causing all sorts of problems. The best way to work with such a problem is to simply make a channel for the prayer to flow down and route it into the nearest church—that way the prayer goes to where it should and does no harm.

The other major problem that can happen to an outer sacred space is desecration. This is where the inner pattern is purposely disturbed or damaged, and beings that are known to be in direct conflict with the space are introduced. This can happen in very powerful magical ways, or in very simple ways.

A good example of a simple way is this: a few years ago I was sat in my local abbey and it had begun to feel really weird and imbalanced. I felt sick whenever I went in and inner contacts were repeatedly telling me to clean and retune it. Because I was not a member of the Anglican faith, I felt it would be an intrusion, so I took no action for a while. But then I noticed that the local villagers who did use the Abbey were manifesting faith issues, illness, and a reluctance to go to services.

This is the point where I have to state that an exorcist should have no judgment on faiths and should be willing to uphold all faiths that people hold—it is an expression of spirituality and Divinity within the people and should be respected. It is also the job of an exorcist to serve all beings and all expressions of spirituality.

I was finally dragged kicking and screaming to the Abbey to sort it out. I sat quietly for a while to get a sense of its inner structure. The Abbey was a thousand years old and had some very impressive structures still operating from an inner point of view, it just wasn't being used actively as an inner spiritual place by the Anglican Church that now owned it. It was the home of psychologised preaching that was divorced of any inner spark.

After a few minutes I started to see a modern Wiccan imprint trying to impose itself on the inner space which got me really curious. I hunted around the church first outwardly and then in vision. In vision I saw seals all over the place. Someone had drawn a variety of magical symbols—mainly pentacles—under some of the benches. Someone had also hidden a couple of small Goddess figures smeared with blood…all very silly stuff, but very effective. I cleaned them all off and removed things. I then did a basic cleansing of the space and all went back to normal. No one has the right to desecrate a sacred space, no matter what they think of that faith.

What happens when a space is hacked and taken over?

This can happen when a space is not properly tuned and protected by guardians—the ritual can be hacked and the energy raised can be stolen. This can also happen if the protection of the space or ritual is too heavily defined. It is very tempting to become a control freak and choose certain named beings to protect the ritual/space and bind how they operate and what they do. By doing this, you do not protect against possible situations you are not aware of, or hadn't thought of. It is not too hard to hack into a sacred space or ritual if you know how, particularly in certain magical traditions where lots of named beings that are bound have been used.

The most protected sites are ones where the builders have allowed beings to do their job without interference, and have called upon an order of being, rather than an individual (individuals have limitations).

The other thing to be aware of is that in magical groups, the initiation joins a person to the collective; but when someone is cast out, they still hold the insignia of the group upon their spirit so the guardians will not see them as hostile. So if a lodge/group is one of those that gets into feuds (which so many do) then any cast-out individual must also be banished from the space, even if she carries the insignia (which is bloody hard to get off once it is on). So, it's sort of like, "Your name's not on the list so you can't come in."

The more sensible way to deal with this sort of issue is that when a person is initiated into a line, it is done in such a way as to place collective responsibility for the upholding of sacred balance and the task of service upon them. If they break that, they automatically carry the effect of dishonouring the temple. Once they have done it and felt the effect upon themselves, they tend not to do it again.

An initiation of that sort—the initiation that includes service and honor—is service and honor to the inner worlds, the land, and Divinity. It does not mean service and honor to a leader, so it does not trigger if the initiate tries to hack for honourable reasons in the spirit of service. So if the leader of a line or group goes off the rails, the initiate is not going to trigger bad dude stuff by hacking if it is for the benefit of the sacred space, or in service to uphold the sacred/group honor. This does not work in magical lines that operate within selfish means, so you are then back to loads of trip wires, defences, and feuds.

Wḥat ḥappens if it is not properly tuneд anд Ɓecomes parasiteд?

If a magical space is not properly built, upheld, and tuned, but is used for powerful things, then it will quickly become parasited. There are certain magical lines that will summon all sorts of beings, use basic protections/seals and conditionally bound contacts. That is a true recipe for disaster. The temple will be full of holes and will become a feeding ground for all sorts of parasitical beings. This normally manifests by conflict, struggles of leadership, break ups, and illness, often mental. The way to sort that out is to de-parasite the space, and then to fully strip and rebuild the inner and outer temple. The working methods should be closely looked at along with ritual methods, contacts, etc, to see where the weakness is and fix it.

Most of the above listed problems can be addressed by using some of the clearing methods discussed in previous chapters: clearing a space, exorcising a space, etc. The real issue is when a magical/spiritual space has been badly violated and the inner structure of the space is damaged. To piece the original space back together can be a nightmare as you will have to know, in detail, how it was originally constructed and what beings were used. If it is not badly damaged, then you can tap into the contacts that are still operating through the space and they will guide you. You will also need to know the magical outer structure that is used (i.e., what tradition, what rituals, etc).

If you cannot access such information for whatever reason, then you will need to reconstruct and graft the inner space, and reconsecrate the outer space. So, for example, if a Western Mysteries temple/lodge, a Christian church, a Golden Dawn Lodge, Freemason temple, or anything that is based upon a structure of Kabbalistic magic is damaged badly, you would use angelic structures and inner adept contacts to reconstruct the space and reconnect the contacts.

If it was a Wiccan or other nature-based magical space, then you would probably use a mix of human inner contacts, elementals, and faery beings to reconstruct the space.

The basic method of reconstruction that I use for either is more or less the same, and it is effective in most circumstances. The idea is to learn the base pattern of work and fit the details around it, so it is pure technique, not magical dogma.

Clearing and reconstructing a sacred/magical space/temple/lodge

If the space has been badly desecrated or damaged from an attack (inner or outer) then it may need partial or full reconstruction. The first step is to take out the magic from anything that is in the room. Altars will need to be 'de commissioned' by ritual cleansing and exorcising. If a magical tool/ritual implement has been fully consecrated, then it should just need a clean off. If it is a dedicated ritual tool, then it will need stripping and rededicating.

Once everything in the room has been decommissioned, then they need to be taken out of the space. This is also a good time to get rid of anything that has no real purpose in the temple space. People these days are very much into 'dressing up' the temple space with wall hangings, pictures, etc, so that it ends up looking like a new age store or a Halloween funhall room. Such clutter is distracting in a magical space and can become very counter-productive really quickly. (It gives spaces for unhealthy things to hide and it also absorbs inner yuck. Try running your hand down something that has no job in a temple...it will feel disgusting.)

So once the room is completely clear, clean it. Consecrate the water before you use it and throw lots of consecrated salt in the bucket along with simple soap and a drop of bleach. Clean the space from top to bottom, and then clean all things that have been taken out and are going to go back in.

Once you have done that, do a simple exorcism of the space and a re-blessing. That has only taken care of the outer temple though—the inner problem will still be there.

So...on to phase two:

Reconstruction

Leave the space clean until the following evening and then go in, place an unused white candle in the centre and light it. Place four more white candles in the directions, by each wall, but do not light them. When you light the central candle, reach into the stillness, to the void to get the flame so that the candle flame is a doorway.

Sit quietly for a while with the flame. This has to be done in defined stages and mustn't be rushed—there are inner dynamics that need to be given a chance to work. When that flame has done its first job, you will feel it. It will shift, and a deep sense of peace will fill the room.

Next, light some frankincense on charcoal and go around the room, making sure you get into each corner. Let it settle in the middle of the room next to the candle once all corners have been done.

Then you need to re-open the gates so that the building process can begin. Start in the east, and light the candle, each time reaching out into the void for the flame. As you light the candle, see the gates beyond the flame and see them opening. You can also use speech to open the gates, just keep it real simple: "In the name of...I open the gates to the east." And so on.

Once the basic gates are open, then the real work begins. The construction work must be done simultaneously on the outer and inner, so it requires a good deal of focus and concentration. You cannot work from a script—you must know the contacts deep within you and be able to work with them without any distraction.

The first step of the rebuilding is the foundation: the builder must mirror the manifestation of the world through the building of the temple. A sacred space is a mini me of the world and therefore has to be built in the same way.

Warning: this work will bring tremendous power through, so ensure you are clean, clear, and have no drugs, meat, stimulants, ritual talismans, etc, upon or in your body. Fast on a clean diet for a couple of days before, take a ritual bath, and take off any magical bling you might be wearing. You have to be the vessel of Divinity to re-create the universe!

Stand before the central flame and still yourself by going into the void. Once you are still and empty, you must call upon the first Keystone to begin the building. There are two keystones (this is part of the inner mysteries of sacred building. Most ritualists believe there is one keystone and that is not so. That assumption comes from the building of archways which is a modern(ish) building method. Very ancient structures had no archways and the lack of arches is one of the indications of very ancient magical constructs.

The two keystones are made up of an archon and an aeon. They are the base foundations of power in sacred construction and allow the power of Divinity to flow through a construct to make it a suitable vessel for Divine power.

Some magical studies specify that archons are evil angels or spirits that destroy man. This is not really correct—the archon is the power that stops a soul reaching divinity before it is ready. They are also the balancing power of the aeon. For power to manifest in the outer world, it must have positive and negative—a balance of power that creates friction and tension, thus allowing matter to manifest.

When you reach this section of the work, you must be ready to plough straight through it and not pause. You are bringing through great power of destruction and regeneration, both of which create disaster if left unchecked, even for a short time.

Ideally this should be done by two people (one male and one

female). Unfortunately it is very hard to find someone nuts enough and capable enough to do it, but also it is important for the full power to manifest from a single source: you take on the role of Divinity with no form (this is why your body gets fried while doing this).

If you are lucky enough to have a working partner able to do this, then the female works to bring through the archon and the male brings through the aeon.

Standing before the flame, and in the stillness, you call out verbally and in vision for the archon named JAO (IAO), Keeper of the seven heavens, asking him to bring into being the heavens above. The reason you use this name of the archon is this is the name tuned to the archon associated with Metatron, who is an archangelic being that has known humanity (that way you don't end up as a pile of crisped cells in a mush on the floor).

As you call upon the name of JAO, see the being emerge out of the void and stand in the ritual keystone position before the flame in the centre of the room to your left (you are stood before the central flame), the keystone position is left foot forward, right arm outstretched, and the many wings stretched up like an arch over the head of the being until the tip of the wings are over the central flame.

Immediately go back into stillness in the void and call upon the aeon ARKHAS, the foundation of the lowest thing, and see that being come out of the void to stand to your right, with his right foot forward, his left hand outstretched, and his wings reaching over his head to touch the wings over the flame with JAO. In vision take the left hand of JAO and the right hand of ARKHAS and join them together over the flame. Then do the same with the opposite hands so that their wrists cross over the flame. (If there are two of you doing this, then you assume the ritual positions yourselves and bring the beings through you...crispy! This is a great way to get a natural perm....)

Once the hands are joined over the flame, their arms will make the figure of eight infinity sign over the centre of the space. Then place the right foot of ARKHAS forward so that it touches the left foot of JAO. So the image becomes two angels on either side of the central flame, with their feet, hands and wings touching to create a vertical figure of eight, and their arms crossed over the flame to make a horizontal figure of eight. As soon as all the bits are connected, the power will begin to flow freely within the shapes. Together in the ritual shape of connection, they are the keystone of the world and the keystone of sacred space.

As soon as the connection happens, then you go to the east and call upon the angelic power of air to flow into the space. Turn with your back to the flame, and, in vision, with your eyes shut, see the power of wind flow into the room. Behind the wind will be inner contacts—reach out to them and verbally as well as silently ask them to offer a contact of communication and recitation to work in service through the temple. This can take the form of a human inner contact, and elemental contact, or an angelic contact. Either way, see the contacts flow into the room from the eastern gate and watch as they pass into the walls and floor of the temple. At this point one of the contacts should give you a word or show you a sigil which will act as a key to connect with them.

Then you go to the south and repeat the process with fire and the fire/solar priesthood. Be very careful with this line of contact as they can be very difficult to control and will easily take over the temple if they are not filtered properly. If you get a human contact, reject it and ask for an angelic contact to come through. The reason for this is that the fire temple inner line has repeatedly degenerated into lines of corruption and misused power. This line brings war, hostility, conflict—all the yummy power imbalances. It is best not to have to deal with that lot, so go straight to the source and reach for angelic contact.

When the temple is up and working, you will draw upon that angelic contact when lighting the flame. It will protect and defend the temple, and provide thresholds to the inner worlds.

Next you go to the west and repeat the process. Again it is best to reach for an angelic contact or elemental contact that can be drawn upon for seership and cleansing within the temple space.

Finally go to the north and call upon the Sandalphon to come through into the space to create the ballast and bring through the wisdom of the earth into the temple. If the temple group works with Kabbalah, this contact is a wonderful one to have connected to the temple to work with. See them merge into the walls in vision, and see how they take on the shape of the room. The Sandalphon can also become the altar.

Remember, with all of these angelic contacts, that you are asking them to work with you in service, you are not commanding them or binding them. It is their job, performed of free will within their job description, and which will open all sorts of doors for expansion and learning. If you command or bind them to work, you immediately limit their range of action—they know more about their ability to do the job in hand than you do. If you command or bind them, then they can only do what you tell them, not what they know needs doing.

Once all the gates have been connected to the elements and angelic contacts, you need to re-establish the working inner contacts, the altar/s, and ritual patterns. If there are ancestral contacts or now-dead inner contacts that the temple works with, then you call upon them to pass over the threshold of the north and come and take residence within the temple. A doorway can be created for them in simple terms, like an object, drawn sigil, or image. If you are going to use an outer expression of the contacts, then it must be made and established within the temple within 24 hours.

Similarly, if you work with contacts from inner orders, beings from the Abyss, etc, now is the time to reconnect them and bring them into the space. If they work through an image, sigil, or object, then it needs to be in position within twenty-four hours.

Now is the time, while all the gates are open and still holding vision, to have the altar/s brought back in. Have it done in silence and have the people carrying it stay silent and leave as soon as they have set it in position. Now you have to bring the power back through into the altar.

Whatever power you use to enliven the altar (regardless of the physical make up of the altar), place your hands upon it and be aware of the two keystones in the centre of the room. If you use a central altar, then be aware of the keystones flowing through it.

In vision and out loud call upon the power that will become

the altar and invite them to flow out of the central flame (thus through the keystones), through you and into the altar. Although you can call upon a specific power to be within the altar (the Catholic Church brings through the Corpus Christi), it is far more interesting and powerful to call the Sandalphon and ask them to bridge the power of unnamed Divinity within substance (the earth, Malkuth).

If you manage to make the contact, you will feel the immense beauty of the power of Divinity within substance as it flows through you and into the altar. It is the true solid foundation of everything and is the basis of all magic—hence it makes the best of all altars.

Once the connection is bridged, place the central candle upon the altar and announce that the building begins. Withdraw from vision and withdraw from the room, leaving all the candles going and let the inner builders get on with their jobs. Go have a cup of tea (no coffee or wine yet, it hasn't finished) and have a little rest. Once you feel that the inner construction is finished (it will feel like a light has gone off), go back into the room and reintroduce the ritual implements. If the temple uses deities, then it is at this point, and not earlier, that you reintroduce and reconnect the deity to the temple. That way, the deity is a guest of the temple and works with you, rather than being the major power source for the temple which will leave the space vulnerable if they should choose to withdraw for any reason or get temperamental.

If the group that operates within the space uses transubstantiation, then a performing of that ritual should be used to seal the work. Don't go in for the 'bread with semen and menstrual blood' thing—simple bread will do. You need a blank slate to work with, even if you normally work that way. The use of simple food stuff allows deeper powers to flow through it, where as the use of human blood and seed defines what power can manifest in the substance, thus narrowing the range of power available to the temple.

It would be a good idea to have a constant flame going in the space to keep it tuned. This can be done by using larger church candles or the candles in long glass which is so often used in Mexican shrines.

€gregores going feral anδ how to δeal with them

When a group works within a sacred space/temple and uses initiations/consecrations, then an inner egregore is built by default. An egregore is a collection of all the inner knowledge of the group coupled with shared energy from all the members. It is like a bank of knowledge and energy, a smaller octave of the inner library that operates within the line of initiates, giving access to a collective of wisdom and strength. When a magical/spiritual group is healthy, the egregore will operate for the good of the collective and will shine through the initiates—"by their fruits shall ye know them."

It will not take away from the initiates' independent thought, but will be a resource to be accessed when necessary. The egregore of a temple can usually be seen upon the inner planes and will often give the exorcist a really good truthful assessment as to the health of the magical group in question.

Sadly, things can go badly wrong very quickly with egregores and it happens much too often. If a leader becomes unstable, he will pull upon the egregore for his own personal energy and knowledge, and will attempt to block the initiates from accessing such power. Sometimes, an imbalanced leader will link the egregore to his own fate and allow the egregore to act as a scapegoat for his own transgressions.

Sometimes, egregores can be 'moved into' and can be possessed almost like a human. When this happens it then starts to control the initiates and leader alike, usually for parasitical reasons—to gain more power and energy. A glaring symptom of such a condition is where the initiates lose the ability to think for themselves and defer everything to their leader. The egregore has to be exorcised and dismantled, which is a hell of a job, as it can sometimes mean also clearing and dismantling the initiate line itself.

If an egregore takes on a life of its own, without being parasited, it then becomes a thought form. This can be a little easier to deal with in that the reconstruction of the temple—coupled with a major change in working practice, along with going into the inner realms and taking it apart—will usually solve the problem.

At the end of the day, the basic rule of thumb is: if you create a magical temple/space/group, do it properly, use your common sense and keep it simple. Have regular clean up sessions for both the space and the workers, and keep in mind that if you do silly stuff in a magical space, it will invite trouble.

Chapter 12
Issues of the land and beings of nature

It is not often that an exorcist will be called out to deal with issues regarding the land, but it can happen, and the land itself and any inner contacts connected to the land can also reach out for help, and often do. Apart from the usual issues of hauntings on patches of land, there are a whole host of things that an exorcist can be presented with in way of service to the land and beings inherent within the land.

There are a wide range of issues that can present as land problems that would need an exorcist—for example, beings trapped in land areas, parasites, and lesser demonic beings (for want of a better word) terrorising an area, sleepers that need help, sacred ground that has been disturbed or built upon, faery beings trapped by building projects, or faery beings getting into feuds with locals, deities awakening in the land or reaching out to humanity for recognition, land imbalances caused by interference that need attending to, feral guardians, desecrated burials...the list goes on and on.

An exorcist who has natural inner sight will be roped into 'jobs' where ever he goes. It is like a little light goes on in the inner landscape that heralds the arrival of the cavalry...the inner powers-that-be just forget to ask and instead manoeuvre you to where the jobs are that need doing. Then they will smack you over the head until you get it and go do the job.

Sometimes these jobs have major consequences for the land, and when you have finished the job and look back over the previous few weeks, you will see how you were gently played chess with to get you into a situation where you would engage and work. Those larger jobs are often echoes of mythical patterns that are deeply embedded within the land, but you do not realise the full meaning of the myth until you have done the job and are then able to see it from a different perspective.

Here is a good example of such a job: a few years ago I moved to Tennessee and went to live in a house that was beside a lake full of poisonous snakes, snapping turtles, and aggressive fish. From the moment I moved there I started to have bad dreams, low energy, and a feeling that all was not quite right. The house was on the land path of the Trail of Tears, so I assumed it was some psychic resonance from that suffering. I went in vision to talk to some of the tribal elders from that time and did a job that they asked of me. But the deeper problems persisted and it became obvious that what I had dealt with was just a symptom of something deeper going on.

I finally got to a deeper level of contact which was pre-human and offered service to do what ever I could to help ease the suffering in the land. I got no reply and assumed that I was being told to piss off politely. Over the following weeks, I began chatting with neighbours who all had a similar experience. Since they had moved to that lake they had become depressed, weak, plagued by nightmares, and overcome with exhaustion. I wondered if it was pollution, I wondered if it was burial grounds (which it wasn't), and eventually I gave up guessing and got on with my day job the best I could.

At work a certain name started to pop up over and over: Beowulf. It was in books my students showed me (they were choosing ideas for a project), a film advert started to appear, and finally a friend, out of the blue, gave me a copy of the poem on a whim. Hmm....

So I read the poem which went in through the eyeballs and out through the ear...I wasn't getting it. In the meantime, I was dumping my ritual implements in a canoe with a friend (complicated reasons) and went out at night at a new moon (it was against the law to be on the lake at night) and dumped the sword, cup, wand, and stone in the lake.

Another wee while passed and in a dream one night, I saw a large tic-like being that was the size of a big house at the bottom of the lake and it was sending out odd-looking creatures that would go into peoples' houses and suck their life force as they slept. The dream repeated itself a few times until I got the hint. I was starting to get quite sick at the time and I didn't know if I had the strength to do such a task. Then I got a call that my daughter would be coming home to stay and she was heavily pregnant. I did not want her exposed to such a parasite while she carried a child.

So at the full moon, I went and sat at the side of the lake and went into vision. I swam down to the bottom of the lake and there glowing in the muck was my sword, all shiny like Excalibur.... Well cheesy!! I got the sword and swam deeper and found the tick with all the parasite beings huddled around it, preparing to go out and feed on people.

I rolled in the mud to cover myself and then went at the big tick. I was obvious it had been operating unchecked for a very long time as it had no defences at all and did not see me coming. I killed it and then got into killing off all the other parasites. Normally I would have worked with various beings to put the parasites back where they belonged, but this was not that sort of situation. It was very clear that they no longer belonged in this realm at all and that they had been prolonging their spell in our world by sucking people to death. Time to go, dudes.

The difference was immediate: everyone started sleeping soundly and getting more energy. The lake took on a different feel and nature began to return. When I first moved there, no birds, no nature (other than the snakes, scorpions, ticks and mosquitoes) were to be seen. Within a month of the work, ducks, geese, herons, all sorts of birds, turtles, raccoons (little bastards), a couple of peacocks, guinea fowl, wild turkeys...the list goes on. It was like everything came out of the cupboard again...very peculiar!

A few weeks later, I sat down and read the Beowulf poem again—holy shit, now I got it. It took the inner contacts quite a while to get it through to me (I'm a bit slow sometimes) but I found it really interesting reading that poem in light of what I had just been through and I began to see mythical stories in a different light—it is as if they are guide books or maps on how to deal with inner beings that manifest through the land and the people.

From that story you can see how the inner contacts tried to get the information to me many times about a job that really needed doing. Even the inspiration to throw all the ritual implements in the lake was probably part of it, as they worked with me during the vision, and protected me while guiding my actions.

These ancient parasites seem to be a lot more prevalent in the U.S.A. than in the U.K. and that got me wondering about the ancient stories of slaying dragons in the U.K.—if the stories were sometimes relaying information regarding the clearing of some of these very old beings that were not compatible with human settlements.

Bridging work

An interesting form of land work that one can get dragged into is bridging work: literally, building inner bridges for beings to get out. Again, the exorcist is usually called out to a place because of disturbances, or is drawn there by instinct, or led there by inner contacts.

Here is another land story for you (Jeez, I spend so much of my time being dragged from one land disruption to another): Whilst living in Tennessee (which I have to say is the most haunted and weirdest place I have ever lived—Wisconsin was the second), I had a visit from a friend of mine called Peggy, who is a priestess. As is the magical rule, get two magical people together and trouble begins....

Sooo...we made plans to go visit an ancient Indian pyramid burial and as I was going out of the door, the sword (remember the sword? This is the pre-dumping-in-the-lake era) decided it wanted to come too. So off we went, travelling south out of Nashville and we promptly got lost. We looked everywhere for this damn burial and could not for the life of us find it.

We were just about to give up when the sword woke up and the inner contact that flows through the sword said that something of great importance was near by. We parked up and started walking (with sword under arm) until the contact said "stop, look up." We stopped and looked up and half way up the small cliff was a cave entrance. It was obvious that whatever was to be done was in that cave.

So we climbed up into the cave and sat looking at each other. Peggy beamed a big smile. "Look behind you," she said. On the cave wall, just behind me, was a perfect cross indented in the stone. It was either a very old carving or a natural formation. To me it looked natural. We had been talking about cross, anchor, and cruciform magical shapes all the way down in the car. We knew we were on the right track.

We looked around, slightly confused. We knew we were where we were supposed to be (try saying that line when you are drunk) but we didn't know what to do next. In such circumstances, my failsafe is to switch the lights on and see who is home. So we both went in vision deeper into the cave and we found an area that was blocked off in the inner worlds as well as physically blocked. The inner landscape of the place, the inner realm that expresses through that place, was blocked.

So we started to unblock it. We didn't expect much more than that as such a block can cause all sorts of energy problems for an area of land and we assumed that was the job in hand. Wrong.

We dug through the inner blockage and when we cleared it, thousands, and I really mean thousands, of small, amphibian part-human-type beings came out. They were so relieved but shocked. They were looking for the sea and nothing was there— just a small river mumbling past. They were desperate to get to the sea, so I told them that if they went into the river, they would eventually be carried to the sea. They couldn't make it to the river on their own so we bridged them using our bodies—they flowed through us and out into the river.

Now I am not sure if we needed to bridge them because the world was so different and they could not recognise the water, or if they had some magical binding on them. A lot of the time, particularly when working with ancient land beings, things that happen do not make much sense. But don't worry about that, the world tends to not make much sense anyhow.

We were both trashed after it and we sat quietly for a moment in the cave to get our breath back. As we sat silently, a young man walked past, a local young farmer by the look of him. Something made him look up and his face was a picture. From his vantage point, deep in the shadow of the cave, was the outline of a woman covered in a shroud or shawl, leaning on a very impressive sword with a single tattooed arm exposed as it held the blade. He looked like he had seen a ghost, which is obviously what he thought he had seen (TN is the Bell Witch state). He looked like he needed a toilet as he scuttled away, poor man.

For nights afterwards, I dreamed of those strange creatures from the cave and I decided to do some research. I did find local Indian myths about beings who were half fish or lizard and half human, and then loads of ridiculous David Ike poop so I went no further.

To my mind, they are some ancient spirit beings that just needed help to get to where they are meant to be. The land has many levels of being, and if one gets badly out of balance, the whole area becomes problematic. This is reflected in European myths such as the Arthurian myth, to name one of many.

There are many early Norman churches that have reference to the tower pinning a dragon below the church, or St Michael/St George churches sat on top of volcanic or granite outcrops, caves, and circles. These early churches are often pinning an older power of the land down—for good or bad? We don't know until we let them loose....

If you are drawn to or are called out to a land area that is disturbed, you might want to go into the land itself to see if there are any such issues that can be actively addressed. Sometimes what can be a seemingly small issue can have a devastating effect on the surrounding land, conversely something that you think might really impact a land area (like nuclear dumping, etc) can some-times turn out to be no more that a minor irritant. I think the key is to keep an open mind and just do the job that presents rather than sweep the land ready for action!

Sacred ground

Another land issue that can manifest sometimes is where there seems to be an energy stagnation which results in a build up of 'inner goo' (deeply technical term, huh?). Such stagnation or blockage in land energy can often be very pronounced around sacred sites, ancient churches, etc. Sometimes this can come from ritual pinning that was a favourite act of land suppression exercised by the pre-Christian Roman priests (usually to Apollo).

This action of ritually pinning the land is also practiced by some orders of Tibetan Buddhist monks. By pinning the Goddess, they pin and control the power of the land and are able to then channel it through their rituals. The land tends to take exception to such behaviour and it can cause all sorts of imbalances—it is those imbalances that normally draw an exorcist in.

If you are called in to an area where there is a lot of disturbance in the land, the first thing to do is map out what sacred sites are in the vicinity, and what has been done to them. In the U.K., a lot of the Norman churches were built on earlier Saxon sites, which in turn were built on top of Celtic hermitages, stone circles, bur-ial mounds, etc. Some of the churches were built on previous Roman temples (which were built on top of previous pagan bur-ial mounds and stone alignments) and those churches tend to be sat on top of Roman pinning.

Another method of 'pinning' or trapping land power was a Masonic habit in the U.S.A. in the 1700s and early 1800s: sacred Indian burial mounds, usually the biggest and the best, were used to build state capital buildings upon. The power of the ancestral land and its people were overlaid by the central core of civilised power.

If you should take on the task of unpinning or releasing ances-tral spirits, land powers, etc, there are a few considerations that you have to take into account before you take on such a task.

The first consideration is to be sure you know what you are releasing. Some powers just really don't need to be out in the world anymore, and some powers were pinned for good reason. If the land around it is disturbed, it might need retuning, or the inner landscape working on, rather than a massive power of destroying fire releasing.

The second consideration is the pissed off-ness of the consciousness you release. This tends to happen more in European mainland and the U.K. than in the U.S.A. The land beings and consciousness found in the U.S.A. tends to be a wild, ancient nature-based flow of power that takes on forms of strange animals, earth beings, and weird weather.

In the U.K. and mainland Europe, the powers can manifest more in the forms of deities because they have been consciously interacted with by humanity and given human structures to flow through for thousands of years.

When you have a deity consciousness in the land that has been pinned for a thousand or so years, it might be a little pissy when you release it. For example, Pete and I worked on a pinned deity in the land in the U.K. We went through a whole series of steps in visions to slowly release her and restore her to the land. It was exhausting and very demanding work, but we got it done.

The last night of the work this Goddess appeared, her hounds around her, and she was rather put out, to put it mildly. She wanted revenge, she wanted all men dead, she wanted to destroy the powers that had pinned her—she wanted to know where they were. Hmm...raging goddess bent on destroying civilisation. Oops, there goes another red button....

The other major issue that can surface is the inner goo around stone circles. If the circles don't like it, they will call you if you live near or are visiting. For five thousand years those stones have been hanging around and the ones that are still standing are largely unpinned. (Sites were pinned by building upon them and ritually putting a blade in the land upon commencement of building). The stones have had the occasional vicar or bishop 'cleansing them' but apart from that, they have more or less trundled along in life until just recently.

Now, over the last hundred years or so, they have become the focus of every magical group that has an agenda, no matter what that agenda is, so certain stone circles are used for rituals of all kinds, regardless of the land energy or the needs of the land. Modern day Pagan activity at stone circles can range from careful intelligent tending, prayer, ritual of acknowledgement/gifting to the spirits, to all out selfish psychologised parasiting of the stones, vicious cursing, weird sex dramas, and the general dumping of modern shit on an ancient site (along with plastic flowers, nylon ribbons and chemical incense..yum).

Some sites just brush it off, but in other areas it attracts large parasites which contribute towards a land imbalance and it affects all the humans within the vicinity. That is where the exorcist comes in: remove the parasite, clear the site, get the energy flow working in harmony with humanity, and ask if there is anything else needed.

Certain power sites that have not been tuned either too heavily or at all towards humanity (i.e., where there are no stone circles, just an unmarked power centre) often have a strong faery presence. For the people living nearby this can be a good thing or a bad thing, depending on what type of faery being it is, and what their relationship to humanity is, and also how the humans interact with the land.

If there is a faery presence, and you have been called out because there are problems in the area, then the easiest way to try to solve such issues is to go into vision and talk with the beings and ask them what you can do to help the situation. If they ask you to get rid of all the humans, then you have a problem—some form of negotiation and compromise has to be reached so that faery and human can live on the same patch of land without killing each other. This is where the exorcist becomes politician and conflict manager—it is great fun getting between faery and human, particularly when neither side believes in the other one and both have a sense of their own sovereignty to the land. Then you have to really work on your negotiating skills.

A good example of this in regular working practice is Iceland: the government of Iceland employs faery experts who ensure new building or road works do not infringe on faery territory, and they also smooth over interracial conflicts between beings of the land and the resident humans. This led to an overall better relationship between the old and the new, the civilised and the wild. Now buildings and bridges don't fall down, costing the government millions in rebuilding costs, and the faeries get to stake out their territory and only occasionally poke the humans.

When you are working to try and bring some sort of rebalancing to an area, patch of land, or residence, and faeries are involved, sometimes the solution can be very simple: they might ask you to take something away, or move something, or bring something. The other simple solution can sometimes be asking the affected family to change something in their house/garden, or to ask the family to offer regular gifts (rent/payment) like honey, little mirrors (faeries like shiny things), fruit, coins, or a service like making bread for them, or singing to them on a regular basis. It can often be very simple and can smooth a lot of ruffled feathers in territorial disputes.

Sometimes, though, it can be bigger issues that can become violent and when that violence comes from a host of beings who are feeling invaded or slighted, then the choice has to be made: do the humans move out, or do they lock the faery beings out of that area? That is easier said than done (there is a lot of traditional advice that often doesn't work in practice) and having tried it many times under very difficult conditions, the best advice I can give for locking out faery beings is to work with bigger, more powerful beings. But then you can be swapping one problem for another.

Another method of calming faery beings that are infesting a human area and causing chaos is to give them things to do that they will like. Faeries like reenactment of stories and myths. Pete and I were having problems in our home for a wee while with a bit of an infestation that I brought into the house. In the end, I painted mythical creatures and faery people on the walls in bright shimmering colours. They are still busy 'playing out' in those images and have become part of the household. They are not causing trouble now, as they have lots to do and have also become default guardians within the house, willingly telling me when something or someone tries to intrude. It's like having hyperactive naughty children in the house—just give then lots and lots to do.

Vortexes

Vortexes in the land can be very interesting things but can cause chaos for people living nearby if not worked with. Like all natural power, it clashes with modern living a lot, but if it is interacted with, then it can flow through the human world without causing chaos. In fact, when worked with consciously, these vortexes can be very advantageous to the land and the people.

They often act like interfaces for deeper powers in the land that can manifest in strange mythical ways, and that teach the beings living on the land how the power works, and how to work with it.

A recent example was a friend of ours who lives in Cornwall next to a powerful vortex. When I went to visit, the vortex was shouting at me to come and visit. I had no idea what it was, just that a land power was waving its hand wildly at me for attention. It was easy to find: it was like having an inner lighthouse and fog horn all going at once—pretty hard to miss, really.

Out of the vortex, once I got 'speaking' to it, came a large giant who was carrying a little child on his shoulder—the exact image of St Christopher, except it wasn't a Christian saint I was looking at. It was a very interesting land power manifesting through the human image. The most powerful of the two was the little child or dwarf sat on his shoulder. I was told very clearly that if the child was not kept well fed, it would call or sing in the storms that would kill the fishermen, and it would feed off them instead.

So this is obviously a local power of the vortex that works with condensed earth power (hence the big gentle giant and the little ferocious child) which in turn works with the weather patterns that come off the sea. So, having given us this information by way of a visual cue, we now know that the vortex on that land is one that can be worked with to keep the weather in balance. Such knowledge could become very useful in today's climate crisis.

I have come across other such sites in Ireland and Cornwall where the stone alignments are connected to the weather, but I have never had such a strong human-style visual that I got at the Cornish vortex. This means that it is a power that has been worked with by humans for a very long time—the interface is well established and the cues would tell the people exactly what power it is.

When you get called to or come across such a situation, it is a very rare opportunity to make contact with these powers to see what they need and how they work. Just the simple interaction can be enough to make a major difference to the human issues on that patch of land. At that vortex, a little ways off across a stream and up a hill, is a fairly modern chapel. I sat in the chapel for a while and found myself being dragged down into the underworld to a bright sleeping maiden who needed something.

I saw that she was held down by something, not pinned, but blocked in someway. I had to find a way to free her up without waking her, and once I had figured it out, a beautiful light shone out of her and filtered up to the surface world. Again, it is a deep land power that needs to flow freely for the health of all the beings that live there. To me, I felt that she was a version of the land power that some would call Brigh, a deity I have worked with on and off for many years (I grew up next to one of her sacred springs).

Land work can be very illuminating and can teach us a great deal about the powers that flow through the lands where we live. It's the most positive (sometimes) work in the field of exorcism, and it is a branch of the work I dearly love. It is very exhausting, though, and if you make contact with a being that hasn't been listened to or interacted with for a long time, they can really blow your socks off by trying to converse at all power levels at once.

Sleepers, burials and guardians

One of the most common reasons for house problems outside the cities is where the house is on top of or beside a burial or on the path of a guardian. In Britain there are some areas where you just can't get away from the buggers. Wiltshire, for example, is knee deep in burials, sleepers, stone circles, etc, all of which have guardians. So if you live there, chances are you have come across problems at some time or other.

If you get called to a house where there is a disturbance and you trace it to an ancient burial then it is possible that something is happening in the house, or something brought into the house triggered a guardian. Another option is if there is a child or adult in the house who has natural sight or psychic abilities and the burial has been disturbed or the sleeper is waking up. Then they will try and communicate with the house occupants—they will expect the people there to know who they are and to have a spiritual pattern in place to help then do what they need to do.

More often than not, where there are problems in these circumstances, it is a matter of doing the job that is needed, i.e., release the sleeper, change something in the guardian's path, etc, and then it all goes peaceful again. Sometimes these burial sites can be extremely peaceful once they are balanced and well kept.

I was called to one site where the occupants were having really bad nightmares night after night. They were all having the same nightmare, and the children were becoming distressed. I went to the house, which was built on top of a burial mound. I went down in vision to the burial and there was a sleeper beginning to wake up, but there was no one there on the land to bridge the sleeper into death. (The soul of a sleeper stays in the body for an allotted length of time, which can be very long, and then as they awake they would be bridged into death by someone.)

The sleeper was awakening and reaching out for a living human with the knowledge to bridge him and no one was there, so he reached out to any available and receptive human nearby. As there was no active magical or spiritual tradition within the people who were nearby, the messages filtered through in their dreams, hence the 'nightmares.'

The best way to release a sleeper that is ready to go is to build a fire and open a gate within yourself and let her pass through you, which is what I did. The being came up through me, into the fire, and through the fire to the inner worlds. End of problem and end of nightmares.

Guardians that cause trouble, on the other hand, are not quite as easy to manage. A guardian of a sacred site can appear in a variety of ways depending on what sort of being it is. Some guardians are very intelligent, active, and occasionally aggressive. The most common of that type appear as black dogs of huge proportion, sometimes accompanied by a man. Another type of intelligent guardian can appear as a female child, often appearing with crows, and that guardian being tends to observe or nudge you away rather than threaten you.

Some major sites are protected by very large earth beings that walk around the site and knock away anything that gets in its path, but they are not bright and cannot really be communicated with very well. Best to just get out of their way.

Later temple sites can have quite elaborate and complex guardians that are a mix between elemental beings and inner contacts in service—they are the best in that they can be communicated with and learned from. The down side is because they are intelligent and of human consciousness, they can be very temperamental, stubborn, and unwilling to compromise. They do not accept modern civilisation, and they usually want to continue to work under ancient rules. This can be a problem if, for example, they want a blood sacrifice and your offer of a glass of port and a chicken leg is turned down....

The work in general with the land is huge, never ending, and once you get on that merry-go-round, they will not leave you alone and do not understand the meaning of 'burnout.' It also makes it very hard to just go and visit a piece of land. Once you have worked as an exorcist on the land, it is like they put a badge on you that says 'idiot, willing to work'—so it makes tourism and that strange elusive state of 'relaxation' a mythical ideal that you never quite reach.

So if you do get dragged into land work, define your boundaries from the very beginning, and limit what you are willing to take on. There will always be someone else who will come along eventually and do the job that you didn't.

Chapter 13
A tailored divinatory deck for exorcists

One of the most useful tools in the bag of an exorcist is a tailored tarot deck. An ordinary deck is too vague and will not have the contacts and contexts that you need to make a quick and accurate assessment of a situation and possible avenues for resolution.

When a situation presents itself to an exorcist, it can often be not what it seems, or can be magically shielded, in which case you need to get behind the shield and see exactly what is going on, why, by whom, and what help, if any, you can draw upon. You can use the deck to analyse outcomes to certain choices and the long-term consequences of certain actions. This is truly invaluable—being able to look at courses of action (what the short-term outcome is, and then what the long-term effect will also be) can potentially save a lot of suffering. Some short-term answers can have truly horrific longer-term consequences, so both paths must be carefully looked at.

When I use a deck, I look at the victim, his home, the being that is causing the trouble, where it came from, where does it need to go, and what will happen if I do not intervene? I will then look at the outcomes of a choice of certain actions so that I can decide which the best way to proceed is. I don't rely completely on a deck, though. It is only one of a number of tools an exorcist can use and it never a good idea to become too reliant on any one method of work.

The deck Pete and I have created comes from first-hand experience of having our backs up against the wall in dangerous situations, and realising what information we need and why. So the deck has no superfluous cards, no obscurities, no mystique, just a range of the beings you are likely to come into contact with, places, powers, catalysts, realms, and tools—all the things that are involved in the various fields of exorcism and nothing more.

The following chapter lists the cards and how to read them, their meanings/personalities, the realms, layouts, and tips for extracting information from the deck. It is up to you to get blank cards, make them, work with them, and get to know them.

When you create the cards, they do not need to be works of art, in fact, that can work against the deck—it is a tool, not a toy. A card should have only what it needs on it and no more. There is always the temptation to put fancy looking magical sigils, etc, on them when they are not needed (on some cards they are), and that will hamper the contact trying to come through. Making and using a deck like this is good training in how to simplify, focus, and undress true magic so that it becomes a working method instead of a fashion accessory.

Through working simply but powerfully with the deck, you will get to know about and then connect with the many beings that flow through this deck. They are not archetypes, they are real living beings that work with or against humanity in a variety of ways, and they are all beings that you will need to know how to interact with if you are going to stay safe in the role of an exorcist.

The Exorcists Deck

The Characters, who they are and what they do

Note: I call angels 'he' just because they often but not always appear as sort of feminine males, but that is probably my childhood programming—they do not have gender.

Keeper of the Abyss/Metatron: the keeper of the Abyss is your very best friend if you manage to bridge a working relationship with him. He is a massive being, beyond an archangel, and keeps order in the flow of life as it passes in and out of the physical world. He keeps the Abyss in balance and he is the filter through which a soul passes when flowing into manifestation. He is the manifestor of the thoughts of Divinity—through the keeper the thought becomes word, and the word becomes flesh.

The Keeper is the managing director of the boiler room, so you don't run to him with every little problem, but he is one that you go to when things are beyond your comprehension and control.

The Keeper is also the one who gives you access to all the different levels of the Abyss: if he feels it is not right for you to go somewhere, then you are not going to get there, simple. But if you are carrying a being with the compassionate intention of putting it back where it belongs, then he will carry you to that threshold in the Abyss and make sure that you get out safely.

The Keeper is one of two major angelic beings that work directly with humanity. Power-wise, they are each equivalent to a hive of archangelic beings, just to put their size in perspective. But within their immense angelic power, they also have the breath of Divinity within them and are therefore of humanity also. This allows them to work with humanity without crisping people and gives them a human appearance so that they don't give people heart attacks. This links to the legend of Metatron originating in the prophet Enoch, and the Sandalphon originating in the prophet Elijah.

The keeper does not appear to humans anywhere else but the Abyss—the Abyss is the material expression of Divinity and

Metatron is right there, enabling that expression. This is why Metatron, in some rabbinic texts, is viewed as a lesser expression of YHWH.

In practical terms, he can take you anywhere in the Abyss from the highest points up to the threshold of Divinity, down to the depths of the Abyss where the most physical conditional expression of life exists. The Keeper will not take you above or below what you can cope with, but he will take you to the point of absolute stretch. His concern is not to kill you, but beyond that there is a lot of elbow room, so you can expect, in a heavy job, to have your 'toes burned.' You can come out of the Abyss with some serious injuries, so keep in mind that you are responsible for your own safety.

Sandalphon: the Sandalphon are cool dudes and they were saving my ass way before I knew who they were. The Sandalphon are beings that are the other side of The Keeper—the Sandalphon work in a similar way to the Keeper but they operate in the physical world. The difference between the two, from what I have experienced, is that the Sandalphon can go down the Abyss and to other places, but the Keeper doesn't leave the Abyss.

The Sandalphon work with humanity in a protective way and they are particularly helpful to exorcists. They work within the desert, within death and down the Abyss to the realm of the demonic beings. They will give you ballast, they will create armour for you and will cover you with dust to make you look like a stone (which is very useful when surrounded by demons hungry for human energy). They will lend you strength, give you advice and they will also teach you about the mysteries of the Tree of Life. They are the corridor monitors of the Tree of Life and are therefore privy to all its ins and outs.

If you are working to remove a dangerous demonic being, then work with the Sandalphon in all aspects of the job. They do not go 'up' the Abyss to angelic realms, but seem to stay in the operational areas of the desert which are to do with humanity and the physical world. They also work in death and are one of the major angelic beings that work in that realm.

To work with the Sandalphon, go into the void and call upon

them as you step out of the void back into the physical world. Another option is to go through the void into the desert of the Abyss and call upon them there.

Angel of Death and Destruction: the angel of death and destruction is an interesting huge hive being that does have names, but the use of those names limits his expression. This is due to generations of magical binding of this hive, and using that bound angel to destroy nations. This is one of the problems when dealing with angelic beings: when do you use their names (which is a key) and when do you not? I have figured out over the years that an angel that has the power or potential to do destructive things, or things that are linked to sovereignty, is best dealt with without the use of its name.

This is because such skills are coveted by humanity and therefore it is very likely that some group of humans at some time in the last 10,000 years has figured out how to bind that being and misuse it. Some groups will have used this being to attack and kill, some groups will have bound its action to stop epidemics or disasters, which are all part of the natural flow of life. Therefore most names connected with that order of being are corrupt and connect the exorcist to that bound angelic manifestation.

The angel of death and destruction is a being that sweeps the land clean when the population has gotten out of control, or the land is out of balance. It cuts away overgrowth, degeneration, contamination, and corruption. We fear this angel because we do not want to die. But without death, the world becomes 'overgrown' and is slowly choked to death. If this angel is working unbound, it will take only what is necessary and will destroy that which needs rebuilding. It is a difficult truth to swallow, but the difficulty comes from the lack of understanding of what we are, who we are, and what happens after death.

The world works in a harmonic balance but we have become far too disconnected to understand that as a species. People are scared, and they blame God for disasters. Planes fall out of skies for human reasons. People die from tidal waves because they build close to the sea and do not listen to the ocean. People die because they are mortal, not because any god in a white frock and Birkenstocks has forgotten them.

Anyway...practicalities....

He is sometimes summoned by sorcerers to attack someone and rain down disaster upon them. If this happens, it is because the sorcerer has tapped into the bound aspect of this being and is trying to use him to kill someone. When this happens, the key to success is for the person attacked and the exorcist to do everything that they can, but to leave what they cannot do to the hands of Judgment. It would also be wise to offer service to take off the binding from the angel—it puts you in their good books....

So if this card appears in a reading, chances are your victim is on the wrong side of some very nasty magic and you both may need to do some visionary unbinding and rebalancing to save lives. I have seen people killed with this stuff, so it is not to be taken lightly. Such binding is bloody dangerous, but it can be sidestepped if you use the laws of Divinity—you have to appeal to Divinity to put them in motion, it's not an automatic action. Which leads nicely into the next angelic being to work with.

Keeper of the scales/angel of judgement: this angelic being fascinates me and has taught me a great deal about myself and how humanity operates. As far as I am aware (and that is not too far) there is not a named version of this angel in the listed Monotheistic hierarchy. The simple reason for this, in my opinion, is that this angelic being (which does exist and will work with you), throws one of the major foundations of Monotheistic dogma out of the window: there is no reward and punishment, there is only balance and learning.

The angel of judgement is called upon whether when you are giving your life over to Divinity for service, or you/the victim are in overwhelming danger from angelic beings that have been bound into action by magic or magical patterns in the form of curses. Basically this angel balances the odds when a non-human being interferes with human business. It stops all action, weighs the good and bad, and then instigates situations that will bring about rebalancing. So if a victim has been badly attacked or cursed repeatedly and is dying, if called, the angel will block all current attacks, weigh the scales of the victim (and the attacker) and bring about situations which will rebalance scales and teach lessons.

The angel of Judgement is a being that holds the scales upon the tip of its sword and brings the scales into balance. So if you call upon this being, it will weigh up all that you have done and learned, and it will highlight what still needs learning. If you have done bad things and not really learned why it is bad, the angel will put you in circumstances where you have the opportunity to learn the lesson in this lifetime—that often means you will be on the receiving end of the 'bad' thing until you learn to not do it to others.

Interestingly, the angel will also balance out too much 'good.' Energy must be kept balanced, if too much it outputted, then the angel will stop it. This can manifest by being blocked from doing things or if you are bright enough, by the angel teaching you when to not take action/output energy. This in turn teaches someone when to step back and allow others to 'do' for themselves, and also to step back and let the inner flow of energy find its way naturally (and more powerfully) rather than being forced (and limited by human ability).

If this angel appears in a reading, it will indicate either the need to invoke this angel (ask the keeper at the Abyss to take you to him) or the fact that there is a need for balance, or that a rebalancing process is happening. It depends on the card's positioning in the layout.

If this card appears in a reading repeatedly, then the message is not getting through and the victim is suffering unnecessarily, or there is a major rebalancing coming and needs to be actively engaged. Inaction when this card appears in an active position is not a healthy option.

Barakiel: the Barakiel are an amazing and powerful angelic hive being that have a wide-ranging effect on humanity: they champion the innocent, are teachers of deep mysteries and bridge between the power of the stars and the earth. They have the ability to filter magic off of humans and will come to the aid of innocent victims.

They are a great source of learning if you are in the middle of a major demonic/bound angel job and have exhausted all avenues you can think of. The only problem with their information download methods is that it can be very intense and it would be wise to consider slowly building a working relationship with them so that when you need help, you have a framework ready for them to operate through. Get a method of communication going with them in 'peacetime'—that way you both work out what the volume setting should be so that when crunch time comes, you don't get fried.

They have a strong connection with the stars, with alignments and with lightening powers. They would be good to work with, for example, if a person's destiny has been cursed or blocked by interfering magic that uses the victim's astrological chart as a frame for the curse, i.e., a magician can use the details of an astrological chart and then bind that fate.

They work through electricity, lightening, the angelic sound of the stars, and the star power itself.

I have worked with them by asking them to intervene in a very serious curse situation where the victim was innocent. They offered protection through vision and by way of a lighting sigil to be used. If this being appears in a reading, it will most likely be a prompt to work with them. Methods of working with this being are in Chapter 3.

Ariel: I came across this being many years ago and did not understand for the longest time what it was. The first time I found the Abyss, I was prompted to cross the Abyss and I knew that if I didn't, then my wish to be of magical and spiritual service would stop right there at that moment. I also knew that the crossing could go wrong and I could quite easily die as a result of the vision.

After a terrifying crossing (where I also first met Metatron/The Keeper) I found a lion lying injured on the other side. It had a massive thorn in its paw and I knew I had to take it out. I remembered reading about this sort of myth in my childhood, so I realised this was an important step I was taking.

After getting over my fear of a roaring lion with big teeth, I pulled out the thorn which released a heavy flow of pus and blood. The flow made me weep because he had suffered so much and my tears cleaned the wound. The lion then stood and said that he would carry me on his back.

This lion being that sits on the Divinity side of the Abyss is an angel that is also a deity. It appears as Sekhmet, Tefnut, Durga, plus many other deity beings that are a connection between lions, justice, demon slaying, and healing.

This being is Ariel. Ariel is an angelic being that will work with you to fight demons, and also to heal injury and illness that is a product of magic. Ariel demands great courage and strength from you before this being will work with you. As is the case with most angels, they will only assist you in things that are truly beyond you—they will not do anything that you could remotely do for yourself, as such an action would weaken you and withdraw learning from you.

If this being appears in your reading, depending upon the position in the layout, it could signal that there is a need for this being which, in turn, means that the situation has a load of demons involved and is very dangerous.

It could alternatively mean, depending on the reading, that the victim is in need of powerful healing at a soul level and this would be the best angel to work with in that situation.

Angel of Air: I work with this angel by calling it out of the void. I purposely avoid using a name for this being as so many versions of this angel have been bound into magical service, usually for no good. It is an angel of swords, words, recitation, binding, cursing, and blessing.

It is most often worked with by stepping into it so that you can see magical bindings upon a victim, or it can be worked with in the void to dismantle and cut away curses and magical binding. A fragment of this angel is sometimes bound to a person as part of a nasty curse (a kabbalistic favourite) and will often appear as ropes of sigils or text/words, or as a platonic solid.

If it appears in a reading, it is usually an indication that the form of magic used to curse or attack someone is a form of magic that is in the family of Judeo/Islamic/Christian traditions. If it is, then it can also be worked with a cure.

Angel of Fire: the angel of fire is unnamed for the same reason as the angel of air: those two angels are the most used when it comes to western magical attacks and curses and can be approached and worked with the same way—unnamed, identified by the element, and summoned through the void (which wipes out any cultural expression).

The angel of fire operates through the immune system in the form of fevers and infections and literally by fires. It carries the magic of the 'fire temple' which is an Atlantean and more recently Persian/Mithraic magical form. It is a dangerous angelic being when bound and ordered to attack someone. It will cause untold damage to a person's immune system, often irreversible, and can also cause dangerous fires.

If it appears in a reading, then it is an indication that this being has been used in an attack and needs to be removed. This is best done by working in the void with this being to take off any fire magic bound to the victim.

Bound Angel: this card is an unnamed angelic representation that covers the appearance of a magically/ritually bound angel in a possession/attack situation or an aggressive guardian situation. If this card appears, the reader can deduce that a bound angel has been used in the situation and its bound function can be ascertained by using the minor cards to describe the outcome of its function. The choice to unbind the angel is with the exorcist, but it should only be unbound if it is directly attacking the victim, or if guided to so by other contacts.

If the bound angel is one that has been placed in the desert of the Abyss and has no direct influence over the victim, then it may well be best left well alone. The majority of bound angels that are stuck in the desert are there for good reason: they have been bound into inactivity, not bound to action and there is a major difference.

Unknown Angel: I have thrown this card in because there are bloody loads of angels and most of them do not need listing in this work. It comes in useful where there is an angel involved either to help or is in a hostile position and along with the minor action cards it can be identified by its effect upon the victim. You don't always need to know the angel if it is being hostile or helpful, you just need to know what to do with it and that is where the layout comes in.

Beings You Will Encounter

This section of the cards is all the various beings that an exorcist comes up against in one form or another. They don't need quite as much explaining as the angelic lot do, just a basic background so that you know what you are looking at.

Greater demons: Big nasty demons, on a level power-wise with archangels which equates to danger potentially on a massive scale. They only come into our realm where there is serious stuff going down. They operate either through large structures, i.e., organisations or through individuals who can wield a great deal of power. In general though, they are very rare. If this appears in a reading, double check the reading and if it continues to show up, then the chances are the victim is deeper in the shit than anyone probably realised. Make sure you get proper backup and a good working plan of action before you take these dudes on.

There are times when these beings come into our world, usually at a time of major change, and they do have a role to play. If that is what is happening, just try to stay out of the way as these are not beings to tussle with in any form. If you are dragged into a situation with them and it is not a possession, do not get into a situation of wants and needs with them. Just do your part and get out.

Lesser demons: Still nasty but slightly less dangerous—again, not often seen in our realm, but they are becoming more frequent, which is a bit worrying. They are very powerful, tend to operate through a human, usually are very intelligent, and often have a reason other than feeding for wearing a meat suite (human). If this shows up, prepare to do a full exorcism with appropriate back up. If this card turns up in a helping position, well, it does happen and these beings can be helpful, just very conditional. You need to be very balanced and able to sidestep any mind games they might play.

Parasite: These guys are very common and come in all shapes, sizes, and power settings. In general they do not belong in our world or in us, so it is just a matter of finding them, identifying them, and getting them out. If it turns up in a reading, then the message is probably clear. If it is in the future, that means that whatever path the victim is on, they are going towards a period of imbalance that will attract parasites. That can be changed by identifying what is taking the victim there and changing it.

Scapegoat: This is a complicated category as it can be an angelic being, a demon, a parasite, a human—whatever, really. It is a being that has been bound by magic and is carrying the fate of someone else. If this appears in a reading, it probably means that the victim is being attacked by someone who has a great deal of knowledge and who probably cannot be traced energetically because the scapegoat will be on the end of all magical interactions—they get the shit from the attacking action rather than the magician.

If this comes up, find the scapegoat and disconnect it from the sorcerer/magician who is using it. Look for chaining, binding, etc. It might be a thought form in which case you will need to dismantle it. If you don't know where it belongs, ask the Abyss keeper.

Faery being: Great fun, they are like working with manic-depressive pickpockets. They can cause all sorts of problems for us, but often they do not realise the effect of their actions. Tread carefully and compassionately with these beings that are wonderful expressions of nature. This card covers all types of faery beings as it is unnecessary to list individual types. They can all be treated the same way and bribery works wonders with them.

Elemental: This card represents beings that are made up of an individual element and are usually found in the path of an exorcist in the form of a guardian. They usually do not display intelligence as we understand it, but they are powerful. Once you have figured out which elemental type it is, then put it back into the appropriate inner form, i.e., a rock or fire, and send it home.

Shapeshifter: These are a tricky form of inner predator and can change form or host at the drop of a hat. They are not parasites per say but they often display parasitical tendencies. Once you have figured out what it is—i.e., looks like an angelic being but doesn't feel like it—then just grab it and take it to the Abyss Keeper. If this appears in a reading, you will have to figure out its various presentations and act accordingly. Usually by its presentations you can figure out what it is after.

Ghost: This represents a being that was once human but has now become a composite, usually with a parasite. It does not usually represent just a dead person, but represents a haunting of a composite. It can occasionally simply represent a dead person and you will have to assess by its action which type of ghost it is (composite or not).

Human inner contact: This card shows up when a human inner contact (not living) has either gotten involved in a situation or is trying to make contact to teach/assist.

A god: This is a male deity that can take many forms. If it has appeared in someone's situation you need to get into a dialogue to find out what he wants.

A Goddess: This is a female deity that can take many forms. If it has appeared in someone's situation you need to get into a dialogue to find out what she wants.

People

This section of the cards expresses the variety of humans that can come into a reading regarding a situation that needs an exorcist.

Priest: A male human who is active, who is trained within a magical or spiritual tradition, and who is in a role of service. He usually represents someone who can help, but if he appears as a protagonist, then usually he has a good reason (in his eyes) for his actions. Either way, he needs to be dealt with in a non-hostile way.

Priestess: A female human who is active, who is trained within a magical or spiritual tradition, and who is in a role of service.

She usually represents someone who can help, but if she appears as a protagonist, then usually she has a good reason (in her eyes) for her actions. Either way, she need to be dealt with in a non-hostile way.

Sorcerer: A male magician/ritualist who is actively working magic for selfish and often dangerous ends. If this appears, it usually represents the person who is attacking, or who has brought an unhealthy situation into being. He is often clever and dangerous, and should be treated with extreme caution. If he is knowledgeable, he will know if you have become involved in the situation as an exorcist and will try to stop you. He sometimes uses groups to operate through, and is often very difficult to isolate energetically.

Sorceress: A female magician/ritualist who is actively working magic for selfish and often dangerous ends. If this appears, it usually represents the person who is attacking, or who has brought an unhealthy situation into being. She is often clever and dangerous, and should be treated with extreme caution. If she is knowledgeable, she will know if you have become involved in the situation as an exorcist and will try to stop you. She sometimes use groups to operate through and is often very difficult to isolate energetically. Another word of caution is that if the sorceress is fertile, i.e., she is still ovulating, then she can be far more deadly than a sorcerer, as she can draw upon deep primal powers connected to menstrual blood. If this card appears, the victim may need protection by way of working with a female deity to counter/negate the feminine destructive power—like treats like.

Witch: In this deck, this represents a magical worker of either sex who uses nature beings, powers, and spirits to do magic for good or bad. They can operate on a 'work for hire basis' and often show up when tribal magic is being used. Tribal witches sometimes use scapegoats, so tread carefully and make sure you have a full understanding of what beings he or she is using and why. In a helpful situation, he or she will show as someone who has a deep understanding of nature magic and can be consulted as a resource or helper.

Exorcist: this represents a human who is nuts enough to take on magical service in the area of possessions, attacks, and hauntings. If this shows in a reading, then either it is showing the exorcist's role in the problem, or it is advising that an exorcist should be consulted to solve the problem.

Teacher: the teacher is a human who holds knowledge about the situation and can offer learning, advice, and help that no one else has the ability to offer.

Family: this represents either the family as a unit, or an individual who is a member of the victim's family. You would be surprised (or not, if you knew my family) how many family members are willing to instigate an attack on a fellow member. It can also represent a member of a magical lodge/temple.

Lover: the victim's lover, past, present, or future—or someone who has a very close business partnership with the victim (where there is energy exchange).

Sleeper: a dead human who is sleeping in service to the tribe or land. These burials are pretty rare these days as so many of them have been dug up. If this shows, it can mean that a sleeper needs help, is emerging, or is in distress. It can also simply mean the sleeper is sleeping and needs sidestepping in the job. In such a case it will only show if you really need to know it is there so that you can avoid waking him or her up.

Human male: a man who falls outside all the other categories but is involved somehow in the situation. Further reading can usually identify who he is and what he wants. It can sometimes represent a sorcerer who has managed to shield his identity and thus projecting a blank id.

Human female: As above.

Places

The Upper Abyss: this section of the Abyss is anywhere from the human level all the way up to Divinity without form. It usually represents angelic realms from individual angels up to the archangels, archons, and aeons. The other cards that fall with it will usually differentiate between the two, or alternatively if not sure, you can expand the readings to pinpoint exactly which part of the upper Abyss it represents.

The lower Abyss: this section of the Abyss is anywhere from the human level all the way down to Divinity in full physical form. It normally represents realms that include the ancestors, parasites, demons, and ancient deities. The other cards that fall with it will usually differentiate between the two, or alternatively if not sure, you can expand the readings to pinpoint exactly which part of the lower Abyss it represents. This card is basically a big arrow pointing down.

The Desert of the Abyss: this is the human realm of the Abyss and expresses the inner landscape of our lives and our world. It is a form of the tree of life and is often littered with bound angels, odd people, and ghosts. It is also our way to the Abyss, and falls in a reading when the help we need can be found in that realm.

The hall of elders: this is an inner realm where adepts, teachers, and magical workers who have pledged service to the world can be connected with. It is 'up' in the Abyss from our standpoint and is a place where we can go to learn, get advice, or a good telling off.

The desert of death: this is an area of the desert of the Abyss, usually as far away from the Abyss as you can get, which leads to the river of death. It is best approached by going into the underworld, and will show in a reading if the problem is stemming from an issue related to a dead person or an imminent death.

Void: the void from which all comes and to which all goes. It is a state of nothingness that is filled with potential. It is a good place to use as a threshold to other worlds as it prepares the spirit for the journey and is a place where things can be dropped or gained.

The underworld: the underworld is 'down' from our standpoint on the earth. It is where our ancestors lie, where the past landscape is, and is a 'front door' to many deeper inner places including demonic realms, death, ancient deities, and massive titans.

The faery realm: the faery realm sort of overlays our physical world and the inner landscape of our world. It can be accessed by our physical land (rocks, caves, trees, etc) and will show in readings if the veil between these worlds has been breached, or if a being needs to go back there. It can also come into a reading if the healing of the victim can be done in that realm.

The ancient landscape: this is a part of the underworld and is like the inner resonance of the land from a very long time ago—ancient spirits, creatures, and earlier forms of humanity can be reached in this realm. If a reading shows that a being needs to go back there, it means something has bridged time quite heavily, and that breach might need closing.

Inner temple: this shows the inner structure of a temple, the structure that was built before the outer structure was constructed. It can show the magical system of a place and indicate what is wrong with an outer temple.

Outer temple: the outer temple is literally just that, a temple, magical lodge, church, etc. This represents any physically constructed magical space.

Grove: this card represents a natural sacred place or power spot. It can also represent stone circles, barrows, vortexes, sacred caves, etc.

Burial ground: place where there are lots of dead bodies… clever, huh? Usually a sacred burial ground but can also be a body dump, burial mound, or single grave.

Home: the place where the victim usually resides.

Work: the place where the victim usually works. (Duh....)

The Minor cards

These cards give the details or outer expressions of the inner powers—these cards depict how powers manifest in our world and our lives. They work with the four elements and each element has seven cards that progress the power of an element and how it can manifest in the situations an exorcist or victim might find themselves in. I have avoided numbering them just to annoy all the numerology freaks and to avoid unnecessary deep ponderings over the numbers, meanings, and hidden messages. They are what they are and no more.

The element of fire

Sacred flame: the flame at the centre of all being, at the centre of life, and the flame within. The core threshold of Divinity within Humanity, it can be used to access anywhere, to tune sacred spaces, and to light the way forward in extreme spiritual darkness.

Threshold of fire: the threshold of fire is a wall of fire that is the presence of an angelic being which can be used to pass from one realm to another. In vision it literally appears or is visualised as a wall of fire with no other attributes. Even though it is an angel, the lack of any other attributes renders it safe for use as a threshold. This is one of the basic functions of an angel, to allow something to pass from one realm to another (hence divinity must pass through an angel to manifest).

Healing: the healing power that flows as heat—it can often represent the need for hands-on healing, or the healing action of a fever.

Agitation: this card often comes up when the power levels are starting to rack up. When fire power starts to build, it can create an intense agitation or irritation in the victim or exorcist and is a clue that fire power is being used. It is important to recognise where this agitation comes from and to bring it under control. If it is given free rein it can become very destructive—usually once someone knows where the agitation comes from and that it is coming from magic, then it is easier to disengage from it and just observe. This card can also represent the agitation that builds up within a magical worker just before a download of power or a job of immense power.

Argument: this can appear when there is fire magic or a being that has fire as its central energy expression and it is poking the victim, trying to instigate disharmony. A fiery argument is supper to a parasite, so another option can be that it is a reaction by a being that is within someone. If it feels threatened it will become aggressive, which will initially manifest as heated arguments, usually over nothing.

Fever: literally, a fever—when someone is possessed, or on the receiving end of magic that uses fire as its energy/construction, then most people will react by getting a fever. The body reacts to the attack as if it was a bacteria or virus and the immune system can go into overdrive. If there is a known attack and the victim manifests a fever without any other physical symptoms (i.e., cough, discharge, etc) then it is a pretty good indication of fire magic.

Danger: literally, danger—if this appears in a reading then the danger is imminent and needs identifying as quickly as possible. If it appears in the action/advice position of the layout, then it means that a chosen course of action is dangerous.

Fire attack: this card shows an all-out magical attack using fire as the main fuel. It is common with magicians working in Atlantean, Mithras, Egyptian, Persian, Azteca, and Polynesian magic. It will need fire to dismantle it, usually working with an angelic being of fire.

The element of Water

Pool: the pool or bowl of water is an access point into the inner worlds, usually the underworld or other parts of the human world. It can also be a tool to 'soak' up impurities in a room and can be consecrated as a tool. When this card shows in a reading, it could indicate an access point if it falls in a position, or it could mean that the exorcist needs to use consecrated water (and salt) to cleanse somewhere or someone.

Compassion: when this card appears in a reading, it would be advisable to step back and look at the overall situation and ensure that you are being truly balanced in your approach—to put something where it belongs or where it needs to be, without emotion entering into the decision—is true compassion. True compassion can also mean walking away from a situation if it means that your input as exorcist is going to undermine the victim's gained knowledge from bitter experience. It is easy to make it all better—it is much harder to do the right thing, particularly if it will appear that you are heartless or uncaring. Being able to act under those conditions takes true compassion.

Replenishment: this card is a warning that the victim is in serious need of energetic replenishment. Sometimes magical attacks can drain the vital life force from a human, leaving their spirits to look grey, thin, and shrivelled. That is an extremely dangerous state for a spirit to be in as it weakens its connection to the physical body. It can also leave the body vulnerable to cancer (many cancer patients look like this when viewed from an inner point of view). The replenishment must be in the form of healing energy, nothing fancy, but the exorcist can put hands upon the victim and go into stillness. The exorcist calls upon whatever is necessary for the healing of the victim to come through.

Vision: this is a loud hint that the major part of the work must be undertaken in vision.

Emotional collapse: this will appear when the emotive spirit of the victim has been breached and has been destroyed or is being fed off. It is important to attend to the victim by working with him in vision and also energetically feeding him. It is often the darkness before the dawn and if the victim is going through this, he will need someone to keep vigil with him and help him in the short term. It would be a good idea to help him rebuild emotionally, by working with him in vision with deities or land beings to reestablish a sense of wholeness with the land, the powers, and himself. This can only be done once the problem that caused it has been removed (i.e., attack, possession, parasite, etc).

Sexual Union: this will come up in a reading if the sexual activities of the victim have been hacked by a parasite or a being trying to use the energy to manifest itself. It will indicate that sexual energy is its main food source and its probable port of entry.

Emotional attack: this form of magical attack is the favourite of magicians/witches that use earth/nature magic. It is usually used to destabilise a relationship, isolate a person, or get her to leave a certain emotive situation. If the emotions are being attacked, then usually the attacker is emotively connected to the victim so you should not have to look too far.

The element of Earth

Rock: the rock is a storage place, a resting place, and a place of transformation. Large chunks of rock are great at storing beings, particularly land beings that have become destructive. Rocks can hold people, dragons, demons, parasites, etc. The only problem with storing beings in rocks is that someone else can come along and let them out. Rocks are also good for putting strange energies into: they are then put out onto the land where they recycle the energy.

Nourishment: an appearance of this card indicates that the victim's body has become depleted of physical nourishment and should be attended to immediately. It can also represent a gift of food (usually a power food like honey, wine, etc) to a being.

Payment: this card represents a payment given or needed in an interaction with a being. It will usually appear when there are faery beings involved or human inner contacts, which are the beings most likely to ask for payment.

Pattern: the use of a pattern in magic is very common and can be a great tool to use for either access to a realm or inner temple, or to give protection by acting as an interface for a being. Metatron's cube is a very good example of this as it can be used for protection against demonic beings and bound angels. The cube is a complex expression of Divinity (the 13 spheres) and an initiate's relationship with Divinity that develops as the human walks the pathways (lines) that connect the spheres.

There are many sigils and patterns that can have a powerful protective quality and it would serve an exorcist well to have a good grounding in pattern development. It is best to do it alone, freehand, and with inner guidance as opposed to reading some of the theoretical bullshit that is out there.

Construction: the construction of an inner structure can be done to contain something, hide someone, or to repair a damaged inner temple. If that card appears, then it is time to roll the sleeves up and get to it.

Obstruction/overgrowth: depending on what context this appears in, it can mean that a positive destroying power has been bound or suppressed, hence the overgrowth, or it can mean that a similar process is happening in the human body of the victim. If this is the case then the inner cause needs to be found and dealt with quickly as it can possibly lead to cancer (worst scenario...which I am adept at) or getting very fat, or getting very fat. This happens to a lot of adepts who learn to override a natural protective shutdown that blocks people out of the inner worlds who do unhealthy or very stupid things. It is also known as humanity's magical 'self cull' mechanism. This is usually stemming from either 'abundance' magic or just plain greed for substance or energy/power. It can also happen when the inner body is being repeatedly depleted by attacks/curses/heavy inner burdens and the endocrine system tried to replenish the body by getting energy from food (which is a very poor source of inner energy). In my opinion, this is what happened to Dion Fortune—her work of inner service was such a major burden that her body began to buckle under the weight quite early on. Because it was not attended to, it fatally weakened her.

Greed: this can refer to a human, an inner being, or the energy needs of an inner construct. Either way it will indicate selfish imbalanced energetic wants rather than needs, and action must be taken energetically to cut the umbilical cord that is feeding such greed. If the greed is in the victim, then chances are no matter how hard you work, they will probably get themselves right back in the same situation pretty soon by not being able to control or find balance between want and actual need.

The element of Air

Breath/word: air is the power of the first utterance and when it appears in a reading, it can indicate that going back to the very primal expression of Divinity through breath/sound will form a foundation for the resolution of the problem at hand.

Recitation: a lot of magical binding and cursing is done through recitation, and if this card appears, it would indicate a probable structure of the attack. In a possession, it can indicate that the use of recitation will unseat the unwanted guest, or clear a space.

Learning: sometimes we need the inner hint to get us off our asses and this card is one of those hints. It is saying, 'this is a learning process, either simply from experience or by nature of the studying you will have to undergo to complete the job successfully.' If this does appear, it means that the knowledge needed for the job is within your reach, you just need to figure out what it is, where it is, and then write it down so that you don't forget it!! See, speaking from experience, drawing a blank in front of a tooth-gnashing demon is not a good idea—they tend not to be accommodating if you ask them to pause for a moment while you go check something.

Fight: this means you are going to get your hands dirty or that you are stepping into the middle of an unseen battle. This can either mean hidden agendas/details that the victim didn't tell you about, or it can also mean that there are much bigger forces that are playing out through the victim/s and the picture could be much bigger than you realised.

Pinning: this one is simple. If it appears, it means that someone or something is pinned, or needs pinning. It can be read in context of the layout and other cards but usually it is pretty straightforward.

Revenge: now there is a deeply spiritual concept. The revenge card makes an appearance when some human somewhere wants their pound of flesh and they will do anything to get it. When you see this, you know that somewhere there is someone with a major axe to grind and could possibly be willing to do anything to get her revenge. The problem with this is that if someone is magically developed enough to create magical havoc, then she is probably intelligent, which means that they are not attacking out of stupidity—she is probably becoming or is mentally ill. This can very dangerous and you need to make sure that you have all your bases covered.

Ritual attack: pretty basic and straight forward. If this card appears, then the problem stems from a ritual attack of some sort, and you will need to track back and find out what was done, why, when, and to whom.

Situational cards

This small section deals with the basic situations and do not really need much, if any, explanation. They just make the readings easier and more straight forward. This can be really helpful when you are trying to isolate a situation and get quick informa-

222 | *The Exorcist's Handbook*

tion out of a reading, and there is a bound angel that has been programmed to rip your soul out (yummy). Make a simple card for each title.

Possession, Haunting, Curse and Communication

Communication is probably the only title that needs any explanation. Sometimes what can appear as a haunting or attempted possession is actually an inner contact, angel, or ancestor trying to communicate something to the victim. If this card appears, then step back and take a second look at what is happening, and see if it could possibly just be a bodged communication attempt.

I have had this experience, many years ago, when an inner contact tried to speak to me and I thought it was trying to take me into death (I was a youngster and not ready for such fun). In the end the contact found someone else who could listen and relay the information to me. Needless to say I felt like an idiot.

Layouts

The information that you need in such circumstances needs to be straightforward and to the point. In the middle of a serious attack or possession emergency, you do not have time to ponder deep philosophical hints—you need to know what, when, how, and why.

The layouts reflect this need for simplicity, and if you are used to using tarot in a more abstract way, it may take some adjusting to. Saying that, the skills acquired over years of deeper tarot readings can really come in useful for more obscure answers which can sometimes come up. This happens when the situation is not quite as straightforward as it seems and certain magical situations can be very complex indeed. One has to take into account the spiritual journey of the victim and be acutely aware that the situation he faces can be part of that path; you need to be able to help without short circuiting his magical/spiritual development.

This is another reason why the role of an exorcist does not usually come into someone's life until she is older—she needs a series of magical/spiritual crises and revelations before she can intervene in the life situation of another person. I always wanted to be an exorcist when I was a young un, and I did work in that role in a number of ways: I thought I knew it all and I was very evangelistic about what I knew. Now I don't have a bloody clue, but I can still manage to be evangelistic about it if I try really hard....

The first layout that is used is a simple diagnostic and can give quite a lot of information about the situation. It goes as follows:

4	5	6
3	1 / 2	10
9	8	7

1–This is the victim and will often show how his body is reacting.

2–This crosses the victim and represents the being. It will show you what type of being it is.

3–What happened in the past that brought about the situation.

4–Where has the being come from, what realm, what race of being.

5–The greatest thing the victim has to overcome. Can often show the body's immune or emotional struggle.

6–Beings that will help.

7–Warnings, what to be mindful of, or not to trust.

8–Things that are hidden from the situation, usually purposely by the attacker, sometimes hidden by circumstance.

9–Advice—a hint on where to put your attention or work method suggestion.

10–The future.

One of the ways to work with the deck and layout is to first look at the situation and write down the reading. Then from the information you have, choose some options for courses of action and read to see what the outcome would be if you took that course of action. Then choose the one with the best outcome. Sounds straightforward? Ha! If only life were that simple.

Once you have narrowed down a couple of options, then it would be a good idea to either use this deck or an ordinary deck

224 | *The Exorcist's Handbook*

and look at the long term outcome of the action for the victim. The reason to do this is sometimes an action can seem straight forward, but it can have negative affects longer down the line, so it is important to track the affects of your actions over a few years, just to be sure. I use a tree of life layout among others, but anything that you are used to will work.

The other thing that you need to check before you swoop into action is how the action is going to affect the health of the victim. I also check this in the first round of investigations using a health layout (see appendix).

Look at the health of the victim while she is under attack, and it will give you warning areas to watch out for or hidden health needs that you need to keep an eye on while you work. Then you can track the body reactions to certain courses of action by looking with the health layout to see what the health reaction will be, which will also be a deciding factor in choosing what method of work to use.

Once you have narrowed down how you are going to approach the work, you can track the progress through readings. Be aware, though, that certain orders of beings can interfere with readings and if they don't look or feel right, it may be that they are being messed with. A way around this is to simply ask to be shown the real truth as you are shuffling and asking a question—it can be that simple and straight forward.

It is always best, though, not to do the readings near or even in the same building as the victim. Do it in your work area and be aware that the reading can pull a contact with the being into your space—any sort of divination when a hostile being is involved carries risks. Make sure you seal your space before the readings, cover the surface you are reading on with a ritually marked cloth and cleanse your space, your deck, and your hands after finishing the readings. I put my deck in a bowl of dry salt and wash my hands with salt, soap, and water after the readings. I also smudge them regularly with various disgusting smelling incense mixes that are guaranteed to send everything out of the area, including all humans!

When you are not using the deck, it should be placed where it cannot be casually handled or messed with. It can potentially link to any hostile being you are working with and any sensitive person or child can become entangled just by handling such a deck. The decks themselves also have a very short shelf life, hence the lack or artistic input into them. They are simple working tools and they can get burned out very quickly so you might want to make a couple of decks at a time and burn a working deck after it has been used for a few months. You will feel when it is time to destroy them—they will be sticky, dirty to touch, and will give you a headache every time you go near them. Make sure you burn them so that no unsuspecting person can come along and find them.

The more you work with the deck, the more they will personalise to you, and you may feel the need to add other cards/beings/actions. This is good and means that you are developing your own working style. Use the deck as a starting point and let it grow with you. The more situations you use the deck for, the more chances there are for it to expose any inadequacies the deck may have and the beings that do connect through the deck can guide you to other beings that may be willing to work closely with you.

Eventually you will have a full deck that is specific to you and your working methods and that will include every being that you have encountered. It can take years to develop such a deck and it does become an invaluable tool for your work.

Chapter 14
Long-term management of the exorcist

When a magical worker takes on the role of an exorcist there are many things the person has to consider, most of which are covered in the chapter 1. But as the work progresses into a long-term commitment, there are things that an exorcist may have to address as the work progresses.

The most basic consideration is the 'shelf life' of an exorcist, which in reality is quite short, just a few years. It is one thing to come across the occasional job over the years, but once the intention to focus on that specific path comes into play, then the intensity and regularity of the work increases—the lights go on, the queue forms outside the door and your life is no longer your own. It can become increasingly isolating when you find that the many people who are put in your path are 'jobs,' not social contacts, which can make for a difficult social life!

The key to avoid burnout is to realise when you are coming to the end of your service time and back out quietly. Often at that time there is a call to teach or guide other exorcists, or to do work that doesn't involve people such as structural work and land work—there is only so much each human can give and you need to know your limit. If you push beyond the limit of your capacity, then serious damage can occur at both a physical and spiritual level. The ability to say no becomes very important—there will be jobs that present that you know others can deal with and you must be willing to let other people step in and take over the work.

Entanglements

Once an exorcist has been working in the field for a while and has dealt with a variety of issues, lines of connection form which link one being to another, and the exorcist can become burdened with a variety of entanglements that link them to various victims, beings, and places.

The net result of these tangles is that when something major happens to one of these beings/victims/places, the exorcist is drawn upon as an unconscious resource which can become quite a serious burden. This is another reason not to take on every single job in the world: you will eventually end up carrying the net results of those jobs and the human spirit is not designed to undertake such a burden.

In the past, a human who took the role of an exorcist would work with a very small amount of people within a defined community and a limited pot of beings. With the advent of world travel, the dissemination of various spiritual traditions, and the beings that are incorporated in those traditions has widened considerably, and with it the field of work that an exorcist has to undertake has expanded. There are no longer small isolated communities that are all a part of one tradition—an exorcist may have to cross oceans to deal with 'foreign' beings that they have very little true experience of.

Our natural 'immunity' to certain beings and magical situations is passed down in the ancestral blood line from one generation to another. Since the industrial revolution, people are no longer deeply connected to a specific area or land mass, nor are they usually a part of a spiritual tradition that spans generations. We choose our homes and we choose our spiritual paths. That brings an amazing freedom and a broadening of spiritual knowledge, but it also brings uncharted territory and opens doorways into worlds that we have not had such wide access to before.

This situation is what brings about such a fast burnout rate in exorcists: the range of beings and worlds that are navigated today is unparalleled in modern history, and the lot of an exorcist is akin to a local family doctor suddenly having to work on call around the world in obscure areas and treat strange tropical diseases without having any inoculation protection, natural immunity, or known medications to hand. It's a steep learning curve for the human body and spirit, which has its limitations.

The good side is that by passing on to others what you have found, the next round of exorcists do not have to reinvent the wheel: they can focus on new situations and find inventive ways to overcome novel problems. And by absorbing the experiences of those who have gone before, coupled with the study of more ancient writings, the next generation develop a strength and flexibility that works in tandem with our ever changing world.

Patterning of the soul

This section can relate either to the exorcist or to a victim who has been very badly magically assaulted. Through constant serious attack, or through intensive working with demonic influences, the spiritual pattern that the soul expresses through can be badly damaged, and if it is not attended to it can result in an early death. It can also affect the spiritual expression of the soul beyond life, which is a very serious matter.

This can be worked with but is not something to undertake lightly, nor is it something that is appropriate for a magical beginner or new initiate to attempt. For this reason alone, I have not written out the vision, but the details and writings that follow should be enough of a guideline for an experienced worker to be able to construct a working that will be effective.

The vision works at the Abyss and works on the manifestation of Divinity into life before it takes on a specific form—it is the blueprint of life that is built out of the entirety of angelic consciousness. When you get back to that level of the blueprint, it still has the potential to manifest as a rock, a tree, an animal, or a human. Once the blueprint is plugged into the tree of life pattern, then it is narrowed down to human expression and it is at this

point, standing with your back to the Abyss and solar sphere/
Tiphereth of the tree of life before you that the damage will show.
Without a complete blueprint at this level, the different facets that
make up our human expression begin to crumble and that crum-
bling separates the life form from its inner pattern.

It is unusual for damage to occur at this level, but if an attack
or an interaction is powerful enough or prolonged enough, damage can occur and must be detected and dealt with before the
damage becomes permanent.

The 'blueprint', so to speak, is the full breadth of angelic patterning and appears as a large construct of platonic solids
arranged in a geometric pattern. A known example of such patterning is the Metatron Cube which is 13 spheres of Divinity,
linked by pathways that create platonic solids which interconnect
to create a holism. This pattern sits at the edge of the Abyss and
interacts with the patterning of the tree of life to create humanity.

In vision, the exorcist or ritualist reestablishes the original
untainted pattern on the far side of the Abyss and then bridges it
to the realm of humanity by carrying it across the Abyss and
down to Malkuth. As the pattern progresses down the three of
life, the various spheres of human expression are reconnected
with and re-established to create a vessel that the blueprint can be
contained within. It takes on human form as the structure of the
tree of life integrates with the blueprint, thus becoming a whole
physical expression.

Once the pattern reaches Malkuth, the structure is complete
and the human expression is fully operational. The path through
the desert beyond Malkuth is the life path of that human.

This work does not get rid of magical attacks, bindings, etc, but
what it does do is to reestablish the physical and spiritual integri-
ty of the human structure which in turn enables it to withstand
strains or attacks. It is also an opportunity to gain a deeper insight
into the nature of the human soul, of the soul's inherent Divinity,
and the deeper aspects of our role within the fate pattern of our
world.

It is not something that can really be intellectualised upon. Like

the Metatron cube, it must be experienced in its own environment for its deeper secrets to become apparent and be understood. For example, if you sit down to draw a Metatron cube with
a ruler, you will miss a massive part of what it has to tell you.

I know, because I did just that—I sat down with a coin for the
spheres and a ruler for the lines. The spheres were fine but when
I reached for the ruler, it vanished. I hunted all over for the
bloody thing and in the end a contact that had been following me
around the house all day said, 'just do it...the spheres are of God,
but the lines are of you and must be drawn free hand from point
to point: you cannot draw through points to make a long line, it
must be approached a connection at a time.'

So I did just that and I was astounded at the information that
came through as a result of working from point to point. I began
to see how different angelic beings supported certain aspects of
Divinity and how they interconnected across the pattern to support the manifestation of humanity—it just blew me away.

The wider pattern at the Abyss can be approached the same
way: once the flawless pattern has been established on the far side
of the Abyss and then merged with the broken pattern, the most
intricate and beautiful lines appear to reestablish themselves and
you begin to see how the whole pattern weaves itself in a multi-
dimensional cloth that makes up our existence.

Once that pattern has been worked with, the practitioner
begins to feel more 'whole' and 'connected' as the weave with life
is reestablished.

Once the repair work has been done, the exorcist must then
make specific choices regarding her ability to continue, or
whether it is time to retire. It is a difficult choice to make, but
more often than not, the inner contacts and beings that an exorcist has worked with for years will help the exorcist find the
appropriate way forward.

In the end, we do what we can and when we can do no more,
we pass on the tools with support to the next generation and
hope for the best!

Appendix 1
Understanding and working with the Abyss

The Abyss, like angelic beings, has been the territory of mystical Kabbalah to the point of almost exclusivity. The complexity of real Kabbalistic training has so many tangles, filters, and dead ends that it can encourage the practitioner to become focussed upon patterns to the extent of truly missing what they are attempting to work with.

Some of that structure was originally woven into the training methods as a safety valve, not only to discourage idiots and casual glances, but also to create a 'firewall' from an inner point of view. When you work with an angelic being, you are potentially playing with a 'nuclear' type of power. The names, attributes, patterns, shapes, and rituals that are connected to the contact and interaction with such a being filter and form the power that you work with.

So you get a focussed, filtered, power controlled contact that does specific things and does not move out of its structure. Although that is still powerful and dangerous, it is much safer to work with as a magical practitioner.

If you do not use these filters, shapes, and patterns, then you are faced with the true power of the angelic being in all its glory and you have to be extremely focussed, unconditional, and balanced. You also have to be willing to die if it is necessary.

This rule is also true for working in and with the Abyss. If it is approached with its magical filters then it can be worked with safely but in a limited and filtered way. The more patterns, attributes, and rules we apply, the less of the Abyss we are able to access.

And yet accessing the Abyss without such filters is asking for trouble, unless you know what you are doing. Many a hapless magician has been burned to a crisp by reaching down or up the realms of the Abyss in pursuit of power. If you reach into the Abyss for power, it will destroy you in one way or another eventually.

When you reach beyond the surface world in magical practice, you reach into worlds of beings and power. If you reach beyond that level, you begin to touch upon the workings of the universe and the structures/beings that ensure the universe exists and functions (the universal boiler room). If you are stupid enough to think that you can reach into the boiler room to tap into that power for personal gain, then you are an idiot.

If you want to reach into the boiler room to be of service, then you are still probably an idiot (it is extremely dangerous) but at least you are a worthy idiot and with such selfless intent, you will probably be protected to an extent. If humanity does not create its own filters, then the inner worlds will do it for you, and theirs tends to be far more workable.

The inner filters work to protect you from complete destruction, but they will allow enough power though to do the job and teach you something—bear in mind that humanity always learns the hard way. So it can be a very difficult lesson, though usually a very important one.

So what is the Abyss? If you strip all the formal padding away that has been attributed to it, you are left with a multi-dimensional freeway for power and consciousness. The way that we see it when we look at it from an inner point of view is just the way our brains perceive it—it has no real form as such.

The Abyss is a highway from the highest form of consciousness to the lowest: the two extremes meet one another and are of one another. It is mirrored in the tree of life with Divine Being at the top and Humanity at the bottom, so the Abyss is Divine consciousness without form at the 'top' and the densest of beings at the 'bottom.' If I try to describe the shaping too much I will really get my knickers in a twist, because the dimensions of this structure are many and are beyond our ability to grasp. But here is a simple(ish) pattern to follow (then I can get on with discussing what it does).

<pre>
                    I
                    I
          _____

                    I
                    I
</pre>

Divine Being is at the top, then archangelic and angelic beings, at the line is humanity, below the line is demons, bigger demons and then Divine Being in its densest form (which is also humanity). In between those levels are lots of interconnections, levels of consciousness, and a wide variety of beings. The structure also bends in on itself, so that the top and bottom are the flip sides of one another. Humanity in the middle is our balanced state between good and bad, no form and density—we are the fulcrum in the tree.

When magicians figure this out (that humanity is the fulcrum) many tend to trip out on being the master species. Those tend to be the stupid ones. At the fulcrum is also the rest of our physical world—the animals, plants, etc. Everything that is physically manifest is in our realm of the fulcrum. The other levels are different worlds/states of consciousness—hence shedding your humanity is one of the keys to exploring and working with the Abyss.

In reality humanity tends to veer from that centre line in both directions—so the Satanists dive down and the messiahs reach up (they tend to get nailed to bits of wood if they go too high up...). The goal of Humanity is to stay at that midline—to keep the balance of substance/non substance, good/bad in perfect harmony, and to stay in their own realm.

That is why it is so important when you work deeply in the inner worlds that first you go through the void and shed your everyday world. Then you approach the Abyss unconditionally, without selfish intent, and with proper focus—that way you cannot be dragged to one extreme or the other. This is also the reason why, when you first begin working in the void, you are often asked if you are willing to give up your life. You have to be willing to let go of everything, therefore nothing can be used to seduce you, and nothing can hold you back. If you can shed life within life, then you are a step further on in the mysteries (this is the root of the death-within-life initiation).

Another point to look at with this pattern is what happens at conception—the act of making love reaches through the worlds in search of a consciousness to bring into form. If you imagine that the couple is making love at the bottom of the structure (and also at the fulcrum) they open an inner vortex that stretches up through the Abyss until it reaches as far as it can go. Then a soul tumbles in from that level and falls into conception.

This is the basis for the sacred union: the sex between priest and priestess, Queen and King, etc. Their lovemaking would be focussed with the spiritual intent for bringing through a sacred child. They would go through a variety of preparations for both mind and body, and the act itself would be held in a sacred space. The method used is also mirrored in the mysteries of Tantra.

The flip side of the sacred union is debauched, unhealthy, and unconnected sex, where the vortex does not reach very far up and brings through unhealthy beings.

Faery children are born when the Vortex reaches to the faery realm—one or both partners mediate a faery being while making love so the Vortex reaches up to that frequency.

It is like tuning a radio: whatever frequency/wavelength you are on, that is what you will bring into your body. And it does not have to be a physical child—this can also bring through inner beings when done with intent.

So, back to the Abyss. Not only is Divine Being 'up,' it is also 'across.' When you cross the Abyss, you are into the realm of Divinity in the process of polarisation and preparing to manifest. To understand this better, look at the Tree of Life: you cross the Abyss and you hit Divinity split into Male and Female (Hochmah and Binah), beyond that is God without Form but in preparation (Kether).

This split into Male/Female is purely for the fulcrum/human realm—we are by nature polarised beings (male/female/positive/negative) as is the world around us. Divinity filters through that polarisation, so that Divinity and Humanity can be aware of each other. The further away a being is from the Fulcrum, the less aware of Humanity it is.

The dimensions and twists of the Abyss can be mind bending: God is up and also across. And Divinity is also down in its most dense twisted form, as is the human form—which brings about the reflection of the ability within humanity for great good or great evil. It depends which part of the pole you are sliding down (or up). The best way is to get blindingly drunk, then it all makes sense.

In practical terms you would work in the boiler room (remember the boiler room?) for specific reasons rather than sightseeing, or personal gain. If you are in the business of creating a sacred or faery child, if you are working with Angelic consciousness, if you are working within the realm of death, if you are an exorcist, a worker in Universal service, or if you are stupid enough to want to stand at the foot of God, or connect with a demon, then the Abyss is for you.

The closer to the fulcrum a being is, the more aware it is of humanity and it is either 'friendly' towards humanity or 'unfriendly.' The further a being is away from the fulcrum the less aware of humanity it is and is therefore neither 'for' nor 'against.' Also, the further away from the fulcrum a being is, the more powerful and less physically formed it is, and the less ability it has to manifest in the physical realm. It has to pass down the Abyss towards humanity to appear in our world—hence the angels and demons taking human/animal form.

To work with true angelic form without a human filter, you have to go up the Abyss to its own realm and meet it as an inner being. The same is also true for what we call demons. The two sides of the Abyss beyond the fulcrum reflect for us the two sides of power—threshold mediation power becomes angels and demons, the extremes become Divinity in dense form or formless.

All the levels in between have their own 'fulcrums' that appear as tunnels and as the beings of those levels come to the edge of the Abyss, they have their own 'up' and 'down.' Many a magician has been pulled off track by getting glamorised by the 'tunnels' and the beings that exist at those levels. All of the tunnels/levels have a glamour that can draw a human in and trap them in endless meaningless communications, therefore holding them back from evolving. Our spiritual evolution is about being cast 'down' and finding our way back 'up'—falling into physical manifestation and striving to move back to formlessness.

As an exorcist, this boiler room can be especially useful as it enables one to commune with beings at their own level in their own realm as opposed to how they express themselves when they are in our polarised worlds. It is also safer to approach some of these beings this way. The rule of the Abyss is as always though: be focussed, be in service, and have no wants or needs. True clarity and the void within keeps a worker safe in the deepest realms and keeps the inner filters in place.

That is not to say you won't get the shit hammered out of you—you probably will. But that is just the side effect of working at such depth; it is not from any being attacking you. The deeper or higher you go away from your own realm or the fulcrum, the more of an impact it is going to have on your body. Even though you are working through your mind, the power filters through the physical body and you will feel like you have just built a house single-handed while being beaten with a cricket bat.

So what can go wrong? Oh lots! If you are a skinny, spotty, black clothed, chain-festooned luciferian intent of communing with demons to expand your power over women/groups and get a bigger willy, then one of three things will happen:

1) You will not manage it but will end up connecting with bottom feeder parasite-type beings. This will take you down a path of feeling terribly important and very depressed at the same time. You will become paranoid, depressed, withdrawn, and even spottier (the power flows through your body and will enhance any imbalance, therefore if you were spotty to begin with, it will get worse).

2) If you should happen to have natural abilities and are able to connect with beings, then you may, in fact, connect with a lesser (nearer to our realm) demon who may offer you just what you want and have a good amusing time at your expense, and your willy will not get bigger.

3) If you are truly naturally able to connect with beings you may reach a very deep 'demonic' or titan consciousness that will look at you in complete fascination, being unable to work out exactly what you are and what the hell you want. These beings can be disastrous for humanity, not because they are 'bad' but because of the sheer power they mediate.

The same is true of going 'up.' Angelic beings closer to our realm tend to be worked with in the Kabbalistic patterns (among others). You can also work with them out of those patterns but you do need to be focussed with your intent and concentration (otherwise all that will be left of you is a pair of slightly burned shoes).

If you have natural talent for connecting with beings, you might also reach up quite far and come face to face with an archangelic being (well, not quite face to face; as with the deeper demons, they are rather large) which, like the deeper demon/titan, will look at you with total astonishment before trying to communicate with you. If it does, not even your shoes will be left.

There are methods for working/communicating in both directions with these beings and the methods are simple, direct, and very hard to maintain. If you chose to toss aside the magical structures/patterns and don't do it via drugs (which is the worst possible way), then working through the void or carrying the void within is your best option.

If you are working from an intention of universal service, then you will have the natural inner filters in place and working through the void will bring you to a fraction of the being you need to work with. (Note the use of the word 'need.' When you go through the void, you are connected to what you need for the job, not necessarily what you want.)

If you work through the pattern of the Abyss, take the void within you and the same filters will be in place. You have to try to maintain a balance though—if you are working in the Abyss, work in both directions. This not only ensures that you gain working knowledge of beings on both sides of the 'fence,' which is handy in any deep work, but it also maintains a sense of inner balance, which is also important if you are engaging in deep, useful magic.

Those workers who constantly reach up and work only with angelic beings, climbing higher and higher up the ladder of angels eventually stretch too far away from the fulcrum and 'cease to be.' This is known as 'ascending': the prophet Enoch 'who walked with God and was not' for example.

It has become a very popular term in new age circles: "Oh Trudi White Light Angel Flower? Yeah, she ascended after the third workshop." (She actually went to go live in Wisconsin....)

And what happens if you only reach down the Abyss, going deeper and deeper? Well, I dunno really. I guess you become a conservative politician.

But for sensible, balanced, and powerful work, work on both sides and up and down. Work for true intent and with focus. And by true intent I don't mean 'good' or 'bad.' I mean true intent, for a job, something that is not selfish. Good and bad is relative to your culture/religion—it depends on which end of the action you are on. But the difference between selfish and non-selfish acts is a big difference in the inner worlds. Selfish acts will work, but they only work to a point. Unselfish acts that are a part of service to the Universe have almost limitless access to power—it is all down to what you are capable of holding.

Appendix 2
Tarot layout for looking at the health of a person

Tarot, as we know, has many applications, and one of the more interesting ones is as a tool for looking in depth at the human body. Not only does it tell you what is going on with the body, but you can, with the right layout, look at the influences that are bringing about changes in the body, be they organic or inner.

Before we go any further, I have to point out the common sense thing that everyone knows but it has to be said anyway: using tarot as part of healing is not a substitute for going to a doctor.

You can use an ordinary deck but, if this is something that you are going to use often, I suggest that you make your own deck, maybe based on an ordinary deck, but with the minor cards adjusted more towards body matters.

When you look at the body using tarot, you begin to see some very interesting things that relate to illness, body changes, and the minute reactions to things that have long-term consequence but few outer symptoms. You start to see the impact that inner work has on the body, how magic sometimes changes things within the body, and how various parts of the body react to power in various ways. It also maps out the passage of inner power through the body, which in turn gives the magical worker clues as to how to care for the body while doing powerful work.

The other interesting thing that begins to emerge is the pattern of illness. Normally we see only the outer symptoms, which are treated and we get better. Using tarot, we start to see the profound implications of a virus or bacteria, how it can change things at a deep level, and we also start to see the inner manifestation of the outer virus. Every living thing has an inner expression and through the tarot we can look at these illnesses to see their inner 'personalities.' This, in turn, can change how we approach an illness and how we get rid of it.

When you start to track the progression of an illness using tarot it quickly becomes apparent that some illnesses, while they may make us miserable, have positive uses for the body. I used to hate the occasional cold—I very rarely got them but when I did they made my life a misery. But when I started to look at them from an inner point of view, using the tarot, I saw that the body was using the cold to 'dump' a whole load of toxins that it had in storage. The cold virus was actually a positive thing for me, so I stopped trying to treat the symptoms, and let the body get on with it.

In fact, the more you look at the body and illness using tarot, the more you see positive sides to illnesses that the body can use to avoid deeper and more troublesome problems. You also start to see the positive and negative affects of certain types of magic and how the body copes with such power—it changed the way I did magic.

It also began to become very clear that the endocrine system processed the heavy impact of magic—too much heavy work, or the burden of a serious attack/curse could seriously damage the endocrine system. This was something that Dion Fortune wrote about from her own body observations, and to see it expressed within a spread is fascinating.

I also began to look closely at the immune system and tracked how magical attacks trigger the immune system. The body treats the energy as an invasion, which, in reality, is what it is. The immune system kicks in and tries to fight the attack. If it cannot succeed, the reaction becomes chronic and manifests as an auto immune disease. No amount of treatment can cure it because it is not an outer illness. There is no virus to subdue—it is purely an inner attack and has to be dealt with using inner work.

It really helps if you are doing a lot of magical work to be able to differentiate between ordinary illness and illness that is a manifestation of magic. Too many people think their body problems are the result of magic and the reading will very clearly point out if it is or not. Mostly it's not—but it is always good to check, particularly if someone is just not getting better. If someone is sensitive, then his or her body will react to all sorts of things and you can track that reaction all the way through the body—it's fascinating!

The layout is the key to working in this way. The layout has to be specific so that you can pinpoint certain things that you need information about and the layout has to have no ambiguous parts to it: it must be precise. I put together a layout that I have used for a few years now: it's not perfect but it does its job and I am constantly trying to improve it. Maybe it will come in useful for others to use as a starting point which they can expand upon and develop.

The layout

```
              1
     5        2        4
     7        3        6
              8

    10                 9
    12       13       11
             14
             15
```

1 = the inner powers: what is coming in from the inner worlds
2 = the inner landscape: the threshold between the body
    and the soul
3 = the brain/head
4 = what is taken in (food, drink, drugs): what feeds the body

    5 = emotions: What are the emotions doing? How do they feed
      the person?
    6 = short term immune system: primary immune reactions
    7 = longer term immune system/thymus: chronic problems
    8 = core of energy/central organs
    9 = male bits/hormones/male power
    10 = female bits/hormones/female power
    11 = digestive system/ processing of food
    12 = sleep/processing of thoughts
    13 = nerves/muscles/bones (motor system)
    14 = skin
    15 = near future pattern

The layout works in a sequence so that as powers come into the body, you begin to understand how the body processes certain types of power. So, for example, if you look at the pattern of the layout, you can see that food comes in, affects the primary immune system (feeds it, triggers it, etc), is processed through the digestive system, and then exteriorises.

Emotional power is processed through the thymus gland which is the seat of the long-term immune system, which in turn processes it through sleep. The central pillar is the flow of energy from the inner worlds, through the landscape, through the endocrine system in the brain, through the central organs and glands, through the musculoskeletal system to finally exteriorise out on the skin. Hence 'a rash is good!'

When inner power impacts the body, it always shows first in 1 and 2. Then it will go straight to the centre or to the two polarities of hormones to play itself out there. When the illness comes from a virus/bacteria, it will show in 6; the primary immune system. You can track the progression over the days of the illness, seeing if it alters the deeper parts of the body in any way.

I have watched things in my children, seeing how an illness has caused a change, and then watching that change emerge over the years. At first I used to panic and try to put back whatever had been altered using homeopathy, cranial work, or inner work.

Eventually I learned not to do that: we are the sum total of constant change within ourselves, and the changes that come from the viruses are all part of our maturation and growth. Nothing stays the same, everything is always changing and moving.

As a person who uses a lot of homeopathy, this method of using tarot to look at the body became invaluable. I was able to look at the possible progression of a specific remedy to decide the potency or even if it was the right remedy. What I learned over the years is that sometimes even though it's the right remedy picture, the remedy would wreck havoc in the body if I took it or gave it. For me, that was not too much of a revelation. When you do a lot of magical work, the 'blood' changes—the way that the body processes power and substance becomes inextricably altered so that normal everyday remedies, medicines, and herbs do not work, or have an opposing effect. You have to approach a magical body in a totally different way.

So I began to use the layout to help choose a remedy in a difficult situation, or to look at possible treatments and their potential outcomes.

It also becomes useful to look at a person's body rhythm. By becoming familiar with someone's processing pattern, you can the make better decisions regarding recovery/treatment. By a person's rhythm I mean the way that the particular body in question processes power, food, and illness. Everyone's body has their own unique way of doing things, and that 'way' is borne out of the body's previous experiences, its miasms, and its personality. By tracking certain behaviours through the readings, you begin to see the individual pattern of action/reaction in the body and such information can be invaluable when trying to help them.

To sum up, be clear with your questions—this is always the cornerstone of good reading. Develop the work to fit what you do—quite a few doctor friends of mine have taken this layout and quietly use it in their diagnostic work with some adjustments. And finally, allow your curiosity free rein—that is how we discover things!

Bibliography

It would be impossible to list all of the books that are of use to an exorcist as the range of information needed is wide indeed. But the following list is an example of the sorts of books I have found useful in this work, and will demonstrate the range of subject matter that can be needed as an exorcist. It is important that an exorcist knows the historical, mythical, and archaeological roots of the cultures and religions that he or she might come into contact with—such information can be the key to many seemingly impossible situations.

I have purposely listed the books by title so that it is easier to browse the subject matter.

Abbeys, Monasteries, and Churches of Great Britain by Frank Bottomley

A Brief History of Ancient Israel by Victor H. Matthews

A History of the English Church and People by Bede

Amulets and Superstitions by Sir E. A. Wallis Budge

Ancient Jewish Magic: A History by Gideon Bohak

An Encyclopaedia of Occultism by Lewis Spence

A New Eusebius by J. Stevenson

Archaeology and Language by Colin Renfrew

Clinical Neuroanatomy Made Ridiculously Simple by Stephen Goldberg M.D.

Complete Works of Tacitus edited by Moses Hadas

Culpepper's Herbal Improved: A New Family Herbal of all the British and Foreign Herbs, Plants, Roots Useful to Man by Nathaniel Brook, Richard Culpepper

Dictionary of Angels by Gustav Davidson

Dictionary of Fairies by Kathleen Briggs

Douay Rheims Bible

Early Christian Doctrines by J. N. D. Kelly

Early Christian Writings by the Apostolic Fathers translated by Maxwell Staniforth

Earth Rites: Fertility Practices in Pre-Industrial Britain by Janet and Colin Bord

Encyclopaedia of Witchcraft and Demonology by R. H. Robbins

Excavations at Tepe Guran in Luristan: Bronze and Iron age Periods by Henrik Thrane

Hermetic and Alchemical Writings of Paracelsus: v. 2 by Paracelsus and Arthur Edward Waite

Homeopathy in Epidemic Diseases by Dr Dorothy Shepard

Illustrated Symbols and Emblems of the Jewish, Early Christian, Greek, Latin and Modern Churches by H. J. Smith

Living Mysteries by John Plummer, PhD

Lyke Wake Walk by Bill Cowley

Magic and the Qabalah by W. E. Butler

Magical Christianity by Coleston Brown

Magical Ritual Methods by W. G. Gray

Megalithic Tombs and Long Barrows in Britain by Frances Lynch

Myth and Ritual in Christianity by Alan Watts

Myths of the Sacred Tree by Moyra Caldecott

Natural Magic: Potions and Powers from the Magical Garden by John Michael Greer

Palestine Before the Hebrews by Emmanuel Anati

Practical Guide to Qabalistic Symbolism by Gareth Knight

Prehistoric Astronomy and Ritual by Aubrey Burl

Scandinavian Folk and Fairy Tales edited by Claire Boos

Seals, Finger Rings, Engraved Gems, and Amulets in the Royal Albert Memorial Museum, Exeter by Sheila Hoey Middleton

Star Myths of the Greeks and Romans: a Sourcebook by Theony Condos

Tales of Greek Heros by John H. Walsh

The Babylonian Legends of the Creation and the Fight Between Bel and the Dragon printed by the British Museum

The Book of Enoch translated by R. H. Charles

The Book of Spiders by Paul Hillyard

The Cathedrals of England by Alec Clifton-Taylor

The Complete Enochian Dictionary by Donald C Laycock

The Dragon, the Warrior, and the Raven: The Magic and the Mythology of the Standards and Symbols of the Saxons, Vikings, and Normans in 1066 by C. R. Kelly

The Essential Talmud by Adin Steinsaltz

The Four-Minute Neurological Exam by Stephen Goldberg M.D.

The Gods of Egypt by Claude Traunecker

The Golden Bough by Sir James Frazer

The Golden Dawn: An account of the Teachings, Rites, and Ceremonies of the Order of the Golden Dawn by Israel Regardie.

The Histories by Herodotus

The Jinn in the Qur'an and the Sunna by Mustafa Ashour

The Magical Training of the Initiate by Josephine Dunne

The Magick of Aleister Crowley: A Handbook of Rituals of Thelema by Lon Milo DuQuette

The Malleus Maleficarum of Heinrich Kramer and James Sprenger

The Oxford History of Ancient Egypt by Ian Shaw

The Republic by Plato

The Sacred Tree in Religion and Myth by Mrs. J. H. Philpot

The Secret Commonwealth of Elves, Fauns, and Fairies by Robert Rev. Kirk and Andrew Lang

The Training and Work of an Initiate by Dion Fortune

The Towns of Roman Britain by John Wacher

CPSIA information can be obtained
at www.ICGtesting.com
Printed in the USA
LVHW050248120623
749491LV00001B/84